DEWS

∽ OF ∽

HEAVEN

To Barbara –
Christmas 2012

[signature]

DEWS
⚬ OF ⚬
HEAVEN
⚬ ANSWERS TO LIFE'S QUESTIONS FROM THE ⚬

DOCTRINE
&COVENANTS

BRECK ENGLAND

ISBN 13: 978-1-4621-1138-1

Published by CFI, an imprint of Cedar Fort, Inc., 2373 W. 700 S., Springville, UT 84663
Distributed by Cedar Fort, Inc., www.cedarfort.com

LIBRARY OF CONGRESS CATALOGING-IN-PUBLICATION DATA

England, Breck, 1952- author.
  Dews of heaven : answers to life's questions from The Doctrine and Covenants / Breck England.
    pages cm
  Includes bibliographical references and index.
  ISBN 978-1-4621-1138-1 (alk. paper)
  1. Church of Jesus Christ of Latter-day Saints--Doctrines. 2. Mormon Church--Doctrines. 3. Doctrine and Covenants--Criticism, interpretation, etc. I. Title.

BX8635.3.E535 2012
289.3'2--dc23

2012032207

Cover design by Brian Halley
Cover design © 2012 by Lyle Mortimer
Edited and typeset by Whitney A. Lindsley

Printed in the United States of America

10 9 8 7 6 5 4 3 2 1

CONTENTS

PRAISE FOR
DEWS OF HEAVEN

"In *Dews of Heaven*, Breck England applies the teachings of the Doctrine and Covenants to our most heartfelt challenges. Neither a history nor a study guide, this book is a beautiful meditation on truths revealed for our day and time. Teachers and students of the Doctrine and Covenants will benefit immensely from the author's painstaking attention to the words of the scripture and his reliance on trusted authorities."

—ARDETH G. KAPP

Former general Young Women president

"Many voices call out to us in this workaday world. But Breck England's *Dews of Heaven,* a thoughtful study of the messages in the Doctrine and Covenants, brings fresh insight and clarity to questions that keep us from feeling close to the Lord and receiving his love. Breck unpacks these teachings of Jesus Christ that have shaped latter-day understanding in a way that points clearly to the Savior and his ways. With his warm, kitchen-table-talk style, he shares personal experiences, scriptures, prophetic messages and eternal truths that can help each reader reach for higher ground."

—HEIDI SWINTON

Author of *To the Rescue:
The Biography of Thomas S. Monson*

THE DEWS OF HEAVEN

When I go for an early morning walk in the springtime, often the sun is just coming over the mountains and there's a fresh coating of dew on the grass. I love the scent of the dew. Every drop is so pure that I want to drink it in with the clear morning.

But the dew doesn't last.

We live in a parched world. Information flows like never before, but little of it refreshes spirits that are searching and thirsting for answers. People send thousands of messages into "the cloud" and get back little that can fulfill their longings for love or belonging or meaning. It's a dry cloud. The flood of electronic pleas is answered with yet more urgent pleas.

Some people try to satisfy their cravings from wells that are empty—or worse, fouled with sin. And when they do drink, it's bitter drink. In the spiritual desert of the twenty-first century, the dews of hope have long since evaporated with the loss of faith. The psalm says, "my soul thirsteth for thee, my flesh longeth for thee in a dry and thirsty land, where no water is" (Psalm 63:1).

But the questions of life are more urgent than ever.

Chris Anderson, a top influencer online as head of TED.com, is both troubled and tantalized by life's biggest questions, those he calls "the questions with no answers":

> "I used to puzzle about a lot of things as a boy. . . . Is there a God? .
> . . Why do so many innocent people and animals suffer such terrible
> things? Is there really a plan for my life? Is the future yet to be written,

or is it already written and we just can't see it? But then do I have free will? And who am I anyway? Am I just a biological machine? But then why am I conscious? What is consciousness? . . . I kind of assumed that someday I would be told the answers to all these questions. . . . [but] most of those questions puzzle me now more than ever."[1]

Although we as Latter-day Saints have marvelous modern revelations to rely on, we are part of the larger culture, and many of us struggle with these same questions—perhaps for different reasons. Some don't understand the revelations; others reject them.

And then other questions about life are unique to Latter-day Saints. We know a lot of things, but some thoughts, such as those following, generate sometimes deeper, more complicated questions:

I know I should love and cherish my spouse, but he/she is so difficult . . .

I know the gospel is true . . . at least I *think* I know it . . . so how can I be sure? . . .

I know I'm supposed to balance family, church, and work, but I'd like to see *you* try it . . .

I know I should forgive others, but after what I've been through . . .

I know I should use "persuasion, long-suffering, and gentleness and meekness" with my teenager, but how can I do that when she's never here? . . .

I know every member is a missionary, but I don't know how to be one . . .

I know I should be on top of my family history, but do you have any idea what I have to do this week? . . .

I know I'm supposed to go to the temple more often, but I'm already overwhelmed . . .

I love my family so much, so why do we have such a hard time communicating? . . .

I know I should study the scriptures, but there's no time, and I can't concentrate long enough to get anything out of them . . .

I know I need to be smarter about money, but it's hard to be smart about something you don't have . . .

I live the Word of Wisdom, so I'm supposed to be healthy. Why do I feel so sick and exhausted so much of the time?

I've done everything I can to stay healthy, so why do I have to get cancer? . . .

I know I'm supposed to be "forever learning," but when would I have time to even read a book? . . .

I know what I've done is unforgivable, so . . .

I know that as a woman in the Church, I should be a sparkling wife and a perfect mom, but I'm just not. Sometimes I want to scream . . .

I know I should be more involved in the community, but politics turn me off . . .

I know I shouldn't look at certain things on the Internet or see certain movies, but . . .

I know I should be magnifying my Church calling, but I'm not even sure what that means . . .

I know I'm inadequate, so why try? . . .

I know I should apply the Atonement of Christ to my life, but in my heart I don't know how to do that . . .

These are often the problems on our minds during Sunday School or Relief Society or sacrament meeting—but it would hurt our hearts to say them aloud. Some of them are embarrassing questions, and we may not have much hope of getting answers anyway.

Some of the problems only chafe at us, and others leave us in a spiritual wilderness. I know people who weep over them, sometimes until there are no tears left.

Taken together, these problems create arid places in the soul. Beneath them lies the contagious culture we live in that long ago abandoned hope in anything beyond itself. Our culture will do anything—work, drink, shop, shoot up, fight, joke around, indulge any urge no matter how repellent—to avoid confronting the real questions of life. They are too hard to bear. A calamity of hopeless denial has overtaken our civilization.

> *Doctrine and Covenants 1:17. Wherefore, I, the Lord, knowing the calamity which should come upon the inhabitants of the earth, called upon my servant Joseph Smith, Jun., and spake unto him from heaven, and gave him commandments.*

The Doctrine and Covenants is the Lord's merciful response to that calamity.

My friend Sean Covey once told me that although he loved all the scriptures, he was especially fond of the Doctrine and Covenants. I asked him why, and he said, "Because it's the only book of revelations addressed directly to us, in our time and in the world we live in, rather than to ancient time and a long-gone world."[2]

The Doctrine and Covenants is a collection of answers from God to the questions and problems and concerns of Saints in the latter days. It's the Latter-day Saint answer book. In most instances, the revelations are actually responses to the Prophet Joseph Smith's many "why" questions: "Why are we here? For that matter, why *are* we? Why all the pain and suffering? Why death? Why so much contention? Why can't we get along? Why is life hard?"

President Joseph Fielding Smith wrote:

> In my judgment there is no book on earth yet come to man as important as the book known as the Doctrine and Covenants, with all due respect to the Book of Mormon, and the Bible, and the Pearl of Great Price, which we say are our standards in doctrine. The book of Doctrine and Covenants to us stands in a peculiar position above them all.
>
> I am going to tell you why. . .
>
> This Doctrine and Covenants contains the word of God to those who dwell here now. It is our book. It belongs to the Latter-day Saints. More precious than gold, the Prophet says we should treasure it more than the riches of the whole earth. I wonder if we do? If we value it, understand it, and know what it contains, we will value it more than wealth; it is worth more to us than the riches of the earth.[3]

As President Smith indicates, we often grossly undervalue this book, which is "worth more to us than the riches of the earth." Hugh

Nibley once said, "The Doctrine and Covenants and the Pearl of Great Price are addressed to reluctant audiences."[4] The Doctrine and Covenants is not just a collection of answers (doctrines) but also a collection of challenges, as its name indicates; and those challenges—called covenants—are daunting

A doctrine is a sacred truth; a covenant is a commitment to do something about that sacred truth. A book of doctrines is reassuring; a book of doctrine *and* covenants is both reassuring and demanding.

Where doctrines give us the map to follow, covenants require us to perform the journey faithfully. It's a difficult journey but a blessed one, and the outcome of the journey is the embrace of our Father in Heaven and a welcome to his glorious family for eternity.

I was once asked, "Why covenants? Don't they restrict you, tie you down, take away your freedom? Why make a marriage covenant, for example?"

I thought about this and answered, "Actually, my covenants set me free—totally free. I am free to give everything I have to my wife, all my love, all my body, all my soul, without holding back for fear that she or I might have second thoughts and withdraw. Without a covenant, I can never give everything. I have to hold back because there's no guarantee. Every expression of love has a doubt behind it. Within a covenant, there are no limits to our devotion to each other."

The same is true of all of our covenants with God. They free us from the chains of the devil, in which we would otherwise remain bound. Made possible by the Atonement of Jesus Christ, the covenants liberate us to drink freely from the waters of life: "By the blood of thy covenant I have sent forth thy prisoners out of the pit wherein is no water" (Zechariah 9:11).

The gospel satisfies a thirsty soul with "the foundational principles of the gospel of Jesus Christ—the simple and beautiful truths revealed to us by a caring, eternal, and all-knowing Father in Heaven," says President Dieter F. Uchtdorf. "These core doctrines and principles, though simple enough for a child to understand, provide the answers to the most complex questions of life."[5] Many of these doctrines and principles are found in the Doctrine and Covenants.

Those answers are like precious drops of dew that refresh the dry earth. The Lord once made a promise to his people as they wandered in the desert: "My doctrine shall drop as the rain, my speech shall distil as the dew, as the small rain upon the tender herb, and as the showers upon the grass" (Deuteronomy 32:2).

In our day, the Lord has made the same promise to his people as they exercise faith in Him and keep His commandments:

> *Doctrine and Covenants 121:45. Let thy bowels also be full of charity towards all men, and to the household of faith, and let virtue garnish thy thoughts unceasingly; then shall thy confidence wax strong in the presence of God; and the doctrine of the priesthood shall distil upon thy soul as the dews from heaven.*

Like heavenly rain, revealed doctrine has been poured out on the latter-day prophets, and now we can drink deeply from the eternal source of all wisdom as we seek answers to life's challenges. This living water is never exhausted.

Dews of Heaven asks twenty questions that are on the minds of many LDS people. It is not a study guide, a history, or a compendium of doctrine. Instead, it's an attempt to bring the refreshing and healing insights of the Doctrine and Covenants to the real problems we face in our lives. Each chapter addresses one spiritual question or concern. I have highlighted passages of the Doctrine and Covenants in each chapter so readers can distil out the essential principles that apply to the question or concern. I have also quoted heavily from modern prophets and Apostles to add their inspired perspective. Insights I've included from my own experiences might help others as well.

For my purpose, I have lifted quotations out of their full context. Many other books are available to provide the background and context that can enrich your study of the Doctrine and Covenants. Also, because the sources I draw on are most easily accessible online, the endnote references mostly lack page numbers, which usually don't apply to electronic documents.

Obviously, although I've tried hard to align closely to official Church teachings, I alone am responsible for the contents of this book. It has no connection whatever with The Church of Jesus Christ of Latter-day Saints. For authoritative doctrine, readers should go to the scripture itself and to the official pronouncements of the First Presidency of the Church.

According to its introduction, the Doctrine and Covenants is an invitation to all people everywhere to come unto Christ. From its pages "one hears the tender but firm voice of the Lord Jesus Christ," inviting all to come unto Him "preparatory to his second coming." (Doctrine and Covenants "Introduction.")

Through an ancient prophet, the Lord said, "I will be as the dew unto Israel" (Hosea 14:5). Ultimately, Jesus Himself is the Refresher who sends the dew to refresh the earth and His doctrine to refresh parched souls. If this book can help people to come unto Him, it will have fulfilled its purpose.

NOTES

1. Chris Anderson, "Questions No One Knows the Answer To," http://ed.ted.com/lessons/questions-no-one-knows-the-answers-to

2. Personal conversation.

3. Joseph Fielding Smith, *Doctrines of Salvation.* 3 vols., compiled by Bruce R. McConkie (Salt Lake City: Bookcraft, 1954–56).

4. Hugh Nibley, *Approaching Zion*, Don E. Norton, ed., (Salt Lake City: Deseret Book, 1989), 600.

5. Dieter F. Uchtdorf, "Of Things That Matter Most," *Ensign*, November 2010, 20.

ONE

THE ATONEMENT OF JESUS CHRIST

I try to keep the commandments and take care of my calling and keep up with my family, but I know I fall short. Sometimes it's discouraging. My flaws and failings are so persistent that I don't know that I'll ever be able to overcome them. When I try to talk about this, I often hear people in the Church say, "Apply the Atonement." What does that mean?

We often hear varied versions of this question in the Church. I believe a lot of members have concerns like these:

"I feel so inadequate so much of the time. My efforts are just crumbs compared to what I ought to be doing."

"I know the aim of the Church is to help us become like the Savior, but in my case, that's not a likely prospect."

"I feel so guilty so much of the time. I know there are people all around me who need help. I could do so much more in my calling. Frankly, thinking about it all makes me tired."

"We don't have a perfect family—far from it. And we're not exactly examples of unconditional love. Well, except maybe the dog."

"I know the Savior paid the price of my sins, but I just keep adding to the debt, then repenting, and then sinning again. I'm hopeless, aren't I? I mean, really?"

To understand the full meaning and scope of the Atonement of Christ is probably not possible in mortality. It is an infinite and eternal subject; thus, we'd have to see beyond the veil to grasp all of its consequences. For that reason, it seems a lofty doctrine, high up and far away. But the Atonement is the remedy for these deep, often-expressed worries *here and now.*

The Doctrine and Covenants helps us understand how to *apply* the Atonement of Jesus Christ to our lives today.

APPLY THE ATONEMENT OF JESUS CHRIST TO YOUR LIFE

The very purpose of the Atonement is to help us become like the Atoner. It is the great enabling act that permits us to have peace in this world and eternal life in the world to come.

We started out like Him in some respects. He is the Firstborn of all God's children. We are also God's children, and Christ prepared this mortal home for us:

> *Doctrine and Covenants 76:24. That by him, and through him, and of him, the worlds are and were created, and the inhabitants thereof are begotten sons and daughters unto God.*

His Father is our Father . . .

> *Doctrine and Covenants 93:21, 23. I was in the beginning with the Father, and am the Firstborn. . . . Ye were also in the beginning with the Father.*

He went through many of the same stages we go through, relying on the grace of our Father in Heaven to become as He is:

> *Doctrine and Covenants 93:13–14. And he received not of the fulness at the first, but continued from grace to grace, until he received a fulness; and thus he was called the Son of God, because he received not of the fulness at the first.*

So the Savior Himself went through a process of perfection, "from grace to grace," just as we must do until we too receive the kind of "fulness" that He has received:

> *Doctrine and Covenants 93:20. For if you keep my commandments you shall receive of his fulness, and be glorified in me as I am in the Father; therefore, I say unto you, you shall receive grace for grace.*

APPLY THE ATONEMENT BY RECEIVING "GRACE FOR GRACE"

The purpose of our mortal life is to continue the process of becoming like the Firstborn—a daunting goal, but one that is achievable because of His Atonement.

Some who have only the Bible to read might not fully understand that we began where the Savior began and belong to His race and family. There was no inherent difference between His premortal self and our premortal selves, and He not only expects but pleads with us to follow Him, "that where I am, there ye may be also" (John 14:3).

This truth revolutionizes our understanding of ourselves. I believe that to a great extent we are discouraged by the "cultural religion" that surrounds us. For many who don't have access to these revealed doctrines, the Savior is a being wholly different from us: We are not sons and daughters of God but wretched creatures, "corrupted, distorted versions" of what God intended.[1]

Our culture copes in various ways with this old idea that we are sick, stunted, inadequate creatures. Some recoil from it, some find odd satisfaction in it, and some even accept it as the basis for a whole theology of our existence.

The revealed understanding that we are literally offspring of God with divine potential should erase these incapacitating notions from our hearts. We are capable of receiving "grace for grace"—that is, divine understanding added upon by more divine understanding until we receive a fulness of truth.

Because of this understanding, we also know that we are taking part in a great mortal school whose object is to form us into beings like our Savior. Like all analogies, the school analogy goes only so far, but in literal reality we are children who have been sent away to school:

Doctrine and Covenants 50:40. Behold, ye are little children and ye cannot bear all things now; ye must grow in grace and in the knowledge of the truth.

This simple revelation beautifully and precisely describes our situation in this life. Our task here is to grow and learn. Everyone knows how excited and nervous a little child is who is just starting school for the first time. We adults also know that it's only the beginning of a long, sometimes difficult quest—but that promising child can mature and be capable of great things in the end.

We also know that there is no other way to get to the fulness of glory that our Savior enjoys. If we want the fruits of an education, we must endure the laborious but exhilarating process of schooling. The child starts her schooling with simple things, for she "cannot bear all things now," but with experience and training, she will grow in knowledge. In this process, she has to put forth her own effort or the school is useless to her. She must do all she can, or she will not fulfill the mighty potential she was born with.

In this school of mortality, we children grow not only in knowledge of the truth but also in grace.

Because of the Atonement of Christ, a great compensating power applies to those who do all they can. That power is called the "grace of God." The term "grace" comes from the New Testament word *charis*— also the root of the word "charity." Fundamentally, *charis* meant something like "to favor, to lean over, to hover."

APPLY THE ATONEMENT BY ACCEPTING THE CHASTISEMENT OF A LOVING LORD

Grace is what we experience from a loving Lord who hovers over us, watching and guiding, stepping in to help when needed. We've all seen dedicated teachers at work: they literally stand over or with their students, attending carefully to their progress. God in His grace is like that.

Once when I injured my shoulder, a physical therapist was a lot of help to me. He showed me how to lift weights to build strength around the weakened joint. He corrected my stance and guided me on how to balance the weight for maximum effect. I grew in strength.

In one sense, my therapist's approach to me is like the grace the Savior shows us. He is attentive. He does not lift the weight for us or we wouldn't get stronger, which would negate the exercise; He teaches us carefully how to bear the weight. He corrects our efforts so we can benefit the most from the exercise.

> *Doctrine and Covenants 136:31. My people must be tried in all things, that they may be prepared to receive the glory that I have for them, even the glory of Zion; and he that will not bear chastisement is not worthy of my kingdom.*

In our culture, the word "chastisement" means "punishment." But that was not the original meaning of the word at all—it comes from the Latin *castigare*, "to correct or make pure."[2] The Lord's chastisement is intended to guide and purify our efforts until "doing it right" becomes habitual. So my therapist was always correcting my routine until I mastered it; when I got there, we both celebrated.

I noticed other patients in the gym who didn't take correction well. Some of the men disputed the therapist's counsel, especially those who had been "going to the gym" for years. They'd say, "That's not how it's done" or "How will *that* help me?" Then they would do it their own way. Once the therapist got alarmed when a patient tried something with the exercise machine: "Please!" he yelped. "You'll injure yourself." Still others wouldn't put forth the effort and gave up.

These people didn't fully trust the expert's eye. For one thing, he didn't ask us to do very much. I was a little skeptical at first myself. The early exercises he prescribed didn't seem strenuous enough to do any good. I too thought, but didn't say, "How will *this* help me?" I was a little child; I couldn't "bear all things now." But over time, I was amazed at how much better I felt, how much more flexibility I attained in my shoulder.

In time, the therapist gave me more demanding exercises, but because I had followed counsel, I was ready for them. Some days I lifted the weight until I could lift no more; at that instant, he would catch the weight so it wouldn't fall on me.

He explained that the muscles around my shoulder needed to be stronger to compensate for the weakened joint. He also showed me that the more strain on the muscle fibers, the more they would grow to compensate. For my own good, he taught me, I *needed* the heavy weight; I *needed* to be pushed to the breaking point in order to improve.

But he was always there to catch the burden I could no longer carry.

The grace of God is the favor, attention, guidance, and careful discipline provided by a loving Savior who hovers over us and who meticulously steers us toward our best selves. And who welcomes us to "cast our burdens" upon him (see Psalm 55:22).

Elder Neal A. Maxwell said, "We should regularly *apply the Atonement for self-improvement*, while enduring to the end. If we choose the course of steady improvement, which is clearly the course of discipleship, we will become more righteous and can move from what may be initially a mere acknowledgment of Jesus on to admiration of Jesus, then on to adoration of Jesus, and finally to emulation of Jesus. In that process of striving to become more like Him through steady improvement, we must be in the posture of repentance."[3]

APPLY THE ATONEMENT THROUGH REPENTANCE AND IMPROVEMENT

"The posture of repentance" is not to punish us but to help us improve. The New Testament word for repentance is *metanoia,* which literally means "change of mind." When we repent, we accept the Lord's correction and resolve to improve. We abandon our way and trust His way. The true purpose of repentance, according to Elder Bruce C. Hafen, is "not because we must 'repay' him in exchange for his paying our debt to justice, but because repentance initiates a developmental process that, with the Savior's help, leads us along the path to a saintly character."[4]

The way to apply the Atonement in our lives is to accept the grace of God. To do that, we "choose the course of steady improvement" and "endure to the end" of the course, as I tried to do with my therapist. The grace of God, which the Atonement makes possible, is, as Elder

David A. Bednar explains, "the divine assistance or heavenly help each of us desperately needs to qualify for the celestial kingdom."[5]

Of course, Christ the Atoner does far more for us than teach and guide us. In his atoning sacrifice, He carried a burden for us—a burden we create through our sins—that would crush us under its infinite weight if we were forced to carry it. If we turn away from Him and refuse to accept the Atonement, we will collapse under that weight ourselves:

> *Doctrine and Covenants 19:15–18. I command you to repent—repent, lest I smite you by the rod of my mouth, and by my wrath, and by my anger, and your sufferings be sore—how sore you know not, how exquisite you know not, yea, how hard to bear you know not. For behold, I, God, have suffered these things for all, that they might not suffer if they would repent; but if they would not repent, they must suffer even as I; which suffering caused myself, even God, the greatest of all, to tremble because of pain, and to bleed at every pore.*

APPLY THE ATONEMENT BY ALWAYS REMEMBERING HIM

We have a sacred duty to "always remember Him" and to repent of our sins continually (see Doctrine and Covenants 20:77, 79). We apply the Atonement at the sacrament table when we make a covenant to remember Him and keep His commandments. We honor His Atonement only if we take full advantage of the gift of repentance. It is the key to our growth, but it is only part of our growth. As Elder David A. Bednar says,

> The enabling power of the Atonement strengthens us to do and be good and to serve beyond our own individual desire and natural capacity.
>
> In my personal scripture study, I often insert the term 'enabling power' whenever I encounter the word *grace*. Consider, for example, this verse with which we are all familiar: 'We know that it is by grace that we are saved, after all we can do' (2 Nephi 25:23). I believe we can learn much about this vital aspect of the Atonement if we will insert 'enabling and strengthening power' each time we find the word *grace* in the scriptures."[6]

An "enabler" is a person who makes it possible for someone else to achieve a goal. This is what Jesus does for us. He opens the way, clears the path, provides the map and the provisions, teaches lessons to make the path easier, and redeems us when we fall from the path. He does all of this because He is also our dearest friend:

> Doctrine and Covenants 93:45. I will call you friends, for you are my friends, and ye shall have an inheritance with me.

From Christ, we receive the perfect love, loyalty, and compassion only a perfect friend could provide. He does not take the journey for us, but He takes it with us every step of the way.

Christ is not waiting impatiently for you on the dais at your graduation to see if you will show up or not; He is by your side, late into the night, helping with each test and each assignment. He is the stabilizing force on the path of life, the Iron Rod, which is the "word of God" that will safely guide us through.[7] Please remember that He *is* the Word (see John 1:1).

Our divine Atoner—our Teacher, Provider, Stabilizer, Redeemer, and Friend—is also our Great Enabler, making it possible for us in every way to graduate successfully from the School of Mortality. Nothing we experience is beyond His reach or comprehension:

> Doctrine and Covenants 88:6. He descended below all things, in that he comprehended all things, that he might be in all and through all things, the light of truth.

No matter how often you stumble along the path, He will come down and help you get up and keep going if you will put your hand in His. The strength of that Hand is unlimited. No matter how discouraged you get or how far down you fall, He can pull you up if you reach out to Him. Elder Jeffrey R. Holland says, "It is not possible for you to sink lower than the infinite light of Christ's Atonement shines."[8]

The true meaning of the Atonement will not come clear for you until that moment—foreshadowed in the temple—that was promised in the Doctrine and Covenants:

Doctrine and Covenants 6:20. Be faithful and diligent in keeping the commandments of God, and I will encircle thee in the arms of my love.

The Old English word *atonement* literally means "at-one-ment"—being made one with Christ. In this life you can feel that warm embrace through your faith and diligence; and when the journey is over and you have done what you can do (which for the best of us isn't much), He will take you in His arms in a loving embrace. This is the moment of Atonement, when you become one with Him.

I've asked myself what I would trade for that experience of being enfolded in the arms of a loving Savior and receiving His blessing. The answer—I wouldn't trade anything. I know something about that feeling of being enfolded in His arms, and in my weakness and unworthiness I really long for it. That's why I keep at it, not giving up despite my failings: I know Jesus is there to enable and enfold me. As Bradley Wilcox says, "When we do finally pass through the veil, . . . it will not be as individuals who have done our parts; it will be, literally, holding hands with Jesus. On that sacred day, there will be no Him and no me—only We."[9]

NOTES

1. David Buschart, "Human Nature and the Purpose of Existence," Patheos Library. http://www.patheos.com/Library/Baptist/Beliefs/Human-Nature-and-the-Purpose-of-Existence.html.

2. See "castigate," Online Etymological Dictionary, etymonline.com. http://www.etymonline.com/index.php?allowed_in_frame=0&search=castigate&searchmode=none.

3. Neal A. Maxwell, "Testifying of the Great and Glorious Atonement," *Ensign*, October 2001, emphasis added. Church satellite broadcast on conversion and retention given at the Provo Missionary Training Center on 29 August 1999.

4. Bruce C. Hafen, *The Broken Heart: Applying the Atonement to Life's Experiences* (Salt Lake City: Deseret Book, 1989), 149.

5. David A. Bednar, "The Atonement and the Journey of Mortality," *Ensign*, April 2012, 42.

6. Ibid., 42–43.

7. "The Iron Rod," *Hymns of the Church of Jesus Christ of Latter-day Saints*, no. 274.

8. Jeffrey R. Holland, "The Laborers in the Vineyard," *Ensign*, May 2012, 33.

9. Bradley Wilcox, "The Atonement After All We Can Do," BYU Education Week, August 18, 2009. http://byutv.org/watch/ adab2746-ea97-466b-bd62-468b1dce7d76/ byu-education-week-brad-r-wilcox-2009.

TWO

FORGIVENESS

I know I should forgive others, but it's so hard for me. Some people I just can't forgive—one of them is myself. How can I possibly forgive?

Some time ago I taught a Sunday School lesson on the topic of forgiveness. We explored the scriptures and particularly this verse:

> *Doctrine and Covenants 64:9–10. Wherefore, I say unto you, that ye ought to forgive one another; for he that forgiveth not his brother his trespasses standeth condemned before the Lord; for there remaineth in him the greater sin. I, the Lord, will forgive whom I will forgive, but of you it is required to forgive all men.*

That afternoon, I answered the telephone to a tearful call from a fellow ward member. She could barely speak between sobs. She told me that it was easy to talk about forgiveness but almost impossible for her to do it.

She explained that years before her little granddaughter had been violently abused by a criminal. The man was caught and convicted, but the girl grew up with profound brain damage and would never live an independent life. Years of sorrow for her granddaughter and hatred for the criminal who so cruelly attacked her had deeply marked my friend's life. She could not forgive that man and was in deep spiritual agony over it.

I was speechless. It had been easy enough for me to quote a few scriptures about forgiveness and lead a discussion, but for my friend, this was the hardest issue of her life. Now I didn't know what to say. So I just listened.

The injury done to my friend was so contemptible. She got me thinking about the people in my own life who had hurt me over the years and whether I had forgiven them. I supposed I had because I didn't think much about them.

Not long afterward, I was skimming over the newspaper at breakfast, and an obituary caught my eye. It announced the death of a schoolteacher I had as a boy, a man who had taken a dislike to me and tormented and humiliated me in his class—not once, but repeatedly. All the fear and heartache I had buried so long before instantly flooded up to the surface.

In the newspaper picture, he was smiling. He had grown old. There was an account of his wife and children, his long career in education, and his service in the Church—I hadn't known he was LDS. It was the brief story of a man loved by others and honored in death.

As I pondered the article, I thought about the lasting injury this man had done to me. Some things still hurt, things that remain hard for me to this day because of him. I developed a strong aversion to the very subject he taught. I thought of how with his expertise he might have helped me in my weakness and had compassion on me, a twelve-year-old boy, instead of mocking me.

At that moment, I felt a little of what my neighbor felt about the man who had hurt her family.

Still sitting at the breakfast table, I then pondered the words I had taught in Sunday School: "It is required of you to forgive . . . If you don't forgive, you're the one condemned . . . The greater sin is in you."

For my own sake, I needed to forgive this man. I sent up a prayer and asked the Lord to forgive me for holding such a deep and ancient grudge against a man who was imperfect like me. I realized he had raised a nice family, had tried to serve, and in some ways really made a mess of things. I knew the same could be said about me. So I prayed for him. I tried to mean it. I meant it as much as I could.

These words of President Dieter F. Uchtdorf applied to me in that moment: "We must recognize that we are all imperfect—that we are beggars before God. . . Because we all depend on the mercy of God, how can we deny to others any measure of the grace we so desperately desire for ourselves? My beloved brothers and sisters, should we not forgive as we wish to be forgiven?"[1]

As I opened my eyes and saw his picture once more, I closed the newspaper; at the same instant, my wound seemed to close. It was done. I could let it go.

FORGIVE UNTIL SEVENTY TIMES SEVEN

The Lord's requirement that we forgive each other is absolute.

Doctrine and Covenants 98:40. And as oft as thine enemy repenteth of the trespass wherewith he has trespassed against thee, thou shalt forgive him, until seventy times seven.

Doctrine and Covenants 82:1. Verily, verily, I say unto you, my servants, that inasmuch as you have forgiven one another your trespasses, even so I, the Lord, forgive you.

This is a high and difficult standard to reach, but we must reach it for our own benefit. Obtaining forgiveness for our own sins depends on our forgiving others when they offend us.

Personally, I don't believe that forgiving a person is the same as trusting him or her. Anyone who sins against me may require my forgiveness, but I'm not obliged to give him or her more opportunities to hurt me. No one who is being mentally or physically abused is under any obligation to let the abuse continue. On the contrary, it must stop. A woman who forgives her abusive spouse is compassionate and obedient to the commandment; but if she lets him keep on abusing her, she is foolish.

President Gordon B. Hinckley taught this about the spiritual benefits of forgiving others: "When we forgive, our own wounds begin to heal. As we faithfully surrender to the Savior the pain caused us by others, the power of the Atonement heals our wounded hearts, lifts our burdens of sorrow, and brings peace to our neighborhoods, to our families, and to our own souls."[2]

In addition to the rewards of peace and healing, forgiving others enables us to continue our progression toward the kingdom of God. As long as we fail to forgive, we are blocked from proceeding. The Lord once commanded Emma Smith to show forgiveness to Joseph for his faults, and made her a promise if she did:

> *Doctrine and Covenants 132:56. Verily I say, let mine handmaid [Emma Smith] forgive my servant Joseph his trespasses; and then shall she be forgiven her trespasses, wherein she has trespassed against me; and I, the Lord thy God, will bless her, and multiply her, and make her heart to rejoice.*

If we don't forgive, there's no multiplying of blessings, no rejoicing heart. At a certain point in holy places, we come to a dead stop in our progress if we have anything but kind feelings for one another. Grudging feelings disqualify us from participating in the perfect unity of heaven.

> *Doctrine and Covenants 64:8. My disciples, in days of old, sought occasion against one another and forgave not one another in their hearts; and for this evil they were afflicted and sorely chastened.*

That sore affliction could have been the catalyst for a great apostasy in the New Testament Church. According to LDS scholar John W. Welch, "Faultfinding, hard feelings, and the lack of forgiveness [may reflect] a widespread condition throughout the church scattered abroad. . . . the primary cause of the apostasy may not have been philosophy, secularization, political corruption, or persecution, as one generally tends to think. . . . It would appear that the trouble began because Christian disciples failed to keep the basic teachings of the Savior regarding humility, love, and forgiveness."[3]

What happened in the early Church can happen to families. Because unwillingness to forgive can tear families apart, the Lord takes it extremely seriously. It hurts Him perhaps more than anything else.

As a parent, I have experienced real pain when my own children have hurt each other and failed to forgive. In my opinion, it's one of the worst things that can happen. The parent's sorrow over the children's bitterness is real and deeply hurtful.

I was touched when President Uchtdorf spoke on forgiveness in general conference because a mother had begged him to talk to her children. He began, "I received a letter from a concerned mother who pleaded for a general conference talk on a topic that would specifically benefit her two children. A rift had grown between them, and they had stopped speaking to each other. The mother was heartbroken." What followed was one of the great discourses in the Church as he addressed her two stubborn children who were ruining not only their own progression but also the happiness of their loved ones.[4]

I have always taught my children that I consider our family an unbreakable, eternal circle, from which other, larger circles will grow with future generations. I like to draw these concentric circles on paper and show them what happens if the inner circle breaks. One small gap in the family circle today will produce a rift that grows larger and larger in eternity.

With his eternal perspective, no wonder the Lord says, "Of you it is *required* to forgive all" (Doctrine and Covenants 64:10).

But how do we forgive?

LET GOD JUDGE

Doctrine and Covenants 64:11. Ye ought to say in your hearts—let God judge between me and thee, and reward thee according to thy deeds.

One step in forgiving others is to develop the "non-judgment" habit. In our litigious society, we can and do sue each other for nearly anything, even for imagined offenses, and we go to court for a judgment. In personal relationships, however, judgment belongs to God, not to us.

For one thing, we never have pure knowledge of the motives of others. People do offensive things out of covetousness, bigotry, fear, or simple immaturity, and we wonder how they can be so malicious. As scientists learn more about the behavior of criminals who offend all of us, they have discovered that small variations in brain chemistry can predispose people to act antisocially. Much of what was once considered criminal behavior we now treat as a psychological disorder. We simply do not know enough to pass judgment.

In one of my favorite stories, "The Last Judgment" by Karel Ĉapek, God Himself is called as a witness in the post-mortal trial of a brutal murderer who has been executed for his crimes. God recounts the man's life in minute detail, describing not only his crimes—but also his sufferings as an abandoned child, as a boy bullied and rejected by society. He describes how the little boy lost the only toy he ever had and how he mourned for it. He tells of the grown man's kindness to animals and his softhearted treatment of the women in his life.

A key point of the story is that human beings cannot judge the hearts of others. We simply don't know their hearts. Therefore, in our own hearts we ought to say, "Let God judge between me and thee." Only God, because of His pure knowledge, can really do that.

FILL YOUR HEART WITH THE LOVE OF GOD

As long as our hearts contain pockets of hatred, we are at one not with God, but with the devil. It is an awful prospect to be Satan's captive, and he can lure us into that position through our unwillingness to forgive:

> *Doctrine and Covenants 10:63. Satan doth stir up the hearts of the people to contention.*

Those who cannot (or, rather, will not) forgive become hardened, more and more embittered "until he grasps them with his awful chains, from whence there is no deliverance" (2 Nephi 28:22).

The antidote is to consciously fill our hearts with the love of God rather than hatred of another person. We do this by constantly reflecting on who we are—children of God—and through intense, regular, frequent prayer. We do this by keeping the commandments, which invites the Spirit always to be with us. The Spirit brings peace to the mind and charitable feelings to the heart, a certain uplift we experience no other way.

About getting to the point of forgiveness, President Uchtdorf asks, "How is it done? Through the love of God. When our hearts are filled with the love of God, something good and pure happens to us."[5]

One young woman who had been raped described how she was able to forgive by filling her heart with the love of God. She had struggled for years with her trauma of being violated by someone she'd thought was a friend:

Not until I had graduated and began dealing with my problems appropriately—going to church for myself, praying intently, and studying my scriptures—did I begin establishing my sacred relationship with Heavenly Father. Realizing that I was a daughter of God was a huge step for me. . . .

Forgiveness was not sudden and was not easy. . . . I sought to understand where this young man was coming from and how he had rationalized his actions toward me. . . . I had to realize that we are all children of our Heavenly Father and that He loves each one of us, even if one of us does do something really, truly awful. Once I let love enter into my heart I was able to move forward. Not until a few months ago, through pleading with my Heavenly Father in prayer, did I finally feel the peace of forgiveness. I no longer felt the hatred in my heart for that young man and I no longer felt hatred for myself.[6]

Through the process of forgiveness, this young woman moved from being encircled by the chains of Satan to becoming encircled in the arms of the Savior:

Doctrine and Covenants 6:20. Be faithful and diligent in keeping the commandments of God, and I will encircle thee in the arms of my love.

FORGIVE YOURSELF

The hardest person to forgive is oneself.

Like anyone else, I have regrets. What I regret most are things I have done that hurt others. I was a sarcastic teenager. I once wrote an ironic poem for the school magazine about a classmate I actually liked and admired very much—I stupidly thought I was being funny, but it hurt her, and I've always regretted writing it. As a schoolteacher, I was sometimes manipulative and harsh. I remember losing my temper and "freaking out," as the students called it, at least once or twice a school year. At home, I threw more than one tantrum over the behavior of my children. I didn't spank often, but I spanked hard.

I don't think I would do those things today. My heart has gone soft, perhaps with age, but I do know I'm more conscious of the Savior in my life than I once was, which in turn makes these tender memories somewhat sore. There are so many things I now wish I could take back.

The same principle applies to forgiving self that applies to forgiving others: It must be done. How?

Elder Richard G. Scott explains:

> If you are one who cannot forgive yourself for serious past transgressions—even when a judge in Israel has assured that you have properly repented—if you feel compelled to continually condemn yourself and suffer by frequently recalling the details of past errors, I plead with all of my soul that you ponder this statement of the Savior:

> *Doctrine and Covenants 58:42–43. He who has repented of his sins, the same is forgiven, and I, the Lord, remember them no more. By this ye may know if a man repenteth of his sins—behold, he will confess them and forsake them.*[7]

For me, forgiving others is comparatively easy; forgiving myself has always been difficult. It's a great relief to know that the Lord will not hold against me the stupid and hurtful things I've done along the way if I pay the price of repentance. I know a little about laying a broken heart on the sacrament table and feeling myself healed there by the touch of Jesus.

"Lay your burden at the Savior's feet," President Uchtdorf asks. "Let go of judgment. Allow Christ's Atonement to change and heal your heart. Love one another. Forgive one another. . . . Remember, heaven is filled with those who have this in common: They are forgiven. And they forgive."[8]

NOTES

---

1. Dieter F. Uchtdorf, "The Merciful Obtain Mercy," *Ensign*, May 2012, 75.

2. Gordon B. Hinckley, "A Mighty Power of Healing," *Ensign*, April 2002.

3. John W. Welch, "Modern Revelation: A Guide to Research About the Apostasy," *Maxwell Institute*. http://maxwellinstitute.byu.edu/publications/books/?bookid=42&chapid=204

4. Uchtdorf, "The Merciful Obtain Mercy," 75.

5. Ibid.

6. Lindsay Papke, "The Trial of Forgiveness," *Exponent II*, Fall 2011, 7–8.

7. Richard G. Scott, "Peace of Conscience and Peace of Mind," *Ensign*, November 2004, 15.

8. Uchtdorf, "The Merciful Obtain Mercy," 77.

THREE

TEMPTATION

How do I overcome temptation? I feel constantly pressured to do and think things that aren't worthy, and frankly, I get discouraged.

Temptation is a harsh but necessary reality. It's necessary because without temptation, we have no spiritual growth. Just as our muscles become stronger over time if we lift weights, our spirits become stronger only if we test them against a repeated burden of temptation. The counsel of the Doctrine and Covenants is to remain faithful (filled with faith) and to apply all our willpower to resist temptation.

Doctrine and Covenants 9:13. Be faithful, and yield to no temptation.

Unfortunately, willpower can be wonderfully weak. Between my twelfth and fourteenth years, I grew about eighteen inches, stretching from childhood pudginess to willowy teenage-hood in just a few months. Along with this sudden height came, unconsciously, bad posture. I curved into a capital *S* whenever I stood up. This really bothered my father, who kept saying, "Stand up straight." I heard this command several times a day for years. It was well intended and didn't annoy me. I believed it needed to be done, and I would respond instantly. But I couldn't keep it up. Within minutes, the commandment was forgotten. I was a slacker—a particularly slack slacker—and no amount of reminding or cajoling or nagging could change that.

But I'm not alone. Scientists who study willpower have found that most of us have a lot of trouble changing our behavior. Most people who have started a diet or an exercise program or tried to correct their posture through sheer willpower know very well what repeated failure is like.

> *Doctrine and Covenants 29:39. And it must needs be that the devil should tempt the children of men, or they could not be agents unto themselves; for if they never should have bitter they could not know the sweet.*

The word *temptation* comes from the French verb *tenter,* which means "to test or to try." All temptations are tests and a necessary part of the curriculum of our mortal life. The Doctrine and Covenants teaches us that our Father has an intricate plan of testing for each one of us, a kind of customized obstacle course designed to expose our particular weaknesses. The Lord has said that one of the main reasons for earth life is to be tempted so that we can learn by experience to distinguish the bitterness of spiritual death from the sweet fruit of eternal life.

FORSAKE ALL EVIL, CLEAVE UNTO THE GOOD

The solution to repeated failures is repeated successes, no matter how small.

A weakness of character, like a bodily weakness, is usually not overcome by a sudden binge of spiritual exercise. If you have little upper body strength, a few quick trips to the gym are not going to sculpt your chest. Resistance exercises like lifting weights or doing pushups make you physically stronger over time. Just as it takes regular, intense, repeated effort to get physically fit, patience and effort are required to become spiritually fit enough to pass the test designed for us. That means we will face temptations, each one an opportunity to increase our spiritual resistance.

This is hopeful news, and it shouldn't discourage us. By the laws of physics, a concentrated, patient, consistent effort at physical conditioning will improve bodily fitness. Equally, by the "irrevocably decreed" laws of heaven, a concentrated, patient, consistent effort at overcoming temptation will provide us with the strength to resist (see Doctrine and Covenants 130:20).

There is no shame in weakness; but there is shame in abandoning ourselves to weakness.

In a fascinating study in Germany, a group of about two hundred people were given smartphones that beeped at intervals. Each time they heard a beep, the participants were to report if at that moment they were feeling a particular desire or temptation and whether they felt conflicted about giving in to it. For example, an individual might at that particular time feel like eating ice cream. If he or she were trying to lose weight, he or she might be struggling with the urge to give in.

It turned out that about half the time people were beeped, they were feeling some kind of urge, for example, hunger or sleepiness or a desire to do some texting. Half of those reported urges caused the participant some inner conflict: "I'm awfully tired, but I don't have time to take a nap right now." The scientists reported that most people were moderately successful at avoiding the temptation if they exercised "active self-restraint." Without active self-restraint, people give in to about 70 percent of their "temptations." With active self-restraint, this number drops to 17 percent.[1]

Doctrine and Covenants 98:11. And I give unto you a commandment, that ye shall forsake all evil and cleave unto all good.

A child can understand the simple commandment to forsake all evil and cleave unto the good. Many of us would try to complicate matters: "I'm built this way. I've always had these urges. I can't help being what I am." And yet the evidence shows that people are not only capable of active self-restraint, but the more they practice it, the easier it becomes.

Doctrine and Covenants 58:28. The power is in them, wherein they are agents unto themselves. . . .

So "the power is in us" to overcome temptation. But how do we exercise "active self-restraint" in the areas of our greatest weakness?

These unwanted wants afflicted everyone in the study. People with so-called high levels of self-control had just as many urges as anyone else, but they were less conflicted about them. Their urges became less powerful and more easily dismissed.

GIVE NO HEED TO TEMPTATION

The people who successfully resisted temptation simply avoided it. One reporter concluded that this is the "banal secret of willpower." He said, "While unsuccessful dieters try not to eat the ice cream in the freezer, thus quickly exhausting their limited willpower resources, those high in self-control refuse to even walk down the ice cream aisle in the supermarket."[2] By sheer avoidance, they increase their powers of resistance and decrease the power of the temptation to seduce them.

Doctrine and Covenants 20:22. He suffered temptations but gave no heed unto them.

This was the approach the Savior took when he was tempted, as the Doctrine and Covenants teaches. No less susceptible to harmful urges than anyone else, the mortal Savior learned to practice "active self-restraint" or avoidance. He "gave no heed unto them." President Thomas S. Monson quotes a father's advice, saying, "'If you ever find yourself in a place where you shouldn't ought, get out!' Good advice for all of us."[3] Simple avoidance is a habit that can be cultivated.

Avoidance is important but not always possible. As a writer, I often go looking on the Internet for pictures I can use as illustrations. It's common to run across an unwanted image, so you know you can't always avoid spiritually harmful influences. Even if you don't go looking for them, they find you.

Decades ago, Professor Walter Mischel of Stanford University conducted a classic experiment. He invited four-year-old children individually into a room and offered each one a marshmallow. Then he said he had to step out of the room for a few minutes. The child could eat the marshmallow right away, but if the child waited till he came back, he or she could have two marshmallows.

The average child waited three minutes before giving in to temptation, although a few kids ate the marshmallow right away. Still, about 30 percent of the children successfully resisted temptation and waited for the promised reward. What was different about these children?[4]

They all found a way to keep themselves from thinking about the marshmallow: "Some covered their eyes or played hide-and-seek underneath the desk. Others sang songs, or repeatedly tied their shoelaces, or pretended to take a nap." Walter Mischel concluded that the most effective way to resist temptation staring you in the face is to focus elsewhere, to do something that diverts the mind away from the temptation.[5]

In a classic address, Elder Boyd K. Packer writes:

The mind is like a stage. During every waking moment the curtain is up. There is always some act being performed on that stage. . . . Have you noticed that shady little thoughts may creep in from the wings . . . *without any real intent on your part?*

Choose a favorite hymn or song . . . one with words that are uplifting and music that is reverent, one that makes you feel something akin to inspiration. . . . Memorize it. . . . Make it your emergency channel.

Whenever you find shady actors slipping from the sidelines of your thinking onto the stage of your mind, put on this [music]. . . . It will change your whole mood.[6]

Like the children who sang songs to resist the temptation of the marshmallow, we can overcome the habit of yielding with a new habit—seeking inspiration through reverent music or, even more effectively, through prayer.

PRAY ALWAYS TO AVOID TEMPTATION

We learn in two places in the Doctrine and Covenants that constant prayer keeps us from yielding to temptation. By far the most effective deterrent to sin is to communicate with the Lord "always," especially when confronting temptation.

Doctrine and Covenants 20:33. Let the church take heed and pray always, lest they fall into temptation.

Doctrine and Covenants 61:39. Pray always that you enter not into temptation, that you may abide the day of his coming, whether in life or in death.

Note that the Lord does not say we can banish temptation from our lives through prayer, but that through prayer we can keep from "falling into" or "entering into" it. Temptation is ever present, but prayer is the ultimate avoidance strategy. Developing the reflexive habit to pray in the face of temptation can save your life.

> *Doctrine and Covenants 29:40. Wherefore, it came to pass that the devil tempted Adam, and he partook of the forbidden fruit and transgressed the commandment, wherein he became subject to the will of the devil, because he yielded unto temptation.*

The stakes are high. If we develop a pattern of yielding to temptation, eventually we risk "becoming subject to the will of the devil." All physical and psychological addictions begin with "just once." So many give in to the temptation to taste the beer or watch the sleazy movie or break the Sabbath—all with the excuse that they are such small things. It's so easy to say "just this once" that we go on to "one more time won't hurt." Then yielding becomes habitual, repentance is cheapened, and before we realize it, we risk becoming the devil's subjects.

As Alma taught, "If ye have procrastinated the day of your repentance even until death, behold, ye have become subjected to the spirit of the devil, and he doth seal you his; therefore, the Spirit of the Lord hath withdrawn from you, and hath no place in you, and the devil hath all power over you; and this is the final state of the wicked" (Alma 34:35). Anyone who has been caught in the desperate trap of alcoholism or any other addiction can testify about that overwhelming power.

CALL ON THE LORD FOR "SUCCOR" IN THE HOUR OF TEMPTATION

> *Doctrine and Covenants 62:1. Jesus Christ, your advocate . . . knoweth the weakness of man and how to succor them who are tempted.*

Of course, the good news is the gospel. If we turn to Jesus Christ, we will find that he understands our weaknesses. He has "descended below all things, in that he comprehended all things" (Doctrine and Covenants 88:6). There is nothing about your most fearful urges and discouraging failings that he does not fully grasp, and his sympathy is infinite. This knowledge enables him to "succor them who are tempted." The old verb *succor* means "to run to the aid of someone, comfort them, and lead them to safety."[7] If we cry out to him when we are tempted, he will come to the rescue—and that's a guarantee.

As a missionary in France, I once stepped into the entry of our Paris mission home to find what looked like a pile of filthy clothes by the door. When I got nearer, I realized it was a person. I had never seen anyone so dirty and smelly. I asked him what he wanted, and he answered in a slurred voice and a language I thought might be Spanish or Italian, neither of which I could speak. I asked José, our Spanish custodian, to come downstairs and see if he could make sense of what the man was saying.

José had a good heart, but he wasn't too pleased at the sight of this derelict. They exchanged a few words, and José told me the man was Italian, his name was Antonio, and he wanted to "change his life." I think if I had been older and "wiser," I would have asked him to leave. Instead, I went to our library and pulled out a copy of the Book of Mormon in Italian. As Italian and French are somewhat similar, I could just make out the verses I wanted to share with Antonio and invited him to read a few—which he did, in a drunken voice, still collapsed at the door of our mission home.

When he finally picked himself up and went away, I figured that was the last we would see of Antonio. To my surprise, he returned the next day and wanted to hear more. Each day for a few weeks, we shared scriptures. Eventually, my companions and I began to teach him the missionary discussions by way of an Italian lesson manual we ordered, and we were awe-stricken as Antonio gradually cleaned himself up.

Antonio did not sail smoothly toward baptism. One day, he came staggering into our offices, sat down by me, and cried bitterly. At first I couldn't tell what had upset him, but it soon became clear he had fallen to some pretty serious temptations. We did our best to encourage him by reading with him some simple scriptures about repentance.

Many weeks later, Antonio stood in the baptismal font dressed in purest white. He had gone from unbelievable filthiness to a kind of radiance I have rarely seen in a person. I still didn't know how Antonio had found his way to our door in the first place, but I believe Jesus literally came to his rescue when he cried out for help. The power of

Christ to succor those who are trapped by temptation became a tangible reality to me.

However, that "succoring" does not necessarily mean that Christ removes the temptation. Remember, our Father has made us "agents unto ourselves" and expects us to exercise our own willpower in the face of temptation. Otherwise, we cannot grow spiritually. Still, our Father also assures us that He will never allow us to be tempted beyond our ability to resist. President Thomas S. Monson is fond of repeating this reassuring passage, 1 Corinthians 10:13: "There hath no temptation taken you but such as is common to man: but God is faithful, who will not suffer you to be tempted above that ye are able; but will with the temptation also make a way to escape, that ye may be able to bear it."[8]

And we can take comfort in the power of Jesus Christ to help us escape to safety if we will rely on Him. "He knows our bearing capacities," Elder Neal A. Maxwell taught. "Though we ourselves may feel pushed to the breaking point, ere long, thanks to Him, these once-daunting challenges become receding milestones."[9]

For those of us who stumble and fall—sometimes repeatedly—in the face of temptation, the whisper of hope that comes from the Spirit of the Lord is ever present. As President Monson has said, "Sometimes courage is the little voice at the end of the day that says, 'I'll try again tomorrow.'"[10]

NOTES

1. Jonah Lehrer, "The Willpower Trick," *Wired*, January 9, 2012. http://www.wired.com/wiredscience/frontal-cortex/

2. Ibid.

3. Thomas S. Monson, "Preparation Brings Blessings," *Ensign*, May 2010, 64.

4. Lehrer, Jonah, "Don't: The Science of Self-Control," *New Yorker*, May 18, 2009.

5. Lehrer, "The Willpower Trick."

6. Boyd K. Packer, "Worthy Music, Worthy Thoughts," *New Era*, April 2008, 8, 11, emphasis added.

7. "Succor," *Merriam-Webster Dictionary.*

8. Thomas S. Monson, "The Lighthouse of the Lord," *Ensign*, November 1990; "Happiness: The Universal Quest," *Ensign*, October 1993; "The Bridge Builder," *Ensign*, November 2003; "Preparation Brings Blessings," *Ensign*, May 2010, 66; "The Three *R*s of Choice," *Ensign*, November 2010, 69.

9. Neal A. Maxwell, "The Precious Promise," *Ensign*, April 2004.

10. Thomas S. Monson, "Living the Abundant Life," *Ensign*, January 2012, 5.

FOUR

TRIALS

I try to live the gospel, but things just don't work out for me. Wherever I turn, there's another trial—it's exhausting and discouraging. Why is my life so hard?

In the fall of 1838, Joseph and Hyrum Smith were arrested and imprisoned in a filthy frontier jail in Liberty, Missouri, where they and a few of their brethren were kept shackled through the winter. Cold, hunger, and fear were ever present. Even worse, the mean-spirited affidavits of former friends had, in part, led to this imprisonment.

Joseph and Hyrum were also tormented by the knowledge that their families and their followers, driven from their homes by angry, bigoted neighbors, were wandering the frozen prairie in search of shelter.

After four anguishing months, overwhelmed with feelings of frustration and abandonment, Joseph cried out in prayer to the Lord:

Doctrine and Covenants 121:1–2. O God, where art thou? And where is the pavilion that covereth thy hiding place? How long shall thy hand be stayed, and thine eye, yea thy pure eye, behold from the eternal heavens the wrongs of thy people and of thy servants, and thine ear be penetrated with their cries?

The trials we face in life often urge us to call out, as Joseph did in the Liberty Jail, "O, God, where art thou?" Illness, doubt, discouragement, and profound loss face every one of us at times in our lives. For some, those times seem to go on forever, and then we cry out, "How long?"

ENDURE IT WELL AND GOD SHALL EXALT THEE

The scriptures teach us that this telestial sphere serves us as a school and a place of opposition, struggle, and adversity, which we must necessarily pass through to attain exaltation and eternal life.

The voice of the Lord comforted Joseph in his trials with this promise:

Doctrine and Covenants 121:7–8. My son, peace be unto thy soul; thine adversity and thine afflictions shall be but a small moment; and then, if thou endure it well, God shall exalt thee on high.

The Lord provided Joseph a full catalogue of adversities that he— or any of us—might have to pass through to qualify to return to his presence:

Doctrine and Covenants 122:5, 7. If thou art called to pass through tribulation; if thou art in perils among false brethren; if thou art in perils among robbers; if thou art in perils by land or by sea . . . and all the elements combine to hedge up the way; and above all, if the very jaws of hell shall gape open the mouth wide after thee, know thou, my son, that all these things shall give thee experience, and shall be for thy good.

The ultimate purpose of our suffering adversity in this telestial sphere is not to punish us but to give us experience that will benefit us in ways we often cannot foresee. A divine law is at work here: Without going through certain experiences that are tailored for our own good, we cannot be "exalted on high." As we review the catalogue in Doctrine and Covenants 121:5–7, we will recognize some of these experiences in our own lives.

For the faithful, trials are a calling from the Lord, as the scripture clearly says we are *"called* to pass through tribulation." These tribulations might come in the form of betrayals by "false brethren." We might be robbed and cheated in our lives. We might be falsely accused. We might be abandoned by someone we love or separated from the bosom of family members by force, by misunderstanding, or by death.

Through no fault of our own, we might see many of our hopes frustrated as "the elements combine to hedge up the way." We might be "cast into the pit" of depression or illness or addiction. In extremity, we might find ourselves literally at the "very jaws of hell"—facing war, disaster, or other tragedies.

As with the Prophet Joseph, the history of the Saints is one of epic trials.

When reflecting on the history of the Mormon pioneers, it is crucial to remember the reason for the sacrifice and suffering they experienced: the endpoint of it all was the blessings of the temple.

The temple is the place where we meet our Savior, where we qualify ourselves for His presence; it was so important to the pioneers that they were willing to give their lives—and often did so—to provide the blessings of the temple for themselves and their families.

The temple also helps us understand why the Saints were required to establish Zion in a desert place, which they of course made to "blossom as the rose."

Anciently, Isaiah prophesied that the Lord would establish his people in the desert: "The wilderness and the solitary place shall be glad for them; and the desert shall rejoice, and blossom as the rose" (Isaiah 35:1).

In the scriptures, the desert is a common symbol. The prophets speak of this earth in its telestial state as a desert, a "lone and dreary world" where much discipline and effort is required to survive and thrive and grow toward perfection.[1] To provide opportunities for spiritual enlargement, the Lord has often called His people to migrate from lush and easy lands to harsh lands. Adam and Eve were commanded to leave the garden and make their way into a wilderness of "thorns and thistles." Adam had to labor hard in this land: "In the sweat of thy face shalt thou eat bread" (Genesis 3:18–19).

God sent Abraham into the wilderness of Canaan from Ur of the Chaldees, a verdant place. Moses brought Israel out of Egypt, another tropical and fertile land, into the desert for forty years. Lehi's family left the prosperous city of Jerusalem for the desert. Even Jesus went into the desert for forty days to be with the Spirit and to be tried (Matthew 4:1–11).

The Mormon pioneers underwent a similar experience, as Elder Russell M. Nelson explains: "The journey from Egypt to Mount Sinai took about three months (see Exodus 19:1). The journey from Winter Quarters to the valley of the Great Salt Lake also took about three months

(111 days). . . . The pioneers turned their wilderness into a fruitful field and made the desert blossom as a rose—precisely as prophesied by Isaiah centuries before."[2] But they paid a staggering price to do so.

Like ancient Saints, the Latter-day Saints were driven from the green lands of the eastern United States into the desert-like West. East of the one-hundredth meridian, farms flourish without irrigation, but in the West crops struggle to grow because of lack of rainfall. Wheat and corn that grew plentifully and without much effort in Nauvoo required elaborate reservoirs and canals in the desert, all of which had to be dug laboriously by hand in hardpan soil. Just getting water and food was an Adam-like challenge for the Mormon pioneers.

But Brigham Young was "less concerned with raising crops and money than he was with helping his people to become a holy nation. He knew from experience that they would grow [in character] from working hard and accepting responsibility. 'This is a good place to make Saints'"[3] he said of the dry, forbidding Great Basin wilderness.

PREPARE TO RECEIVE THE GLORY GOD HAS RESERVED FOR YOU

Doctrine and Covenants 136:31. My people must be tried in all things, that they may be prepared to receive the glory that I have for them, even the glory of Zion; and he that will not bear chastisement is not worthy of my kingdom.

Many Saints were tempted to ease the trial—to go on to other, less demanding places. There was pressure on Brigham Young to settle California, with its richer soil, its mild climate, and its gold fields. Frankly, many refused to "bear chastisement," which is not intended to punish but to purify.

The Lord's purpose in bringing the Saints to the valleys of the mountains, said Brigham, was not to make them comfortable, but to help them increase in humility and understanding. "Go with the giddy, the frivolous, the seeker after gold, to California. . . . I tell you the result of that course. You would cease to increase in all the attributes of excellence, glory, and eternal duration from that very moment.

. . . You decrease, lessen, diminish, decay, and waste away . . . the principle opposite to that of eternal increase from the beginning leads down to hell."[4]

The principle of eternal progression *requires* that we face challenges or we cannot go forward. The pioneer stories of suffering and determination teach us this principle again and again. The Lord's purpose is not to cause his people pain but to help them progress and become as He is. We *must* cross the frozen prairies and burning deserts to move forward. As with Jesus, we learn obedience by the things we suffer (see Hebrews 5:8).

We've all been through our desert times. I remember one such time, in a cold, wintry desert, when I was a missionary. During one winter, I worked in a small town on the gray, freezing North Atlantic coast of France. We had no success. My companion was cranky; he and I were not getting along. The girlfriend I cherished at home was "growing distant," as they say. I wasn't happy with my own performance as a missionary. On top of everything else, our apartment made me ill. I'd wake up in the morning with a nauseating headache that never quite went away (we found out later that our water heater was leaking gas and making us sick).

Late on New Year's Eve, I was driven out of the apartment by a need for air. I sat on the curb, vomiting, trembling with head pain, cold, and loneliness.

However, looking back, I would not trade this time in my life for anything. It was a time when I really needed God, and now I see how He was beside me through it all. Those were the months when I learned to *love* the scriptures because I needed them; when I learned to persevere against the desert; and when I learned to rely on the Lord because I had to.

In such dry, desert places, the people of the Lord learn best. In our own personal deserts, we become strong. Through hunger and privation—physical or emotional—we develop patience and humility. Through trials and plagues, we learn gratitude when deliverance comes.

And it does come. In the grand perspective of eternity, even the harshest trials are temporary and are as "but a small moment" (Doctrine and Covenants 121:7). In my case, spring came at last to that town in France, the wind softened, and the countryside bloomed intensely with green forests and golden fields. I had never seen any place so beautiful. Suddenly, we had more investigators than we could handle; it turned out to be the most successful time of my mission.

The Lord has promised to "comfort Zion: he will comfort all her waste places; and he will make her wilderness like Eden, and her desert like the garden of the Lord" (Isaiah 51:3).

In temporal terms, that prophecy has been fulfilled. As President Gordon B. Hinckley observes of the Saints in the Great Basin, "Notwithstanding the temptation to go to the California goldfields, where the entire world seemed to be rushing, the people accepted their leader's words. They stayed here and grubbed the sagebrush and made their way. Brigham Young's prophecy has been fulfilled. This is now a great and beautiful and fertile area."[5]

In spiritual terms, the prophecy has also been fulfilled. In the desert, the Saints built the house of the Lord, an embassy of heaven in an arid, alien world, where we may meet our beloved Father and feel His embrace.

FORSAKE SIN AND KEEP THE COMMANDMENTS

Of course, some of our hardest trials we bring on ourselves.

In scripture, the desert often symbolizes the desolation of sin. In ancient times, the High Priest of Israel transferred the sins of the people onto a scapegoat, which was then led away into the wilderness (see Leviticus 16:21–22). In the words of the psalmist, sinners "wander in the wilderness in a solitary way, . . . Hungry and thirsty, their soul fainted in them" (Psalm 107:4–5). By disobedience to God, we can find ourselves sorely tried in a spiritual "lone and dreary world."[6]

As Elder Marlin K. Jensen points out, "Not only do we offend God by breaking His laws, we also offend ourselves." Disobedience stops our eternal progression, and the pain of that loss is bitter indeed: "There is no more poignant description of the contrast between the pain of rebellion and the joy of obedience to divine law than the one given by Alma to his son Helaman: 'Yea, I say unto you, my son, that there could be nothing so exquisite and so bitter as were my pains. Yea, and again I say unto you, my son, that on the other hand, there can be nothing so exquisite and sweet as was my joy' (see Alma 36:21)."[7]

That joy comes to those who repent and obey our Father in Heaven We learn in sacred places and from the prophets that "obedience is the first law of heaven."[8] Why? Because without obedience, none of the other covenants of the Lord can have any effect in our lives, and our progress toward our Father's presence is stopped.

Adam's first lesson was about the consequence of disobedience, and as a result of his trial, he committed from then on to strict obedience to Heavenly Father's commandments. The Lord says,

> *Doctrine and Covenants 93:1. Every soul who forsaketh his sins and cometh unto me, and calleth on my name, and obeyeth my voice, and keepeth my commandments, shall see my face and know that I am.*

The redeeming blood of Jesus Christ helps our "deserts"—our sinful hearts—to "blossom as the rose" as we find repentance and obey our Father's commandments.

Our tribulations, as hard as they are to bear, are calculated to help us toward our ultimate exaltation in the intricate plan of the Lord for each of his children. Our task is to "endure it well," meaning to exercise patience and faith in the Savior. The Apostle Paul understood that when we face adversity with patience, the resulting "experience" fits us somehow for eternal progression in the kingdom of God: "We glory in tribulations also: knowing that tribulation worketh patience; and patience, experience; and experience, hope" (Romans 5:3–4).

What reward was the Prophet Joseph promised if he endured his trials well?

> *Doctrine and Covenants 121:26–29, 32. God shall give unto you knowledge by his Holy Spirit, yea, by the unspeakable gift of the Holy Ghost, that has not been revealed since the world was until now; which our forefathers have awaited with anxious expectation to be revealed in the last times, which their minds were pointed to by the angels, as held in reserve for the fulness of their glory; a time to come in the which nothing shall be withheld, whether there be one God or many gods, they shall be manifest.*

> *All thrones and dominions, principalities and powers, shall be revealed and set forth upon all who have endured valiantly for the gospel of Jesus*

*Christ . . . according to that which was ordained in the midst of the Coun-
cil of the Eternal God of all other gods before this world was, that should be
reserved unto the finishing and the end thereof, when every man shall enter
into his eternal presence and into his immortal rest.*

The ultimate reward for those who endure valiantly for the gospel
is *knowledge*—the kind of divine understanding that is prerequisite to
exaltation, the inheritance of "thrones and dominions, principalities
and powers."

President Henry B. Eyring teaches that the Father and the Son
have designed our mortal experience carefully in order to qualify us for
the kind of life they live: "The very opportunity for us to face adversity
and affliction is part of the evidence of Their infinite love. God gave us
the gift of living in mortality so that we could be prepared to receive
the greatest of all the gifts of God, which is eternal life. Then our spirits will be changed. We will become able to want what God wants, to
think as He thinks, and thus be prepared for the trust of an endless
posterity to teach and to lead through tests to be raised up to qualify
to live forever in eternal life."[9]

CALL UPON GOD IN YOUR TRIALS

It is profoundly comforting to understand the divine purpose
behind our trials in this life, and that someday, as Joseph Smith taught,
"all your losses will be made up to you in the resurrection, provided
you continue faithful."[10] Still, the pain of loss or disease or terror or a
broken heart can be overwhelming to us. The only real remedy for the
pain this telestial world can inflict on us is to turn to our Savior here
and now.

When Adam and Eve left the Garden of Eden and the warm,
comforting presence of the Father and the Son, they longed for that
comfort again. As Elder Jeffrey R. Holland observes, "When Adam
and Eve willingly stepped into mortality, they knew this telestial world
would contain thorns and thistles and troubles of every kind."[11]

To help them through their mortal trials, they were commanded
to "call upon God in the name of the Son forevermore" (Moses 5:8).
"Call upon God for what?" asks Elder Holland. "What is the nature of

this first instruction to the human family? Why are they to call upon God? Is this a social visit? Is it a friendly neighborhood chat? No, this is a call for help from the lone and dreary world. This is a call from the brink of despair."[12]

Only the Lord can respond to that call and bring peace and comfort. Tenderly, the Lord reminded Joseph Smith in his cry for help,

Doctrine and Covenants 122:8. The Son of Man hath descended below them all. Art thou greater than he?

We learn from the scriptures that only the Savior can truly "succor his people according to their infirmities" because he has descended below all things and personally experienced the pain that we experience. The prophet Alma taught:

> He shall go forth, suffering pains and afflictions and temptations of every kind; and this that the word might be fulfilled which saith he will take upon him the pains and the sicknesses of his people.
>
> And he will take upon him death, that he may loose the bands of death which bind his people; and he will take upon him their infirmities, that his bowels may be filled with mercy, according to the flesh, that he may know according to the flesh how to succor his people according to their infirmities. (Alma 7:11–13)

The word *succor* means "literally to run to, or run to support; hence, to help or relieve when in difficulty, want or distress."[13] God hurries to our side when we need Him. In contemplating the love of our Father in Heaven, Elder Melvin J. Ballard wrote, "I ask you, what father and mother could stand by and listen to the cry of their children in distress . . . and not render aid and assistance? I have heard of mothers throwing themselves into raging streams when they could not swim a stroke to save their drowning children, rushing into burning buildings to rescue those whom they loved."[14] In the same way, God rushes to our aid when we call on Him.

Many of us are living with real adversity. Elder Quentin L. Cook observes, "Economic crisis has caused significant concern throughout the world. Employment and financial problems are not unusual. Many people have physical and mental health challenges. Others deal with marital problems or wayward children. Some have lost loved ones.

Addictions and inappropriate or harmful propensities cause heartache. Whatever the source of the trials, they cause significant pain and suffering for individuals and those who love them."[15]

Peace of the Spirit can come to those who taste bitter trials if they will endure in patience and call on Father in Heaven for His help. The assurance the Lord gave to Joseph Smith is true for all:

> *Doctrine and Covenants 122:9. Hold on thy way. . . . Thy days are known, and thy years shall not be numbered less; therefore, fear not what man can do, for God shall be with you forever and ever.*

NOTES

1. See Jeffrey R. Holland, "The Ministry of Angels," *Ensign*, November 2008, 29.

2. Russell M. Nelson, "The Exodus Repeated," *Ensign*, July 1999.

3. *Teachings of Presidents of the Church: Brigham Young* (Salt Lake City: Intellectual Reserve, 1998), 9.

4. Brigham Young, *Journal of Discourses* 1:119.

5. Gordon B. Hinckley, "These Noble Pioneers," *Brigham Young University 1996–1997 Speeches* (February 2, 1997), 4.

6. See Holland, "The Ministry of Angels."

7. Marlin K. Jensen, "Living after the Manner of Happiness," *Ensign*, December 2002.

8. N. Eldon Tanner, "Obedience," *Ensign*, January 1974.

9. Henry B. Eyring, "Adversity," *Ensign*, May 2009.

10. *Teachings of the Prophet Joseph Smith* (Salt Lake City: Deseret Book, 1977), 296.

11. Holland, "The Ministry of Angels."

12. Jeffrey R. Holland, "I Stand All Amazed," *Ensign*, August 1986.

13. *Webster's 1828 Dictionary*, "Succor."

14. Melvin J. Ballard, "Classic Discourses from the General Authorities: The Sacramental Covenant," *New Era*, January 1976.

15. Quentin L. Cook, "Hope Ya Know, We Had a Hard Time," *Ensign*, November 2008.

FIVE

COMMUNICATION

I love my family so much, but we have a hard time communicating. We do argue too often, but even more troubling, we don't share very much of what's in our hearts. How can we improve communication between husband and wife, parent and child (and teenager!)?

The Lord's formula for effective communication between family members (or anyone, for that matter) is found in this remarkable revelation:

> *Doctrine and Covenants 121:41–42. No power or influence can or ought to be maintained by virtue of the priesthood, only by persuasion, by long-suffering, by gentleness and meekness, and by love unfeigned; by kindness, and pure knowledge, which shall greatly enlarge the soul without hypocrisy, and without guile.*

Although aimed specifically at the priesthood, these are not only the most effective principles of communication but the only principles a Latter-day Saint should follow in relating to others. My advice to everyone who wants to be a good communicator is to memorize this verse.

We live in a tumultuous time. A sharp tone of incivility, profanity, and contention pervades the air. Influenced by television and the Internet, conversations among friends and family members take on the sarcastic flavor of "one-upmanship." Usually harmless, these conversations sometimes get harsh.

Things have gotten rough in the public forum. Elder Quentin L. Cook decries the "hateful, vitriolic, bigoted communications" that characterize our online conversations.[1]

This coarsening atmosphere seeps into our homes, even into our most cherished relationships. Angry words are the only words spoken by some family members to each other. A spirit of resentment reigns between too many couples. Parents are abrupt with small children and go almost crazy trying to get the upper hand with teenagers (the kids call it "freaking out").

Flying into an incoherent rage is the opposite of the Lord's formula for communication. Satan, we know, is prone to tantrums, which seems to be his natural response when confronted with divine power. Satan "cries with a loud voice and rants upon the earth," demanding his supposed rights; he trembles with anger and weeps and wails and gnashes his teeth when he doesn't get his way. A witness of Satan's outburst, Moses gets fearful and sees into "the bitterness of hell" (Moses 1:12–22).

Some of us do pretty good imitations of the devil. In our homes, President Gordon B. Hinckley says, "There is so much of jealousy, pride, arrogance, and carping criticism; fathers who rise in anger over small inconsequential things and make wives weep and children fear."[2] Persuasion is replaced with force; long-suffering with childish impatience; gentleness and meekness with violence and fury; "love unfeigned" with loud insults; and pure knowledge with blind confusion.

Hot, angry confrontations are one kind of satanic communication; another is cold, bitter withdrawal from our loved ones. Persuasion is replaced with scheming; long-suffering with slow torture; gentleness and meekness with sly remarks; "love unfeigned" with quiet contempt; and pure knowledge with calculated deceit. Guile and hypocrisy reign.

In response to these equally sinful behaviors, the Lord says:

Doctrine and Covenants 121:37. The heavens withdraw themselves; the Spirit of the Lord is grieved; and when it is withdrawn, Amen to the priesthood or the authority of that man.

If I may, I would add, amen to the worthiness of that person, man or woman, to be trusted by others. Unless there is fundamental change, the Lord cannot trust them either.

Let's look closely at the Lord's way of communicating, which we are commanded to learn and emulate ourselves. Latter-day Saints cannot take another way. If we do, we are more likely to succeed in our communication with each other; but even if we don't get the results we want, constant practice of these principles will make us more like Him each time we try.

PERSUASION

Often we understand "persuasion" to be the art of luring people into doing what we want them to do. This is not the Lord's understanding of the word. "Let us reason together," the Lord says (Isaiah 1:18). If you're reasoning together, you're not holding a one-sided lecture full of incentives. You're reasoning upon principles.

Doctrine and Covenants 45:10. With him that cometh I will reason as with men in days of old, and I will show unto you my strong reasoning.

When I carefully reflect on my own communication with God, I hear as many questions as answers. I feel quiet urges rather than dictates. When the light opens in my mind on an insight from the Spirit, it's always accompanied by the impression that He is asking me, "What do you think of this idea? Is it right? Is it true?" I sense a gentle respect for my freedom to choose.

In my profession, I've consulted with many businesspeople on the principles of persuasion. The first principle is respect for the audience. Have I thought through their needs? Anticipated their concerns? Appreciated their viewpoints? Am I prepared to serve them well by sharing *all* the information they require to make a decision? Do I really believe that what I'm about to present to them will be in their best interests, or am I "spinning" my message?

In my world, some people teach persuasion as "the negotiator's art"— various tricks and techniques, such as feigning shock, withholding information, pumping up expectations and slowly deflating them to get a better deal for themselves, committing people in stages until they're in so deep they can't turn around. Frankly, this kind of persuasion sounds vaguely satanic to me.

Too often family members "negotiate" with each other in this spirit instead of reasoning with each other. I know a father who sneaks into his son's room and removes one of his possessions if the boy disobeys him. Another father puts a monetary value on everything he asks his children to do—they have grown up with the attitude that there's a price tag on every family responsibility. One mother wields guilt like an artist, controlling her husband and children by forever reminding them of what is "due" to her because of her sacrifices for them.

By contrast, Jesus was a gentle persuader. He asked many questions, not to cross-examine people but to help them to think along with Him. "What think ye?" often came from His lips. He told stories that helped people reason their way through to their own conclusions. He challenged their assumptions: "You have heard it said . . . but I say unto you. . . ."

In the original language of the New Testament, the word we translate as "persuade" was *peitho*, the same root as the Greek word for "faith." Where the world's method of persuasion invites distrust, the Savior's way builds faith and confidence.

LONG-SUFFERING

Long-suffering was defined in the dictionary of Joseph Smith's time as "patience of offense." Today, it means avoiding defensiveness and declining to take offense even when it's intended. It means patiently overcoming your own weak points and showing tolerance for those of others.

Doctrine and Covenants 63:66. Overcome through patience, that such may receive a more exceeding and eternal weight of glory.

Long-suffering is one of the characteristics of charity, according to Paul (1 Corinthians 13:4). In New Testament Greek, a long-suffering person was *makrothumos*, which means "far from rage." The idea of getting angry could not be further from the mind of the charitable person.

Instead of long-suffering, our culture has become wildly short-tempered. Politicians jump down each other's throats as fast as the

Internet can take them. Sometimes I think they wake up in the morning hoping the "other side" will offend them; and if no offense comes, they manufacture one.

The same thing happens in too many families. I once watched a family I respected gradually fall apart as they became unaccountably nastier and harsher with each other. At first, it seemed just snippy remarks; eventually, it was a full-blown battle ending in divorce.

It hurts me to see young fathers and mothers go into an abrupt rage over some small infraction. The children are frightened; you see real fear in their eyes when the people they love and depend on for everything so harshly turn against them. Little children are loudly ordered out of the room or off to a corner for doing things that I consider, well, *cute*. As President Hinckley said, "So many of us make a great fuss of matters of small consequence. We are so easily offended. Happy is the man who can brush aside the offending remarks of another and go on his way."[3]

Let me be clear. I do not believe a family member should be "long-suffering" if he or she is being physically or emotionally abused. Professional help and a bishop's intervention are absolutely required. Most of the time, though, hurting people just need a patient ear.

Being long-suffering is actually a key to effective communication with anyone. A snarling teenager who won't talk, a pouting child, a wife or husband with frayed feelings—what they really need from you is patient listening.

If you can invite them to talk and then listen to them without interrupting, correcting, imposing your views, or taking offense—*for a long time*—you will be amazed at the miracle that happens. I believe people long to be heard. They want to be able to talk their hearts out, to express themselves without fear of being misunderstood or rejected. It may take long hours of listening, even months or years, but they will grow a bond with you, a bond of understanding and acceptance.

The mother who constantly interrupts with "You can't really feel that way" or the father who chimes in with "Let me tell you what happened to me once" can actually prevent communication. A person with a hurting heart sees these interruptions, no matter how well intended, as impatience, as dismissals of their feelings.

I found with my own children as they grew that it was extraordinarily useful to just sit and listen to them talk. Sometimes what I heard really disturbed me and often compelled me to jump in and correct them, to help them see things my way, or even to defend myself. Too often I did so, but I'm grateful that I eventually learned "long-suffering." My children could solve their own problems—they didn't need me for that—because they could talk freely through their problems.

One night, one of my daughters was really suffering because she didn't get asked to a dance. The night of the dance I took her for a drive to a private place, and a lot of pent-up heartache came spilling out. She berated herself, crying about her appearance, her lack of friends, and her hurting self-image. I was so tempted to contradict every statement she made—in my eyes, she was uniquely lovely and lovable—but I held my tongue, held her in my arms, and listened.

Hours later, once the emotional storm abated, she was ready for a little reassurance from me. But more important to her than my words, which being a teenager she didn't put much stock in anyway, was her knowledge that I loved her enough to hear and patiently understand how much she hurt. Now she is a grown woman, smart and beautiful with a family of her own, but we still share a particular bond of understanding. She knows I know her heart.

GENTLENESS, MEEKNESS, KINDNESS

These qualities aren't much appreciated in our culture. In business, you have to be sharp and sure of yourself. Assertiveness reigns. In our current politics, gentleness and meekness give way to ruthlessness and malice. Genuine kindness gives way to empty courtesy. The culture of arrogance spills over into our families as well.

Doctrine and Covenants 19:40–41. Canst thou run about longer as a blind guide? Or canst thou be humble and meek, and conduct thyself wisely before me? Yea, come unto me thy Savior.

In a way, we are all "blind guides." The Prophet Joseph Smith once asked certain brethren in Kirtland who seemed very sure of themselves, "Why be so certain that you comprehend the things of God, when *all things with you are so uncertain?*"[4]

That's another reason to practice patient listening. As a spouse, you don't necessarily know best; your partner might have something of value to teach you if you will listen meekly with an open heart.

A person can be self-confident *and* gentle and meek. In fact, the most confident people are the ones who don't have to make a display out of their self-assuredness.

It is neither gentle nor meek to talk down to a spouse or children, to "lay down the law" without reasoning together through the law. Children will obey an overbearing parent, but not because they want to. Gentle reasoning is the way of the Christ, who draws people to Him because of His tender voice and touch.

Elder L. Tom Perry says, "Our tone, whether speaking or writing, should be respectful and civil, *regardless of the response of others*. We should be honest and open and try to be clear in what we say. We want to avoid arguing or becoming defensive in any way."[5]

Defensiveness is a common communication pitfall. If you're right, you don't need to be defensive; and if you're wrong, you'd be foolish to defend a wrong position. A spouse who feels defensive might find it more fruitful to let it pass than to argue a case.

It's understandable that we would react strongly when we're contradicted or put down emotionally. It's a natural reaction to want to defend our identity from attack. Neurologists now tell us, however, that these natural reactions arise in the limbic system, which is the primitive lower part of the brain. It acts fast to protect us from external threats, but it isn't the thoughtful part of the brain.

The seat of thoughtful judgment is the upper brain, the cerebral cortex. It takes about twenty minutes for the powerful hormonal reaction of anger to subside and for the upper brain to reclaim control. That's why a person who gets heated up and strikes back at others often feels foolish and regretful before long.[6]

Once when I was under a lot of work pressure, I was kept waiting for an hour and a half in my doctor's office. Finally, I barked angrily at the doctor's assistant and walked out. It took only that twenty-minute interval for the shame to come boiling up in me. I wrote an apologetic note to the woman and have tried to be a model patient since, but I still feel a pang when I see her.

By consciously practicing the principle of gentleness and meekness again and again, you can rewire your brain so that you become less defensive and more respectful. If you feel like lashing out, learn to wait for twenty minutes—pray quietly, think about something else, listen to yourself breathe—and you'll find the moment of anger has passed.

It's tragic what one moment of defensive anger can do to the communication between loved ones. Gentleness and meekness produce far better results than running off blind with fury.

LOVE UNFEIGNED

You might think this is no problem for you—you really do love your family, your ward members, and your friends.

Of course you do. But you can also "feign" love by being less than honest with them or by trying to manipulate them. Eternal marriage partners risk offending each other and their Father if they use "feigned words" with each other.

> *Doctrine and Covenants 104:4. Inasmuch as some of my servants have not kept the commandment, but have broken the covenant through covetousness, and with feigned words, I have cursed them with a very sore and grievous curse.*

It's a sore curse to lose the trust of God and the people you love.

Gary and Joy Lundberg teach us how to check ourselves on this point: "It is important to ask ourselves: What is my motivation for what I do? . . . If I give help to another person for what I think I can get in return, then maybe I am manipulating him like a puppet on a string . . . Do I genuinely care about this person and want to help? Or do I offer help so that when I need something I will not be turned down by this person? Do I help others so people will see what I am doing and give me recognition?"[7]

Anytime we try to persuade others through counterfeit means, we are feigning love for them, no matter how attached we are to them. "Hypocrisy and guile"—scheming words, distortions of the truth, even lies—these are the counterfeits we too often use to get our way.

Straightforward words in a spirit of respect—these are the marks of love unfeigned.

Does this mean we can never talk about the negatives in life? Marriage partners face real problems all the time with money, intimacy issues, differences in child-rearing philosophy, how to spend their time, and so forth. Of course we should talk about them.

What's all-important is the spirit of the talk. We can speak honestly to each other if we do so in a way to keep the Spirit of the Lord in our hearts—and that means by persuasion, long-suffering, gentleness, meekness, kindness, and love unfeigned (Doctrine and Covenants 121:41–43). Even if one partner chooses not to communicate in that spirit, the other doesn't have to respond in kind. Each person decides for himself or herself whether or not to communicate in the Lord's way.

PURE KNOWLEDGE, WHICH SHALL GREATLY ENLARGE THE SOUL WITHOUT HYPOCRISY, AND WITHOUT GUILE

Seeking for pure knowledge means getting past the bounds of our own pre-judgments and biases and learning as much as we can from as many viewpoints as possible. I don't know if we can ever attain absolutely "pure" knowledge of anything in this life, but the quest for it can change our hearts and enlarge our souls.

One day, my twelve-year-old daughter came home from school very upset. Her science teacher had made fun of her, she said. He was requiring every student to do a science project, and he had asked them to present their project ideas to the class. She said she wanted to do a project on time travel, and he had callously rejected the idea and ridiculed her for suggesting it. She felt hurt and belittled.

My fatherly limbic system exploded. I reached for the telephone to call the teacher and tell him in exact terms what I thought of him and what I intended to do to him.

My hand stopped halfway as my upper brain arrived on the scene. I realized that all I knew was my daughter's account of what happened. I had only narrow knowledge of the situation, so I decided to wait until the next day to phone the teacher and find out more.

The next afternoon I got him on the phone and explained to him in calm words that my daughter was upset about the situation. I also explained that she and I had been reading together from a book called *A Brief History of Time* by Stephen Hawking, the great physicist, and had become curious about time travel. She was really interested in exploring it further, and that's why she suggested that topic for her project.

The teacher practically fell over himself apologizing. He told me that many of the students treated their projects as a joke, trying to get away with as little work as possible. My daughter's suggestion of a project on "time travel" struck him as another silly attempt to get out of doing something serious, and he had reacted badly. He admitted it and assured me that he would support her project.

My daughter, the teacher, and I teamed up to help her create a wonderful display about some of the scientific theories about time. This man eventually became one of her favorite teachers and a good friend.

By enlarging my scope of knowledge, I avoided a monumental miscommunication. By seeking out the teacher's perspective before passing judgment, I gained a purer understanding of the situation unclouded by my own biases. And, fortunately for me, I taught my daughter how to resolve a problem in the Lord's way—by showing gentleness and respect—instead of the devil's way—by throwing a tantrum.

We *can* talk about tough subjects if the goal is to seek pure knowledge that enlarges the soul. To do so, we need to work consciously at understanding one another, suspending judgment, and eliminating any hint of guile; and even if we disagree, we will grow in respect and love for each other.

The search for pure knowledge also includes looking for alternatives no one has thought of before. Some people, even experts, say that the aim of communication in marriage is to arrive at workable compromises. In fact, the Lord's way of communicating can take us past compromise to something better—revelation.

People trying to resolve an issue in the spirit of Doctrine and Covenants 121 might find their minds enlightened and their hearts touched by a solution they could not have anticipated nor arrived at themselves. Pure knowledge can flow to people whose hearts are united and who are willing to put their minds to work.

No self-help books on improving communication will ever take revelation into account. Once I was consulting with a group of scientists in Europe, all wonderful people who valued what I brought to them—except for one man. He objected loudly to everything I said; even minor things would set him off. The problem was, he was truly intelligent and well respected by the others. I did everything I knew how to accommodate him, but his combative spirit was ruining the experience for everyone.

One night, I told the Lord that I was exhausted and just couldn't communicate with this man. I needed help or the whole effort would go down in flames.

The next morning I arrived early to get ready for the day. To my dread, the man who had been so difficult also arrived early. But he entered smiling, shook my hand, and told me that the experience so far had been the most stimulating and rewarding few days he'd had in a long time. He was loving the work, loving the give-and-take, and loving me!

From that moment, the entire project changed completely. The most unhelpful man in the room became the most helpful, and we were "edified and rejoiced together." I learned then that all the communication technique in the world can't take the place of the Spirit of the Lord, and I was grateful for the lesson.

Where debates and arguments and contention reign, the devil also reigns, and no one "wins." But the Lord, the source of "pure knowledge that enlarges the soul," softens hearts, changes minds, and opens up new possibilities. When we are having trouble communicating, our best course is to follow with exactness His divine guidelines in Doctrine and Covenants 121 and then trust Him to enlarge our minds and hearts with the pure knowledge we need.

REPROVING BETIMES WITH SHARPNESS

In these verses, the Lord explains his way of communicating disapproval:

> *Doctrine and Covenants 121:43–44. Reproving betimes with sharpness, when moved upon by the Holy Ghost; and then showing forth afterwards an increase of love toward him whom thou hast reproved, lest he esteem thee to be his enemy; that he may know that thy faithfulness is stronger than the cords of death.*

The phrase "reproving betimes with sharpness" is one of the most abused of scriptures. Some people think it gives them license to snap at and even smack each other. I've heard dads who are obviously not moved upon by the Holy Ghost use this phrase to justify some pretty awful measures against little children.

I'm acquainted with a Mormon couple who started out in the holy temple sealed together as the best of friends, but a problem developed. They were both "slappers." They would physically hit each other in anger, later joking about "reproving with sharpness." Today they are divorced.

What is the meaning of the phrase "reproving betimes with sharpness"? If you look in the *1828 Webster's Dictionary*, you'll see that "betimes" means "soon, seasonably, before it is too late." A mother who warns her little son away from the swimming pool before he falls in is "reproving betimes." If she then slaps him or berates him, she is *not* "reproving betimes"—she is abusing him.

Also according to that dictionary, "sharpness" means "acuteness of intellect; the power of nice discernment; quickness of understanding; ingenuity." To reprove "with sharpness" does not mean to scream purple-faced at your family members; nor does it mean to harden your face and heart for the cold "silent treatment."

To reprove "with sharpness" means to be quick and discerning about problems when they arise. Children need to be corrected in time to save them from trouble; this should be done with understanding, not with blows or belittling.

President Gordon B. Hinckley said, "Of course, there is need for discipline with families. But discipline with severity, discipline with cruelty, inevitably leads not to correction but rather to resentment and bitterness. It cures nothing and only aggravates the problem. It is self-defeating."[8] Thoughtful parents will choose a straight, honest talk about behavior over an angry outburst.

SHOWING FORTH AN INCREASE OF LOVE

When I started teaching school, I got some good counsel from my mentor, a veteran teacher who was also LDS: "The best advice I can give you about discipline in the classroom is in Doctrine and Covenants 121. You can be sharp, but don't forget to increase your love for them afterwards, or you'll lose them." When I followed this advice, things went well. When I didn't, I made a few enemies, which I regret today.

When trying to communicate with children and teens, remember that, as my wise principal always said, "You're dealing with a group of people who are inherently irresponsible." Although teenagers can look like adults, their brains are not adult brains; they continue to develop for years. If you as a parent worry that your children don't understand your advice and directions, you're right—they don't. But they do understand love.

One night, one of my teenage children got into minor trouble with the law. A police officer brought him home and explained the situation to me. I know parents who would have exploded or dropped all kinds of bombs about being "grounded FOREVER" or an endless list of punishing chores.

But I remembered how my own father acted when I was seventeen and crashed his car. He'd chuckled softly. He knew how bad I felt about it and didn't need to resort to "sharp reproof" to teach me a lesson. I had taught myself my own lesson.

So I did with my son what my father did with me. I put my arm around him and let him talk through his feelings. He was really scared—shocked, I think, at what he had done. His own sense of shame worked on him far better than my lecturing could have. I'm grateful that from that day he began to mature spiritually: he had tasted the bitter and now understood the value of the sweet approbation of the Spirit.

Sometimes children do need sharp correction, but always under the influence of the Holy Ghost. If we want that influence, we must be open to "pure knowledge"—truly understanding the child and the situation. Brigham Young taught, "Bring up your children in the love and fear of the Lord; study their dispositions and their temperaments, and deal with them accordingly, never allowing yourself to correct them in the heat of passion; teach them to love you rather than to fear you."[9]

Sharp reproof does *not* mean leaving behind "persuasion,

long-suffering, gentleness and meekness, and love unfeigned." These are the tools of the Holy Ghost; they must always be our tools as well.

It also means "showing forth afterwards an increase of love toward him whom thou hast reproved." Long ago, I had a student who puzzled me. He had zero interest in school. He acted defiant but also seemed depressed and lonely. By this time, I was mature enough in my job to apply the principles of Doctrine and Covenants 121. Studying his "disposition and temperament," as Brigham Young advised, I sensed a deep intelligence and reproved him by quietly and repeatedly encouraging him to do better. Any sharper reproof would have been pointless. While other students worked, I often sat down next to him and asked him about himself.

All I ever got from him as he sprawled in his chair was grudging one-word answers. He did the absolute minimum amount of work to qualify for graduation.

Almost thirty years later, I heard from him. It was an email. He told me that he had a family and was doing well as an automobile dealer. He said he was communicating with me to thank me for being the only person who had ever showed an interest in him in high school.

I was surprised and happy to hear this, and glad that what I thought was only one-way communication of love and concern had actually touched him deeply.

When you're tempted to lash out at your family members, to misapply the idea of "sharp reproof," remember these words of President Joseph F. Smith:

> However wayward they might be, . . . when you speak or talk to them, do it not in anger; do it not harshly, in a condemning spirit. Speak to them kindly; get down and weep with them if necessary, and get them to shed tears with you if possible. Soften their hearts; get them to feel tenderly towards you. Use no lash and no violence, but . . . reason— approach them with reason, with persuasion and love unfeigned.[10]

Here is the reward for living by the Lord's standard of communication:

Doctrine and Covenants 121:46. The Holy Ghost shall be thy constant companion, and thy scepter an unchanging scepter of righteousness and truth; and thy dominion shall be an everlasting dominion, and without compulsory means it shall flow unto thee forever and ever.

A father and mother who practice the principles of charitable communication merit the constant presence of the Holy Ghost in their lives; as a result, their children and grandchildren will belong to them in love through the eternities because they *want* to be together.

I have a dozen grandchildren right now. When these delightful little souls run to me, screaming, "Poppy! Poppy!" and throwing their arms around me, I understand a little bit of what it means to have boundless love flowing to me "without compulsory means forever and ever." I don't have to force anything; I don't have to order them to behave. Their love is utterly spontaneous, and it pours over me like a warm stream.

That's how I know the principles in this chapter are true.

NOTES

1. Quentin L. Cook, "What E'er Thou Art," *CES Devotional for Young Adults*, Brigham Young University–Idaho, March 4, 2012.

2. Gordon B. Hinckley, "The Need for Greater Kindness," *Ensign*, May 2006.

3. Gordon B. Hinckley, "Slow to Anger," *Ensign*, November 2007.

4. *Teachings of Presidents of the Church: Joseph Smith* (Salt Lake City: Intellectual Reserve, 2007), 520, emphasis added.

5. L. Tom Perry, "Perfect Love Casteth Out Fear," *Ensign*, November 2011, 43, emphasis added.

6. Lauralee Sherwood, *Fundamentals of Human Physiology* (Cengage Learning, 2011), 124–25.

7. Gary B. Lundberg, Joy Saunders Lundberg, *I Don't Have to Make Everything All Better* (New York: Penguin, 2000).

8. Gordon B. Hinckley, "Behold Your Little Ones," *Ensign*, March 2001.

9. *Teachings of Presidents of the Church: Brigham Young*, 1997, 172.

10. Joseph F. Smith, "Love of Mother and Father," *Ensign*, August 2004.

SIX

MARRIAGE

My spouse and I have a good marriage, but I wish it were better. How do we get past our differences and grow closer? How do we progress toward that eternal marriage relationship that is such a precious goal?

The concerns beneath this question take many forms:

"My husband comes home from work exhausted and has little energy for me or the family. I feel like I'm way down on his list of concerns."

"My wife never says anything to me that isn't critical. I don't know if I'll ever measure up in her eyes."

"He goes through life as if he's the only one in the house. When I talk to him about it, he becomes very concerned and promises to change, but it never really happens."

"Over the years she's become more distant. If I even try a little kiss, I get 'not now.'"

"I wish he'd take more responsibility for things like scripture study and family home evening. I think he has good intentions, but he never 'gets around to it.'"

"She's the best friend I have, but we're not as close I'd like to be. It's nobody's fault—we're just leading separate lives a lot of the time. She has her job, I have mine, and the only time we're ever together is with the kids."

"He loves sports. He just *loves* sports. Sometimes I think that's all he loves."

"We do everything we should, I think. We go to church and to the temple, we have family prayer and scriptures and a lot of fun together. Still, I feel like when we're alone together, we're separate. She seems far away."

"He's a wonderful man, and there's never been a more involved dad, but he's also exasperating. He's always late, he never cleans up after himself, and he puts everything off. 'I'll get to it.' I'm tired of hearing that."

"She's messy. The house is always a mess. I know it's hard with the kids and all, but she's home all day while I break my neck at work. Why can't she hold up her end of the marriage?"

"He's so quiet . . . she's not romantic at all . . . he's always watching TV . . . she's never home . . . he's a workaholic . . . she's a stranger . . ."

And on and on and on.

These are the concerns of ordinary marriage partners. Sometimes the revealed ideal of a couple sealed in a holy bond of unity and love for eternity seems very distant, and our efforts as wives and husbands hopelessly inadequate.

"The first thing to be said of this feeling of inadequacy is that it is normal," Elder Neal A. Maxwell observed. "There is no way the Church can honestly describe where we must yet go and what we must yet do without creating a sense of immense distance. Following celestial road signs while in telestial traffic jams is not easy."[1]

LOOK INTO HEAVEN

Marriage partners in the midst of those traffic jams should always remind themselves of the ultimate destination:

Doctrine and Covenants 132:19–20. If a man marry a wife by my word, which is my law, and by the new and everlasting covenant, and it is sealed unto them by the Holy Spirit of promise . . . it shall be said unto them—Ye shall come forth in the first resurrection . . . and shall inherit thrones, kingdoms, principalities, and powers, dominions, all heights and depths. . . . And if [they] abide in my covenant . . . [it] shall be of full force when they are out of the world; and they shall pass by the angels, and the gods, which are set there, to their exaltation and glory in all things, as hath been sealed upon their heads, which glory shall be a fullness and a continuation of the seeds forever and ever. Then shall they be gods, because they have no end; therefore shall they be from everlasting to everlasting.

God's promise to a faithful husband and wife is overwhelming. Eternal love in the bosom of my eternal companion is the driving force of my life; but how often I (along with so many others) temporarily lose the vision of that love. But when I taste it again, it reawakens and refreshes me like dew from heaven.

Once President Spencer W. Kimball was having his portrait painted, and the artist asked him, "Brother Kimball, have you ever been to heaven?"

> "Why, yes," he responded. "Yes. Just an hour ago. It was in the holy temple across the way. The sealing room was shut off from the noisy world. . . . the drapes, light and warm; the furniture, neat and dignified; the mirrors on two opposite walls seeming to take one in continuous likenesses on and on into infinity; and the beautiful stained-glass window in front of me giving such a peaceful glow. All the people in the room were dressed in white. Here were peace and harmony and eager anticipation. A well-groomed young man and an exquisitely gowned young woman, lovely beyond description, knelt across the altar. Authoritatively, I pronounced the heavenly ceremony which married and sealed them for eternity on earth and in the celestial worlds. The pure in heart were there. Heaven was there."[2]

When President Kimball described heaven like this, I was listening to his address via shortwave radio in a little chapel near Bordeaux, France. I had been a missionary for a few months. The vision of heaven painted by the Apostle made a deep impression on my heart and has never left me. For the first time, I realized what sacred joy must be, and for the rest of my mission I kept that ideal in my heart and mind. I wanted that blessing of heaven with an eternal love more than I wanted life itself.

But when I went home after two years, the young woman I'd hoped to share that blessing with had left me behind. What could I do now? The dream faded. Years passed while I worked and studied quite alone, preparing myself fitfully in the hope of finding again what I'd lost. I met and dated wonderful women I respect to this day; but for some reason, going on dates depressed me. I remember feeling cold and discouraged.

LET THE LORD LEAD YOU ALONG

Meanwhile, something wonderful was happening, almost without my realizing it. One evening I took a date to a play in my hometown— it was called *The Madwoman of Chaillot*. The leading lady on stage absolutely captivated me. She had shining, abundant hair, a resonant voice like a violin, and when she spoke, I hovered on her words.

Her name was Valerie, and she was a friend of my younger brother. I thought about telling her how much I enjoyed her performance, but I had another girl with me and didn't feel comfortable doing that. Soon afterward, I saw Valerie again when she attended my brother's missionary farewell—I kept glancing at her, and I *think* she glanced back at me once or twice. (Again, I had another girl with me, so . . .)

A year or so passed, and I was stunned again when I went to a musical production and this same Valerie struck out from behind the curtain, dancing elegantly and singing to make your heart stop (well, *my* heart, anyway). This time, I worked up a little courage and went backstage after the play, hoping to meet and congratulate her. But she was swamped with admirers, and my courage drained away.

Months later, I was at the university on my way to class, and I stopped for a drink at a water fountain. Suddenly, someone said my name. I turned around, confused—and it was Valerie. How did she know me? I remember to this day her golden hair, her warm, intelligent eyes, and her voice. We exchanged a few words, and that night I telephoned and asked her out (that voice!).

Soon, Valerie had my heart. A kind of peace came over me as if the Spirit were whispering, "She is what you've been dreaming of." It took a long time for her—a year and half—to see things as I did, but the day came for us that President Spencer W. Kimball had described. That day in the Salt Lake Temple, with both our families and all our friends around us and her grandfather bestowing the sealing, matched in every way the vision of heaven I had cherished for so long.

No one can tell me that Heavenly Father was not moving to bring Valerie and me together. Each odd, unanticipated encounter was like a spark in my spirit; by a miracle it flamed up and has warmed me ever since. Splendid, dignified Valerie is the greatest blessing of life for me; the sum of my sweetest dreams is to have her beside me forever.

I know that many don't have the same experience that we have had. I believe, however, that Heavenly Father has an intricate plan for each of us, and that if we are faithful, He will arrange all things in the end. In bringing Valerie and me together, Heavenly Father taught me to trust in His promise:

Doctrine and Covenants 78:18. Be of good cheer, for I will lead you along.

LIVE TOGETHER IN LOVE

Doctrine and Covenants 42:45. Thou shalt live together in love.

I have always cherished this commandment—and it *is* a commandment. In the gift of Valerie, I'm grateful that the Lord made it so easy for me to keep it. My deepest gratitude to the Lord is for her, and my deepest regret is my inadequacy in fulfilling her highest standards and expectations. I've often wished I could get past my limitations and do so much more for her happiness.

I don't think I'm unusual in my feelings. My wife has eight wonderful sisters and three brothers, all married, and I've heard them express the same things about their companions. I believe most Latter-day Saint couples feel the same way I do.

At the same time, we all encounter the kinds of problems I listed earlier. I'm no expert on marriage, but I've heard them all and so have you. Maybe you've felt them too. It's hard to keep your eyes on heaven when earth is constantly getting in the way.

Sadly, our earthbound selves can spoil heaven if we allow it—and

Satan is more than happy to help out. Nothing is more important to the adversary than destroying marriages. By contrast, nothing is more important to our Father in Heaven than preserving them, for without sacred marriage His plan is ruined.

> *Doctrine and Covenants 49:16. Wherefore, it is lawful that he [man] should have one wife, and they twain shall be one flesh, and all this that the earth might answer the end of its creation.*

Our Father's plan depends on the man and the woman becoming one flesh. It is the grand "means to the end" of all creation.

So often, though, the "twain remain twain," or having been one they separate into two. For the Church leaders I know, their greatest sorrow is to have to struggle and counsel and pray with couples that *will not keep the commandments* to live together in love and to be one flesh. Even among temple-married Saints, divorce settles like a plague on far too many homes. Ironically, many of these battling spouses continue to see themselves as perfectly worthy, upright members of the Church while they violate the most primal of God's commandments. They are deluding themselves.

I'm familiar with a couple that lived together for a long time. They were married in the temple, and their children are grown and gone. The husband has struggled over the years to make an adequate living—a few poor business choices and some bad luck can do that. But he's basically a good man. The wife, disappointed again and again in his failures, has grown cold. There is no relationship between them. There is no oneness. He doesn't measure up, and she doesn't forgive him for it.

No one can judge the hearts of either of these people, but one glimpse of heaven provides a blinding contrast to this picture. I'm equally familiar with another couple that has lived together for a long time. They were married in the temple, but no children entered their home. They've had their share of financial challenges too, and both wife and husband have had demanding jobs all their lives. Still, to enter their home is to enter heaven. Peace pervades the house. It's like a mist of light you can feel. Their disappointments have drawn them closer together as they keep the commandments to live in love and become one. I see in them the makings of divine beings.

QUALIFY FOR THE SEAL OF THE HOLY SPIRIT OF PROMISE

I believe that what I experience in that home is the presence of the Holy Spirit of promise. Without the sealing of that Spirit, the temple ceremony becomes a dead work. I've often heard people say, "Well, they're divorced, but the sealing hasn't been canceled." I think to myself, "Then I guess there's hope, but I can't see the Holy Spirit binding together people who don't want to be."

For married couples, the greatest goal in life should be to receive the sealing of the Holy Spirit of promise. President Henry B. Eyring has said, "There is *nothing more important* than honoring the marriage and family covenants you have made or will make in the temples of God."[3] The Holy Spirit of promise, according to Elder D. Todd Christofferson, is the Holy Ghost acting in His role that "confirms the validity and efficacy of your covenants and to seal God's promises upon you."[4]

Doctrine and Covenants 132:18. If that covenant is not by me or by my word, which is my law, and is not sealed by the Holy Spirit of promise . . . then it is not valid neither of force when they are out of the world, because they are not joined by me.

How then do we qualify for the sealing of the Holy Spirit of promise?

When a couple is sealed in the temple, they receive one another *by covenant* as husband and wife. The key to the sealing of the Holy Spirit of promise is to be true to that covenant. Elder Carlos H. Amado teaches, "If you remain worthy and true to your covenants, you will have the constant guidance of the Holy Ghost."[5]

Now, what does it mean to be "true to a covenant"?

Like any earthly contract, the eternal marriage covenant has terms that all parties must fulfill, or the covenant becomes null and void. Here is a good description of the terms of this contract:

Doctrine and Covenants 88: 123, 125. See that ye love one another; cease to be covetous; learn to impart one to another as the gospel requires. . . . And above all things, clothe yourselves with the bond of charity, as with a mantle, which is the bond of perfectness and peace.

SEE THAT YE LOVE ONE ANOTHER

Stephen R. Covey is fond of saying, "Love is a verb." It's as much an action as a feeling. If for a moment you don't feel love, do something loving. Remember what heaven looks like—then do something that will make that vision as real possible in the next few minutes.

Doing something loving is particularly important when your loved one has done something you don't perceive as loving: "We can respond to irritation with a smile instead of [a] scowl," said Elder Neal A. Maxwell, "or by giving warm praise instead of icy indifference. By our being understanding instead of abrupt, others, in turn, may decide to hold on a little longer rather than to give way. Love, patience, and meekness can be just as contagious as rudeness and crudeness."[6] What others do to you may be beyond your control, but you can be in perfect control of what you do to others.

You *can* be in control of your response to the commandment of God: "See that ye love one another" (Doctrine and Covenants 88:123). When I was a child, my mother would give me a chore to do and then she would say, "See to it." It meant that I had the responsibility for that chore and that I would be held accountable for it. Similarly, we are going to account someday for living by the commandment to love one another.

When you do something loving, the Holy Ghost draws closer to you. You will feel differently. Your heart will be lighter, your problems easier to bear because of His comforting presence. His influence might very well warm those around you.

Some of us are so conditioned to react in negative ways that it will take practice—conscious, deliberate practice—to "rewire" our spirits to do loving things for others.

An eminent psychologist, Dr. Steven Stosny has made a specialty out of helping people in troubled marriages change their reactions to each other. He helps them connect back to their "core values"—which for me would be my vision of the heavenly home. Deep down, we all want that vision of a loving companionship. So Stosny asks his patients, "In the history of humankind, has anyone ever felt more loveable by hurting someone they love?" They learn to choose compassion instead of irritation. Dr. Stosny also teaches them to practice doing loving things. He asks them to do hundreds of these things over a period of a month so that love becomes a habit.[7]

Brain scientists now know that when we are provoked, the lower, more primitive part of the brain "lights up" and reacts impulsively. Your wife criticizes you, and you snap back. Your husband leaves dirty dishes on the table, and you say something sarcastic. That is the "natural man" reacting. The higher brain, the more thoughtful part, can control the lower part, but it doesn't work so quickly. How many times have you said something curt or hurtful "without thinking," but then, when the upper brain catches up, you're sorry?

The spiritual can learn to dominate the natural, but the spirit is more thoughtful, less inclined to force; more tender, less abrupt. It takes repeated effort to learn to pause, to "bite your tongue," to hold back the cutting comment or the sudden outburst. It takes even more practiced effort to choose to respond with love instead of bitterness.

CEASE TO BE COVETOUS

The marriage covenant requires that we abandon covetousness. The Hebrew word in the tenth commandment is *chamad*, meaning "desire" or "pleasure"; to covet is to want or take pleasure in things outside the bounds of the covenant to live together in love.

Obviously, the most abhorrent coveting is of another man's wife or another woman's husband; this type of covetousness can destroy trust, the marriage relationship, and the covenant.

Covetousness can also take lesser forms that also infringe on the covenant. To live according to your own pleasure is to "covet your own," as the Doctrine and Covenants puts it (19:26). Too many husbands covet their time off the job and bury themselves in TV sports or hobbies that exclude the family. Wives who long for companionship are hurt when their husbands work all week and then squirrel away their weekends for golf or fishing. Some husbands covet and control money on the claim "I earned it—it's mine." Not so. When I took my wife's hand across the altar, we became one. Any money I earn is "ours" not "mine."

My wife's father is one of the best men I've ever known. A superb outdoorsman, he has often taken the family boating on the mountain lakes of Utah. He carefully observes the rules, such as giving proper signals to other boaters and leaving no wake as he approaches the dock. Many boaters race aimlessly around without regard to others and speed into the dock, leaving turbulent wakes that endanger the boats around them. Everyone resents their thoughtless self-centeredness.

Wherever we go in life, we leave a "wake." The husband who doesn't "watch his wake" plows obliviously through the house, leaving messes, bolting down his food, burying himself in television or the computer, obsessing about sports, and "flying off the handle" when things bother him. He expects everyone to meet his schedule and accommodate his priorities.

By contrast, the husband who watches his wake is sensitive to his wife and aware of the needs of others. He and his wife plan their priorities together. He readily sacrifices things he would rather do for things to do together with his wife. Instead of turbulence and hurt feelings, peace follows him. President Henry B. Eyring teaches that it is "imperative to love your wife. It will take faith and humility to put her interests above your own in the struggles of life. . . . That can at times consume all the energy and strength you have."[8]

LEARN TO IMPART TO ONE ANOTHER AS THE GOSPEL REQUIRES

According to the *1828 Webster's Dictionary*, one meaning of the word *impart* is "to show something by word or token."[9] Husbands and wives should *impart* to one another not just material but also emotional support. The gospel requires us to show our love to each other by word or token—by expressing our love fully and often and by sharing remembrances that symbolize that love.

When a husband brings flowers or a wife plans a special night together with her husband, these are tokens that strengthen the covenant. Often the small tokens are the most meaningful.

Another definition of *impart* is "to communicate," as in "to impart information." Husbands and wives must learn to become rich communicators, not only of their feelings, but even of mundane things—what you are planning, where you are going, when you will be home, and what you propose to spend money on! Although wives and husbands can grow close, they don't necessarily become mind readers.

ABOVE ALL THINGS, CLOTHE YOURSELVES WITH THE BOND OF CHARITY, AS WITH A MANTLE, WHICH IS THE BOND OF PERFECTNESS AND PEACE

In Old Testament times, a "mantle" (*addereth*) was a garment made of sheep or goatskin, like the coverings made for Adam and Eve in the Garden of Eden. The mantle was a symbol of the covenant relationship between God and the first man and woman. It was also a symbol of the call to God's service, as Elijah and Elisha wore the *addereth,* or mantle, of their callings.

When a husband and wife are joined together by the holy priesthood, the robe they each wear in that holy place becomes a mantle to symbolize "the bond of charity" that unites them. There can be no oneness in marriage without charity, which is the "pure love of Christ" (Moroni 7:47). The robe of charity is to remind them to be one, as Jesus Christ is one with the Church through His Atonement. Paul counseled, "Husbands, love your wives, even as Christ also loved the church. . . . For this cause shall a man leave his father and mother, and be joined unto his wife, and they two shall be one flesh" (Ephesians 5:25, 31).

The entirely selfless charity Jesus Christ shows to us should be reflected in the charity husbands and wives show each other. The practice of charity is the key to obtaining the seal of the Holy Spirit of promise.

We show charity to each other . . .

Doctrine and Covenants 121:41–42. By persuasion, by long-suffering, by gentleness and meekness, and by love unfeigned; by kindness, and pure knowledge, which shall greatly enlarge the soul without hypocrisy, and without guile.

This is the revealed formula for action of a charitable person, most especially in a marriage. No husband or wife should ever deviate from this formula. If we cannot persuade our beloved partner, we certainly don't use force. Husbands and wives come to a marriage from different families and cultures—those differences often require "long-suffering," patience, or forbearance. Impatience with differences of opinion has no place in marriage.

If they want to attain that celestial dream President Kimball described, marriage partners must always treat each other with gentleness and meekness. Particularly in the intimate relations of marriage, the Spirit will withdraw if there is roughness, selfishness, or the slightest hint of abusive behavior. A fascinating irony of married life is that if your passion is entirely focused on the happiness of your beloved, your own happiness is multiplied. The tenderest experience of oneness is found in marriage, and the greatest rejoicing, if both partners are patient, gentle, and meek with one another.

Feigned love also drives away the Spirit. The New Testament term for feigned or pretended love is *hypokritikos*. Any trace of hypocrisy or guile darkens the relationship. We don't have to be carrying on an adulterous affair to "feign" love for a spouse. A selfish heart is perfectly capable of putting up a false front for the world to see. I have known over the years of a few situations where a husband or a wife appeared to be totally devoted to the gospel and to each other, but behind closed doors, coldness or remoteness or abuse prevailed.

Elder Melvin J. Ballard taught, "We may deceive men but we cannot deceive the Holy Ghost, and our blessings will not be eternal unless they are also sealed by the Holy Spirit of promise. The Holy Ghost is one who reads the thoughts and hearts of men, and gives his sealing approval to the blessings pronounced upon their heads. Then it is binding, efficacious, and of full force."[10]

I believe spouses should show true, open, guileless love for one another. I believe they should treat each other with the utmost charity, which includes forgiveness and long-suffering. At the same time, I do not believe a spouse should ever tolerate physical abuse. In my opinion, a man who hits his wife should be reported to the civil and Church authorities, and professional help should be sought.

President Gordon B. Hinckley has said,

> Our behavior in public must be above reproach. Our behavior in private is even more important. . . . [The priesthood] is not a cloak that we put on and take off at will. . . .
>
> The wife you choose will be your equal. . . . In the marriage companionship there is neither inferiority nor superiority. The woman does not walk ahead of the man; neither does the man walk ahead of the woman. They walk side by side as a son and daughter of God on an eternal journey.
>
> She is not your servant, your chattel, nor anything of the kind.
>
> How tragic and utterly disgusting a phenomenon is wife abuse. Any man in this Church who abuses his wife, who demeans her, who insults her, who exercises unrighteous dominion over her is unworthy to hold the priesthood. Though he may have been ordained, the heavens will withdraw, the Spirit of the Lord will be grieved, and it will be amen to the authority of the priesthood of that man.[11]

President Hinckley doesn't speak only of physical abuse but also of emotional abuse—demeaning, insulting, controlling behavior.

Once we put on the "mantle of perfectness and peace," we cannot take it off. We wear it at all times, without exception. Of course, differences of opinion arise in marriage. The way to handle them is not to be annoyed and defensive but to seek "pure knowledge which greatly enlarges the soul" (Doctrine and Covenants 121:45).

We do this by hearing each other out. You don't have "pure knowledge" of another's viewpoint until you fully understand it; until then, you have only partial knowledge. Too often, husbands or wives dismiss each other's concerns without a hearing. Pure knowledge requires listening with the intention to understand your loved one, not to argue, debate, or belittle. If we do this, the mind and heart become "enlarged"; we see further than we did before and feel more of what the other person is feeling.

If marriage partners will live by the creed of Doctrine and Covenants 121, a great reward comes:

Doctrine and Covenants 121:46. The Holy Ghost shall be thy constant companion.

With this constant presence in our marriage, the sacred covenant is sealed and the dream of eternal love can be realized. Husbands and wives might bring different expectations to the marriage, but they also bring that shared dream. Isn't it worth the effort to keep trying, to become one in the spirit of Christ?

NOTES

1. Neal A. Maxwell, "Notwithstanding My Weakness," *Ensign*, December 1976.

2. Spencer W. Kimball, "Glimpses of Heaven," *Ensign*, December 1971.

3. Henry B. Eyring, "Families Under Covenant," *Ensign*, May 2012, emphasis added, 63.

4. D. Todd Christofferson, "The Power of Covenants," *Ensign*, May 2009, 22

5. Carlos H. Amado, "Some Basic Teachings from the History of Joseph Smith," *Ensign*, May 2002.

6. Neal A. Maxwell, "The Tugs and Pulls of the World," *Ensign*, November 2000.

7. See Dr. Steven Stosny, as quoted in Stephen R. Covey, *The 3rd Alternative* (New York: Simon & Schuster, 2011), 164–165.

8. Eyring, "Families Under Covenant," 64

9. "Impart," *Webster's Dictionary*, 1828. http://1828.mshaffer.com/d/search/word,impart.

10. Melvin J. Ballard, quoted by Harold B. Lee, Conference Report, October 1970, 111. Cited in Eyring, "Families Under Covenant," 63–64.

11. Gordon B. Hinckley, "Personal Worthiness to Exercise the Priesthood," *Ensign*, May 2002.

SEVEN

SELF-WORTH

I feel like I don't measure up. I feel like I'm lacking as a parent and inadequate as a spouse. I don't feel equal to the challenges of my job or my church calling. I know I'm not supposed to feel this way, but I'm depressed anyway. What can I do?

Some years ago, a major mental health study revealed that Utah was the most depressed state in America, with Idaho, another state with a large Mormon population, not far behind. Also, Idaho and Utah ranked sixth and seventh respectively in the rate of suicide.[1] Utah has an extremely high rate of anti-depressant use.[2]

While people pointed out several problems with the study, and while many cultural and hereditary factors might be involved, the most LDS people in the most LDS place in the world did seem to be disproportionately depressed. This fact struck many people as a huge paradox, given the popular image of happy Mormons in well-adjusted families.

At the same time, most studies show that good mental health, strong marriages, and family stability are also typical of active LDS people. One study ranks Utah highest in the United States for life-satisfaction.

So why the paradox? It could be that educated Mormons are more likely to seek medical help for emotional problems, so they report more problems. It could be that Mormons "self-medicate" with drugs and alcohol less than other people do.

Another explanation might come from the tendency people have to compare themselves with others. For example, New York ranks low on the life-satisfaction scale and has the lowest suicide rate in the US, while Utah scores high on both scales. One scientist theorizes, "Discontented people in a happy place may feel particularly harshly treated by life. Those dark contrasts may in turn increase the risks of suicide." Another scientist agrees: "People judge their well-being in comparison to others around them."[3]

Whatever the reason, there's no denying the problem. Many Mormons, at least in the United States, are seeking help for feelings of inadequacy and depression, and many more suffer from these feelings but don't seek help. Feelings of loneliness, hopelessness, and even despair afflict many. President Thomas S. Monson does not dismiss the problem: "We live in a complex world with daily challenges. There is a tendency to feel detached—even isolated—from the Giver of every good gift. We worry that we walk alone."[4]

At the outset, it's crucial to point out that emotional problems like chronic depression often have a physical cause that can be diagnosed. If you feel depressed for a long time, if you have persistent feelings of inadequacy that affect your performance on the job or your ability to relate to your family and friends, you should seek professional help without hesitation and without embarrassment.

REMEMBER YOUR WORTH IS GREAT IN THE SIGHT OF GOD

In the Doctrine and Covenants, the Lord does anticipate the serious emotional pressures of our time and provides guidance to those who feel they are lacking in some way (and that probably includes most of us).

Doctrine and Covenants 18:10–11. Remember the worth of souls is great in the sight of God; for, behold, the Lord your Redeemer suffered death in the flesh; wherefore he suffered the pain of all men, that all men might repent and come unto him.

This is the Lord's assurance to you if you have feelings of worthlessness. The world we live in is driven by empty comparisons between people. Looks, status, possessions, talents, and abilities—we judge each other on these things almost by reflex. Animals can instantly determine "the pecking order" in any herd; for people, scientists tell us that the primitive part of the brain is involved in these quick, superficial judgments. By such a standard, everybody gets assigned a number on a "worth scale."

I once read a satirical piece of science fiction about a world where people are rated electronically on all of their qualities. In that future world, you carry a screen around your neck that tells everyone how you rate wherever you go: You might enter a room full of people and be immediately labeled the fifth-ugliest person there, but you have the highest credit rating. Or you might be the most boring conversationalist in the room, but you're the third best dancer.

The Lord has an entirely different gauge for the worth of souls—it is infinite. It is immeasurable. The measure of our worth to Him is in the death He suffered for us, in the infinite atonement that He made for us.

When you feel worthless, consider for just a moment the price that He paid for you; you will then have some sense of your true value.

In 1958, a British art collector, Sir Francis Cook, sold some paintings through an auction house in London. One of the paintings, a depiction of the resurrected Christ, went for £45. Eventually, the painting came into the hands of true experts, who carefully cleaned away centuries of accumulated wax and dirt and found a masterpiece: an original work by Leonardo Da Vinci. In 2011, the painting was sold again—this time for £120 million.[5]

Like this painting, beneath the weathered surfaces of our personalities, we are of transcendent worth to our Father. President Thomas S. Monson says, "The Savior provided assurance of this truth when He taught that even a sparrow shall not fall to the ground unnoticed by our Father. He then concluded the beautiful thought by saying, 'Fear ye not therefore, ye are of more value than many sparrows.'"[6]

REMEMBER THAT YOU ARE LITERALLY A CHILD OF GOD

In vision, the Prophet Joseph Smith learned our true identity, a revelation that wipes away any uncertainty we might feel about our unique worth:

Doctrine and Covenants 76:23–24. We saw him, even on the right hand of God; and we heard the voice bearing record that he is the Only Begotten of the Father—that by him, and through him, and of him, the worlds are and were created, and the inhabitants thereof are begotten sons and daughters unto God.

We are *literally* the children of God.

Long ago, the Christian world lost this understanding. The many teachings of the Bible that we are children of God had come to be read metaphorically. It could not be literally true. At best we were on the same level as frogs and worms—"creatures" that might through the unbelievable grace of a holy being be called his "children" in some legalistic, adoptive sense.

The loss of the revealed truth about our true identity has led to a culture of ranking, of comparison, of competition, in which the worth of a human being is measured in economic terms. In the corporate world, people are no longer people—they're "human resources." On the balance sheet, they are liabilities.

Over centuries, the shame and inadequacy of mortal life blinded the world to this sparkling truth: *we are not adopted.* We are not strange creatures brought condescendingly in from the cold. We are of the same family as God, his literal offspring, spiritually begotten sons and daughters of God. When we ponder this realization, we only begin to glimpse the full measure of our worth to Him.

If you are a parent, you have some idea what it means to love a child immeasurably, without limits. When I look at my children and grandchildren, with their stunningly different personalities, gifts, and temperaments, I don't compare them to each other. They do not compete for my love. There's no way any of them could win such a contest—nor is it possible to lose—because there *is* no contest. All the love I have to give belongs to each of them equally.

Our Father in Heaven feels that kind of love, only in a transcendent way, far beyond our comprehension or capacity to love. As a Latter-day Saint, when you sing or say "I Am a Child of God," you mean a real, true, begotten child, a beloved, impossibly valued, irreplaceable member of His family.

BELIEVE IN YOUR INFINITE WORTH

Of course, it's one thing to know the doctrine—and another thing to *feel* that divine love and affirmation of your worth. And it's emotionally difficult to live in a culture that squeezes our self-confidence from us in a thousand ways. "I may be loved at home," you say, "but it's a different world when I leave the house."

> *Doctrine and Covenants 6:34. Fear not, little flock; do good; let earth and hell combine against you, for if ye are built upon my rock, they cannot prevail.*

We know who we are. We know the worth of our souls. Still, we may feel fear and a sense of our inadequacy.

But then the Lord gives us this tender assurance by way of a commandment: *Fear not.* We are members of His "little flock," His family, whom He has sworn to protect against all the combined powers of "earth and hell." Whether we're in the family home or not, His eye is upon us, and He does not forget us. He watches as we make mistakes and feel shame. He feels with us when we stumble and fall. He sympathizes when we fall short of our own cherished goals. He knows how we feel when we're in the company of people who for one reason or another seem "better" than we are. He chastises and corrects and comforts us. But in all of this, as long as we keep trying to keep His commandments, He never turns away—any more than you would turn away from your own children in their tender and vulnerable years.

President Dieter F. Uchtdorf observes:

God is fully aware that you and I are not perfect. Let me add: God is also fully aware that the people you think are perfect are not.

And yet we spend so much time and energy comparing ourselves to others—usually comparing our weaknesses to their strengths. This drives us to create expectations for ourselves that are impossible to meet. As a result, we never celebrate our good efforts because they seem to be less than what someone else does. . . .

God wants to help us to eventually turn all of our weaknesses into strengths, but He knows that this is a long-term goal. He wants us to become perfect, and if we stay on the path of discipleship, one day we will. It's OK that you're not quite there yet. Keep working on it, but *stop punishing yourself.*[7]

At times, each of my children has come to me with doubts about themselves. When they were first growing up, I worried about this. Eventually, I came to expect it. And I realized that every caring parent meets this challenge. Of course, I offered what comfort I could, but mostly I was impressed with the resilience, the faith, and the courage of my own children as they exerted their own efforts to overcome their doubts about themselves. They are building their lives "upon the rock" of Christ.

At the same time, as they talked about their feelings of fear, inadequacy, and uncertainty, I wished deep down that they could see themselves as I saw them. I wished I could express to them somehow what they meant to me and how much I would have preferred to take their pains away from them and bear them myself.

At an even deeper level, though, I began to understand that their self-doubt had a purpose. If they never felt the weight of a challenge, how could they grow? If they didn't taste the fear of failure, how would they ever appreciate success? My heartfelt esteem for each of them led me to welcome their challenges as essential to their eventual triumph over this mortal world.

What was my role? To ensure them that I believed in their infinite worth, that their spiritual and personal growth was the most important thing in the world to me. And to help them as much as I could without "doing it for them." Sometimes they didn't succeed at what they so much wanted to do. But I always sensed that the losses and failures would help their hearts grow tender, which God wants for us above all.

Still, the "combined powers of earth and hell" are strong and, if we allow it, can make our hearts grow bitter or hopeless.

Doctrine and Covenants 29:39. And it must needs be that the devil should tempt the children of men, or they could not be agents unto themselves; for if they never should have bitter they could not know the sweet.

Perhaps the bitterest feeling a human being can experience is a sense of personal worthlessness. I have seen it in all kinds of people, from prisoners to presidents of companies. It's a particular danger to young people who are still developing their own identities.

Many of us are just too hard on ourselves. Elder Neal A. Maxwell says, "Some of us who would not chastise a neighbor for his frailties have a field day with our own. Some of us stand before no more harsh a judge than ourselves. . . . Fortunately, the Lord loves us more than we love ourselves."[8]

Elder Russell M. Nelson asks, "Who has not encountered feelings of low self-esteem because of physique or appearance? Many people wish their bodies could be more to their liking. Some with naturally straight hair want it curly. Others with curly hair want it straight."[9] Almost everyone is trying either to lose weight or to gain it. We all know full well that the glamorous pictures of perfect physiques in the media are "Photoshop phony," but we still compare ourselves against a nonexistent fantasy.

Later in my life, I've come to appreciate the beauty of people, which I hadn't noticed before. Now I'm quite overwhelmed by it. The tall, the thin, the stocky, the strong, the slim, the dark, the blonde—I think it's the uniqueness of each one that's so refreshing to me. I look at my grandchildren: a plump little girl with doll-like eyes; a thin, dark boy, quick as a cat, with a low purring voice; a girl with dimples that flash on and off. They are ordinary children, I suppose, yet each one is exquisite in my eyes. And I wonder more and more as they get older why they don't see themselves as I do.

Instead, our culture is obsessed with physical perfection. I believe our Father in Heaven sees beauty in the variety He has created, not in some impossible ideal of beauty electronically created. What would it mean to our self-image if we could see ourselves as He sees us and delight in that vision of ourselves?

BUILD YOUR SELF-WORTH ON THE ROCK OF CHRIST

Status in the world, and even in the Church, can be another source of bitter comparisons. It's in the nature of the mortal world that some people succeed where others fail. Some are promoted, some get the award, some get all the credit, some win the game—and others lose. All the happy talk about "win-win" sounds hollow when you realize that only one person crosses the finish line first.

At those times, we need to remember the words of Elder Jeffrey R. Holland:

> There are going to be times in our lives when someone else gets an unexpected blessing or receives some special recognition. May I plead with us not to be hurt and certainly not to feel envious when good fortune comes to another person? We are not diminished when someone else is added upon. We are not in a race against each other to see who is the wealthiest or the most talented or the most beautiful or even the most blessed.[10]

Furthermore, those who base their self-worth on status or achievement are not building their lives "on the rock" of Christ. Of course, achievements honestly attained are basic to self-respect. As a wise psychologist observes, "Self-esteem usually results from people's efforts to bolster their images of themselves through accomplishments and achievements. And there's nothing wrong with that, to a point. But when things don't go as planned (and the stress of today's economy has derailed many people's career and life goals), self-esteem takes a hit from which it can be difficult to recover."[11]

The doctrinal admonitions to be diligent and strive for excellence can get distorted in the minds of many LDS people. Some start to expect too much of themselves, and when they don't "measure up" to their own ambitious standards, it can take a serious emotional toll. LDS psychologist Dr. Daniel K. Judd suspects that "perfectionism" might partially explain why so many American Latter-day Saints in particular suffer depression. It is possible to take even good things to excess, to become too driven by the need to excel. "It's not our theology that's at fault," Brother Judd says. "It's our culture, at times. The doctrine isn't 'Come unto me, all ye heavy laden, and I'll give you more to do.'"[12]

Our self-worth must be founded in the rock of Christ, on who we are and what we mean to Him. If we try to build an identity on a foundation of physical beauty or wealth or status or position or the successes of our kids or even a record of personal achievement, we risk bitter disillusionment.

LET VIRTUE GARNISH THY THOUGHTS UNCEASINGLY

Of course, the bitterest blows to self-worth come from sin. I've seen people who can't trust themselves; therefore, no one else, including God, can trust them. Overwhelmed by addictions to drugs or pornography or alcohol, they have lost all self-confidence. Professional help is essential to them. But to one degree or another, we're all susceptible to confidence-destroying sin, and we all need this basic prescription provided by the Doctrine and Covenants:

> *Doctrine and Covenants 121:45. Let virtue garnish thy thoughts unceasingly; then shall thy confidence wax strong in the presence of God.*

For those who lack confidence in themselves, this is the revealed remedy. Those who "garnish" their thinking with virtue avoid vice in their lives. They simply don't indulge vicious music, language, and behavior.

Virtue is the secret to self-esteem. Virtue has been defined in many ways since ancient times. One narrow definition of virtue is sexual morality, but the word encompasses more than that. To the Romans, *virtus* meant "manly courage" in the face of challenges, even in defeat. To certain ancient philosophers, virtue was "moderation in all things."

In the scriptures, however, virtue is moral excellence. In the New Testament Greek, *arête* refers to "reaching your highest human potential." It's the quest for excellence in every important aspect of life. As Paul wrote, a virtuous person "seeks after" the lovely things, the things of good report that are praiseworthy (Philippians 4:8).

A virtuous person listens to the best music, not the worst; strives to enhance his health, not to harm it with drugs and alcohol; dresses tastefully, not immodestly; reads the "best books," not cheap, unchallenging books; uses the Internet for learning, not for crawling into a pit of sleaze and filth.

A "garnish" is a beautiful ornament. When we garnish our thoughts with virtue, we intentionally focus on the beautiful, on the sacred, and on the excellent rather than on the ugly, profane, and cheap things of life. We are commanded to "let virtue garnish our thoughts unceasingly"—as we train our minds in this way, our confidence "waxes," or grows, stronger every moment. We can face our Father in Heaven with increasing self-assurance.

Sometimes, however, low self-esteem is chronic. It's rooted in spiritual depths only the Lord can reach; and like so many other debilitating problems due to mortality, it persists even when we've done all we can to overcome it.

KNOW THAT YOUR FATHER IS WATCHING OVER YOU MOST CAREFULLY

I have a friend who insists that he has a testimony of the gospel, who serves in the Church, who has been a missionary, who has a nice family—and yet who doesn't believe in himself. He sees his life as a long train of setbacks that are his own fault. "I don't blame anyone else for my failures. I don't blame the Lord, my parents, my wife, or anyone. They have all been good to me. I blame myself. I feel weak and fearful and useless." The psychological weight on his shoulders is visible.

He has seen a doctor about these feelings, and medical help has made his life easier to bear. But there's a deep fear in him that perhaps medicines can't reach.

People have encouraged him to "snap out of it," to "buck up," to count his blessings and to think positively. He says he finds some relief in concentrating on his work and being with his family. The gospel comforts him. But underneath it all, the suffering never goes away.

I don't pretend to know how to help him. But I do know that there is One who has an eye on him, who loves him, and who, I believe, will see him through this mortal trial that seems so hard for him.

President Thomas S. Monson was swimming at the gym one day when, by his account,

> Silently, but ever so clearly, there came to my mind the thought: 'Here you swim almost effortlessly, while your friend Stan languishes in his hospital bed, unable to move.' I felt the prompting: 'Get to the hospital and give him a blessing.
>
> I ceased my swimming, dressed, and hurried to Stan's room at the hospital. His bed was empty. A nurse said he was in his wheelchair at the swimming pool, preparing for therapy. I hurried to the area, and

there was Stan, all alone, at the edge of the deeper portion of the pool. We greeted one another and returned to his room, where a priesthood blessing was provided.

Stan slowly recovered, and in later years spoke of "the dark thoughts of depression which engulfed him that afternoon as he sat in his wheelchair at the edge of the pool, sentenced, it seemed, to a life of despair. He tells how he pondered the alternative. It would be so easy to propel the hated wheelchair into the silent water of the deep pool. Life would then be over. But at that precise moment he saw me, his friend. That day Stan learned literally that we do not walk alone."[13]

Father in Heaven had His eye fixed on the paralyzed man who sat at the edge of despair. When you feel truly beaten, He is watching over you most carefully. At those times, if you have been faithful, it might be best to look around for His hand at work. As the Doctrine and Covenants teaches, the combined powers of earth and hell cannot prevail over that Hand.

"Wherever you are," says President Uchtdorf, "whatever your circumstances may be, you are not forgotten. No matter how dark your days may seem, no matter how insignificant you may feel, no matter how overshadowed you think you may be, your Heavenly Father has not forgotten you. In fact, He loves you with an infinite love."[14]

NOTES

1. "Ranking America's Mental Health: An Analysis of Depression Across the States," *Mental Health America*, November 2007. http://www.mentalhealthamerica.net/go/state-ranking.

2. Tad Walch, "Why High Anti-Depressant Use in Utah?" *Deseret News*, July 22, 2006.

3. "Happy Places Have Highest Suicide Rates, New Research Finds," *Science Daily*, April 21, 2011. http://www.sciencedaily.com/releases/2011/04/110421082641.htm.

4. Thomas S. Monson, "The Spirit Giveth Life," *Ensign*, May 1985.

5. Nick Pisa, "The Painting Once Sold for £45," *MailOnline*, July 4, 2011.

6. Monson, "The Spirit Giveth Life."

7. Dieter F. Uchtdorf, "Forget Me Not," *Ensign*, November 2011, emphasis added.

8. Neal A. Maxwell, "Notwithstanding My Weakness," *Ensign*, November 1976.

9. Russell M. Nelson, "You Are a Child of God," *New Era*, July 2008.

10. Jeffrey R. Holland, "The Laborers in the Vineyard," *Ensign*, May 2012.

11. Leslie Becker-Phelps, "Self Acceptance: More Substance than Self Esteem," *Psychology Today*, November 10, 2010.

12. Walch, "Why Anti-Depressant Use."

13. Monson, "The Spirit Giveth Life."

14. Uchtdorf, "Forget Me Not."

EIGHT

BALANCE

I have so much to do, and with work, church, and family, I never feel like I can get it all done. I'm always behind, and it gets more and more frustrating. How can I balance all the demands on my life?

The Doctrine and Covenants provides two basic principles for achieving balance in life. First, we need to lead diligent lives:

Doctrine and Covenants 58:27. Verily I say, men should be anxiously engaged in a good cause, and do many things of their own free will, and bring to pass much righteousness.

Second, we simply must not to overdo it.

Doctrine and Covenants 10:4. Do not run faster or labor more than you have strength and means provided to enable you. . . but be diligent unto the end.

BE ANXIOUSLY ENGAGED IN A GOOD CAUSE

I've worried over the years about the words "anxiously engaged." Are we supposed to be leading anxiety-inducing lives? Then I went to the *1828 Webster's Dictionary* to find out what the word *anxious* would have meant to Joseph Smith when he recorded this revelation. *"Anxious: Greatly concerned or solicitous, respecting something future or unknown."*

Webster didn't say we should be nervous, wringing our hands and making ourselves sick over the pressures of life. He did say we should be "greatly concerned" about certain future possibilities, and that makes sense in light of the revelations. In that sense, we *should* be "anxious" about some things.

But it turns out there aren't as many of those things as we think. And although we should be anxious about those few things, we should not try to spend more energy or resources on them than we have to give.

DO NOT RUN FASTER OR LABOR MORE THAN YOU HAVE STRENGTH AND MEANS

"Do not run faster or labor more than you have strength and means provided" (see Doctrine and Covenants 10:4). The many who violate this commandment end up suffering from what doctors call "exhaustion syndrome." Most of us call it "burnout." It's actually not a symptom of living the gospel—it's a symptom of trying to live as the rest of the world lives. Yet, for Latter-day Saints, this commandment is a "thou shalt not!"

Dr. Edward Hallowell, a prominent psychologist, sees more and more anxiety in his practice:

> For the past 25 years, I've been treating a neurological condition called Attention Deficit Disorder [ADD]. The key symptoms of ADD—distractibility, impulsivity, restlessness, disorganization, trouble planning, procrastination—have come to be key attributes of most people working and living in today's world. Well, interestingly enough, more and more people have been coming to me saying they thought they had ADD, but they didn't. They had what I call a severe case of modern life.[1]

Many Latter-day Saints, particularly Americans, suffer from a "severe case of modern life." We overload ourselves with activity to the point that we can no longer pay focused attention on anything. We schedule our families to the minute. Our to-do lists are endless.

President Dieter F. Uchtdorf has said:

> Let's be honest; it's rather easy to be busy. We all can think up a list of tasks that will overwhelm our schedules. Some might even think that their self-worth depends on the length of their to-do list. They flood

the open spaces in their time with lists of meetings and minutia—even during times of stress and fatigue. Because they unnecessarily complicate their lives, they often feel increased frustration, diminished joy, and too little sense of meaning in their lives.[2]

The larger Americanized culture we live in puts a premium on achievement, and achievement is usually measured in terms of money and status. Henry David Thoreau noticed this long ago: "This world is a place of business. What an infinite bustle! I am awaked almost every night by the panting of the locomotive. It interrupts my dreams. There is no sabbath. It would be glorious to see mankind at leisure for once. It is nothing but work, work, work."[3] Since Thoreau and the invention of email and the smartphone, work has become life twenty-four hours a day, seven days a week.

Mormons are typically "busy as a beehive"; in fact, the beehive is one of the prominent symbols of the Latter-day Saints. But a beehive is not a chaotic place where workers exhaust themselves. It's actually an orderly community where every bee not only has a role to play and valuable work to do but also plenty of time for rest. (I like the fact that bees get to sleep several months of the year!)

In the end, we might not be as wise as the bees are. I have worked in business offices most of my adult life, and I've seen a lot of people being busy about things that don't really matter much in the end (the bees do not waste time). It's important to our self-image to at least appear to be busy, as President Uchtdorf says. Our culture assumes that if we are not breaking our necks to stockpile money and goods or to gain position or to impress others, we are somehow less worthwhile as human beings.

Elder Joseph B. Wirthlin warned us against feeling that "the busier we are, the more important we are—as though our busyness defines our worth."[4]

Of course we want to contribute, to make a difference, to do something valuable. But if for one reason or another we're not clear on what is truly valuable, what is truly worth doing, we tend to fill our lives with activity under the misapprehension that to be busy is to be good.

The cultural expectation that you have to be "crazy busy" at work to be worth anything spills over into the Church as well. Elder M. Russell Ballard observes, "Occasionally we find some who become so energetic in their Church service that their lives become unbalanced. . . . They complicate their service with needless frills and embellishments that occupy too much time, cost too much money, and sap too much energy. . . . The instruction to magnify our callings is not a command to embellish and complicate them."[5]

Recently I attended a ward council meeting. Another council member proposed that we have a meeting to coordinate some of our priorities as a ward. Several heads nodded around the room, until someone suggested that we were already *in* such a meeting.

A friend of mine spent several days going to stores all over the region looking for a certain kind of potato peeler. She was preparing her Relief Society lesson and wanted to present each of the sisters one of these peelers. Then she spent another day carefully decorating the peelers with ribbons and attaching a "special note" to each one.

I admire this woman tremendously, but I wonder if her time would have been better invested studying and pondering the words of the prophets that she was to teach that Sunday.

Maybe the most spiritually rich priesthood meeting I ever attended was in a small branch in Norway, high above the Arctic Circle. There were eight elders in a room that was a bit too cold, while a man who had been a church member for a few months taught the lesson from his priesthood study guide. There were no ribbons, no PowerPoint projections, no showy videos—but the Spirit warmed that cold room as this humble brother read from the words of the prophets and gave his simple testimony of the truth.

The Lord has never commanded us to complicate our lives unnecessarily. Quite the opposite: He expects us to simplify our lives. Elder Richard G. Scott says, "Make sure that the essential needs are met, but do not go overboard in creating so many good things to do that the essential ones are not accomplished. . . . Remember, don't magnify the work to be done—simplify it."[6] The Norwegian brother who taught us that cold Sunday morning focused totally on the essential—and we were richer for it.

In the last few years, the heavy cultural emphasis on being "crazy busy" has been made infinitely worse by the technology revolution that throws people's lives totally out of balance. "You can't stop doing it," one observer says, referring to the Internet, to Facebook, Google,

Twitter, and so forth. Young people exchange tens of thousands of texts a month. Many of us are lured into what amounts to a virtual addiction to the virtual world, staring at our iPads, phones, or laptops for hours a day.

"A new need for endless nuggets of electronic information" has overridden the lives of many. "We search for information we don't even care about." One woman confessed, "My boyfriend has threatened to break up with me if I keep whipping out my iPhone to look up random facts about celebrities when we're out to dinner."[7]

Because our "strength and means" are limited, we can only do so much. Add endless online disruptions to the self-aggrandizing cultural requirement to be crazy busy, and we can find ourselves "fatally distracted."

So what is the "good cause" in which we should be anxiously engaged? And how do we remain diligent without burning ourselves out?

Sister Belle S. Spafford, former president of the Relief Society, said years ago: "The average woman today, I believe, would do well to appraise her interests, evaluate the activities in which she is engaged, and then take steps to simplify her life, putting things of first importance first, placing emphasis where the rewards will be greatest and most enduring, and ridding herself of the less rewarding activities."[8]

In a world that demands we do more and more, the Lord is actually calling us to do less—to focus more of our time and talents and energy on "that which is of the greatest worth" and rid ourselves of those things which are of least worth. We need to "evaluate our activities and take steps to simplify" around those things that are of first importance. Those are the things, in Sister Spafford's terms, "where the rewards will be greatest and most enduring."

We are to be anxiously engaged in "a good cause." A good cause might be somewhat different for each person, but surely it would be a cause that brings great and enduring rewards. One who focuses his best energies on playing the piano will reap a fruitful, lasting harvest of music that those who don't "anxiously engage" will never know. The same is true of all people who invest their time and talents "anxiously" in that which pays off richly in the end. Still, Elder Dallin H. Oaks draws a distinction among causes that are merely good, those that are better, and those that are "best":

> As we consider various choices, we should remember that it is not enough that something is good. Other choices are better, and still others are best. Even though a particular choice is more costly, its far greater value may make it the best choice of all.[9]

The "best of choices" is, undoubtedly, to seek eternal life. Of all the "good causes" we could be engaged in, nothing else compares to it.

Doctrine and Covenants 14:7. If you keep my commandments and endure to the end you shall have eternal life, which gift is the greatest of all the gifts of God.

Clearly, we should do less of what distracts us from this goal, no matter how valuable or praiseworthy it might be. As nothing is more enduring or rewarding than the greatest of all gifts of God, it makes little sense to put eternal life on the back burner of our lives while we obsess about sports or shopping or work or any other earthbound fixation.

Scientists tell us that the human brain is capable of focusing on only one thing at a time. Professor Earl Miller, an MIT neuroscientist, says that trying to concentrate on two things at a time, "such as writing an email and talking on the phone," overloads the brain's processing capacity. "People can't do it very well, and when they say they can, they're deluding themselves."[10] That's why you don't want to be in a car with a driver talking on a mobile phone and eating a hamburger at the same time.

SANCTIFY YOURSELVES THAT YOUR MINDS BECOME SINGLE TO GOD

If it's true that our mental focus is so narrow, the question arises: what should we focus *on*?

In the language of scripture, the mind should become "single to God."

Doctrine and Covenants 88:68. Sanctify yourselves that your minds become single to God, and the days will come that you shall see him; for he will unveil his face unto you.

What would you trade for that day when God Himself unveils His face to you and takes you in His arms as His child? Would you agree that of all the good things in this universe that you could focus your mind and heart on, this would be the best?

If everything we do is measured against this standard, we will do a lot less of the other things that have to do with our status or our wealth or our entertainment. If our minds are "single," that is, focused on God, then our actions become consecrated.

Doctrine and Covenants 88:119. Organize yourselves; prepare every needful thing.

Periodically, we should do what Belle Spafford recommends and "evaluate our activities" and "take steps to simplify life, putting things of first importance first." Literally, this means quietly examining where we are now putting our best energies and then facing reality—are we investing in eternal life or squandering our time on less important things? Are we unnecessarily filling up our days with activity, or are we simplifying our days so that the truly essential things come first? What are the "needful things" around which we should organize ourselves?

President Uchtdorf says, "There is a beauty and clarity that comes from simplicity that we sometimes do not appreciate in our thirst for intricate solutions."[11]

If we are honest with ourselves, we will soon realize that much of what we spend our time on is not really essential and that the simpler, more enduring things are getting little attention. Double or triple vision blurs an eye that should be single to God. The result is this anguished and pervasive sense of overwhelm in our culture; we look in the mirror and see what T. S. Eliot called "strained time-ridden faces distracted from distraction by distraction."[12]

At the same time, we will begin to glimpse the few things that really matter, those essentials that bring eternal life—what God calls "the needful things"—and we can reset our lives around them.

ORGANIZE YOURSELVES;
PREPARE EVERY NEEDFUL THING

I have a good and wise friend who finds solitary time on a Sabbath day to evaluate and plan what he can do during the coming week that will help him keep his "mind single to God." There are a couple of simple things—personal prayer, scripture study—that he plans into his week. He looks at these things not as duties but as rewards. He tries not to let anything interfere with his personal time with his Heavenly Father.

Then he thinks through the few important roles he plays in his life—husband, father, priesthood holder, employee. What one or two "needful things" should he do in each role? He likes to have personal time with each of his children. He plans time with his wife. He evaluates how he is doing in his priesthood calling and what simple thing he could do that week to advance that work. Also, he thinks through his job and what he could do that would make the most difference that would contribute most to his employer.

This consecrated weekly planning time enables my friend to keep himself narrowly focused on those few things that really matter. In keeping with the revealed principle, he organizes his life around those things. He simply doesn't live like so many of the rest of us. Instead of saying "yes" to a thousand little demands, he says "no" to virtually everything that isn't on his list because it's just not as important as the "needful things."

He applies the principle of self-organization around needful things in every aspect of his life. Even at work, where most of us simply do what we're told, he has followed an unusual path. Long ago, he began to reason with his boss about the "needful things"—those things he should *really* do that would be of most worth to the company. Gradually, he began saying "no" to activities that in his estimation didn't really add much value—but not without carefully thinking them through with his employer. Over the years, he has redesigned his job so that he works on one or two key priorities at a time. Instead of doing *more*, he does *less*—but what he does do is of great value to the firm. It took a while, but he—no one else—is now pretty much in control of what he does.

At home, he is fully at home. He likes to cook alongside his wife.

He's not much of an athlete, but his children are delighted when he runs with them or plays football with them, and he gets to enjoy them. He does a good deal of quiet reading, which he loves. As a teacher in church, he prepares his lesson by reading over the material and pondering it, praying for insight—which usually comes.

My friend leads a simple and joyful life, but not a hurried life. Of course, there are times when, like everyone else, he faces emergencies and life falls completely out of balance. But for the most part, he has organized himself around the needful things, as the Lord commands—and he stays in balance.

The harvest of patient planning has been plentiful in his life. His wife and children know they are loved. His employer can count on him to give his best. The Lord can count on him. Elder Richard L. Evans once said, "There seems to be little evidence that the Creator of the universe was ever in a hurry. Everywhere, on this bounteous and beautiful earth . . . there is evidence of patient purpose and planning and working and waiting."[13]

When he was asked about the pervasive problem of balancing work and church and family, Elder Neal A. Maxwell gave this penetrating advice:

> It is important to distinguish between the basic principles involved in the gospel of work and the frantic, heedless busyness that some engage in, which crowds out contemplation and leaves no room for renewal. The thoughtful working person will provide some intervals between his tasks, like the green belts of grass, trees, and water that we often need in our living environment to interrupt the asphalt. Each of us will be more effective if we plan some time for contemplation and renewal, and if we do not feel driven by our work so much as drawn to it.[14]

Taken together, these simple principles from the Doctrine and Covenants are the answer to the problem of life balance (see Doctrine and Covenants 58:27; 10:4; 88:68, 119):

"Be anxiously engaged in a good cause."

"Do not run faster or labor more than you have strength and means."

"Sanctify yourselves, that your minds become single to God."

"Organize yourselves; prepare every needful thing."

NOTES

1. *The 5 Choices to Extraordinary Productivity* (Salt Lake City: Franklin-Covey), 115; *Brain Attack!* DVD (Salt Lake City: FranklinCovey, 2011).

2. Dieter F. Uchtdorf, "Of Things That Matter Most," *Ensign*, November 2010.

3. Henry David Thoreau, "Life Without Principle," http://thoreau.eserver.org/lifewout.html.

4. Joseph B. Wirthlin, "Follow Me," *Ensign*, May 2002.

5. M. Russell Ballard, "O Be Wise," *Ensign*, October 2006.

6. Richard G. Scott, "The Doctrinal Foundation of the Auxiliaries," *Ensign*, August 2005.

7. Emily Yoffe, "Seeking," *Slate*, August 12, 2009. http://www.slate.com/articles/health_and_science/science/2009/08/seeking.html.

8. Belle S. Spafford, cited in *Daughters in My Kingdom*, 2012, http://www.lds.org/relief-society/daughters-in-my-kingdom/manual/preface-something-extraordinary?lang=eng.

9. Dallin H. Oaks, "Good, Better, Best," *Ensign*, November 2007.

10. John Naish, "Is Multitasking Bad for Your Brain?" *MirrorOnline*, August 11, 2009. http://www.dailymail.co.uk/health/article-1205669/Is-multitasking-bad-brain-Experts-reveal-hidden-perils-juggling-jobs.html.

11. Uchtdorf, "Of Things That Matter Most."

12. T.S. Eliot, "Burnt Norton," Athenaeum Library of Philosophy. http://evans-experientialism.freewebspace.com/eliot_burnt_norton.htm

13. Cited in John C. Thomas, "Don't Be in a Hurry," *BYU Speeches*, web.byui.edu/devotionalsandspeeches.

14. Neal A. Maxwell, "I Have a Question," *Ensign*, August 1976.

NINE

WOMEN

I wonder deep down if as a woman I really count. I know the gospel teachings about honorable womanhood and motherhood, but my real life is weighed down with doubts about myself, fears about my family and the future, and, to be honest, feelings of guilt and inferiority.

In President Joseph F. Smith's vision of the redemption of the dead, Section 138 of the Doctrine and Covenants, he describes the radiant beings gathered to greet the resurrected Savior:

> *Doctrine and Covenants 138:38–39. Among the great and mighty ones who were assembled in this vast congregation of the righteous were . . . our glorious Mother Eve, with many of her faithful daughters who had lived through the ages and worshiped the true and living God.*

Mother Eve and her faithful daughters are "great and mighty ones" destined to be clothed with sacred authority. President Joseph Fielding Smith taught, "It is within the privilege of the sisters of this Church to receive exaltation in the kingdom of God and receive authority and power as queens and priestesses."[1]

I've seen my own wife and daughters and daughters-in-law, robed in white, embracing together in the celestial room of the temple. Warmed by love and light, I felt I was looking into heaven and perhaps a little of what our Father must feel about his daughters.

That image of womanhood could not contrast more sharply with the popular image of women.

"Popular culture today often makes women look silly, inconsequential, mindless, and powerless," says Elder M. Russell Ballard. "It objectifies them and disrespects them and then suggests that they are able to leave their mark on mankind only by seduction—easily the most pervasively dangerous message the adversary sends to women about themselves."[2]

Because this dysfunctional image saturates our culture, it's no wonder many women and girls feel deep conflicts about themselves. Many struggle with self-esteem because they feel they don't measure up to the popular image. As Elder Richard G. Scott says, "Many women do not realize their intrinsic worth. That loss makes them vulnerable to those who would convince them that their major role is to be physically appealing."[3]

Another, perhaps deeper source of conflict for women is the question if identity. "Who am I?" many women ask. Women worry about disappearing into their roles, using the word "just"—"Am I just a wife and mother? Am I just a homemaker? Am I more than that?" They mirror the confusion in our culture about the value of women.

Some feel trapped or diminished in roles that can seem tedious; others enjoy their roles but wonder if their lives should add up to "more than this." They love their children, but the intense effort and emotional price they pay for them can be exhausting. For many, the need to get a job takes them from home and children and brings on the guilt. I have to admit that a husband can be a real source of frustration too.

Single women in the Church face their own set of conflicts. They might enjoy their independence and at the same time long for a family of their own. They might feel lonely or rejected, that maybe there's something wrong with them, that they are somehow less than other women.

Because of these conflicts, Elder Scott says, "So many of our sisters are disheartened, even discouraged and disillusioned."[4]

The Doctrine and Covenants answers every woman's question, "Who am I?"

Doctrine and Covenants 76:23–24. [Jesus Christ] is the Only Begotten of the Father—by him, and through him, and of him, the worlds are and were created, and the inhabitants thereof are begotten sons and daughters unto God.

In speaking to the women of the Church, President Dieter F. Uchtdorf said, "You are known and remembered by the most majestic, powerful, and glorious Being in the universe! You are loved by the King of infinite space and everlasting time! He who created and knows the stars knows you and your name—you are the daughters of His kingdom."[5]

As the offspring of God, you are above all an independent individual of unlimited worth and potential. You are free to choose what to do with your infinite endowment of intelligence, talent, and capacity to love.

Because of your divine nature, you are far freer than you might think. You can choose at every moment which of these self-images means more to you—the image of a daughter of God or that of a daughter of Babylon.

LAY ASIDE THE THINGS OF THIS WORLD

In the revelation to Emma Smith now known as Doctrine and Covenants 25, the Lord gave counsel that applies to the choices facing all women:

> *Doctrine and Covenants 25:16. And verily, verily, I say unto you, that this is my voice unto all.*

> *Doctrine and Covenants 25:10. Thou shalt lay aside the things of this world, and seek for the things of a better.*

Latter-day Saint women have an advantage so many women don't—they can make better-informed choices. Women without the revealed understanding of who they really are might have only a vague idea of the "things of a better world." Through revelations, LDS women are empowered with a clear vision that distinguishes this world from a better one. Rather than having a self-image imposed on them, they have the knowledge to *choose* their own self-image.

I have an image in my mind of my beautiful wife, Valerie, kneeling with me at a sacred altar, glowing, all in white. I believe she sees herself that way, as a strong and confident yet meek woman of God. There could be no greater contrast with women objectified, demeaned, and even starved into submission to a squalid media image.

President Gordon B. Hinckley said, "Of all the creations of the Almighty, there is none more beautiful, none more inspiring than a lovely daughter of God who walks in virtue . . . who honors and respects her body as a thing sacred and divine, who cultivates her mind . . . who nurtures her spirit with everlasting truth."[6]

This is the great question facing women at every moment: "Which image will you choose for yourself? Will you lay aside the things of this world and seek for the things of a better world?"

If you choose the Lord's path, His promise to you as a woman is clear:

> *Doctrine and Covenants 25:2. If thou art faithful and walk in the paths of virtue before me, I will preserve thy life, and thou shalt receive an inheritance in Zion.*

That inheritance includes the holy calling of a priestess and the royal calling of a queen. A priestess has sacred knowledge and administers salvation; a queen is a sovereign authority who rules a kingdom. In the eternities, a faithful husband and wife become consorts, a king and queen who reign as one, like Adam and Eve, among a beloved posterity. This can be your glorious inheritance.

Sarah Hogan, a wise woman, has written,

> Eve entered into mortal life with two clear goals: to gain knowledge and to multiply and replenish the earth. As her children, however, we too often experience these as two separate goals women must choose between. Eve chose between eating and not eating the fruit. However, *her role as nurturer and her desire to grow and develop herself are clearly linked.* She reflects on her choice in Moses 5:11: "Eve . . . was glad, saying: Were it not for our transgression we should never have had seed, and never should have known good and evil, and the joy of our redemption."[7]

SEEK LEARNING

The goals of self-development and nurturing the family are actually one goal (by the way, this is just as true for men as for women. A husband's self-development enables him not only to provide but also to grow personally).

Doctrine and Covenants 109:7. Seek learning even by study and also by faith.

Eve's first choice was to seek knowledge. Of course, faithful LDS women learn a great deal through their unique experiences as nurturers of families, but they also have the opportunity and responsibility to continue to learn in both sacred and secular fields of knowledge.

Doctrine and Covenants 93:36. The glory of God is intelligence, or, in other words, light and truth.

Unless we grow in intelligence, we will fall short of the glories we might enjoy. I'm surprised that women in the Church don't take more opportunities for education. In some of our communities, there seems to be plenty of time for shopping but not much for reading and classwork. Are we laying aside the things of this world or holding on to them at the expense of better things?

Many women get tired of the tedium of housework and motherhood, and there's plenty there to get tired of. But with less focus on materialism and more sharing of work between marriage partners, a woman can invest time in awakening her mind. I'm pleased that my wife valued herself enough to get her college degree even while raising our small children, and I tried my best to support her in it. A husband who doesn't encourage his wife's education needs to take a hard look in the mirror, where he will see a self-centered man.

President Hinckley said, "Any man who denies his wife the time and the encouragement to develop her talents, denies himself and his children a blessing which could grace their home and bless their posterity. . . . I am offended by the sophistry that the only lot of the Latter-day Saint woman is to be barefoot and pregnant. It's a clever phrase, but it's false."[8]

In speaking to a women's conference, President Hinckley said, "You have an obligation to refine and improve your minds and your skills, for each of you is a daughter of God with a divine birthright and with an obligation to grow toward His stature."[9]

Each woman can "grow toward the stature of God" by seeking knowledge as Eve did; gaining intelligence is to share in the glory of God.

BRING UP YOUR CHILDREN IN LIGHT AND TRUTH

In another place, the Lord defined his work and his glory as "to bring to pass the immortality and eternal life of man" (Moses 1:39). The gaining of intelligence and the nurturing of God's children are intertwined "glories." Our chief nurturing responsibility is to help children increase in "light and truth":

> Doctrine and Covenants 93:40. I have commanded you to bring up your children in light and truth.

It's not enough to bear, house, and feed children; we must also teach them, provide a righteous pattern of living for them, and help them cultivate their hearts ("light") and their minds ("truth"). Unless women grow in light and truth themselves, they won't be able to bring up their children as the Lord has asked.

Eve's second choice was to "multiply and replenish the earth" (Genesis 1:28). The Hebrew word *ma-lay*, translated as "replenish," can also mean "refresh" or "consecrate." We refresh the minds of our children by reading to them, sharing insights with them, learning together with them. We consecrate their hearts by telling them stories of Jesus, helping them learn to serve, and serving alongside them.

The Lord has commanded women to be not only the models of light and truth but also the teachers of light and truth:

> Doctrine and Covenants 25:7. Thou shalt be ordained . . . to expound scriptures, and to exhort the church, according as it shall be given thee by my Spirit.

Every Latter-day Saint woman is called "to expound scripture." The dictionary of Joseph Smith's time defined *expound* this way: "To explain; to lay open the meaning; to clear of obscurity; to interpret."[10] Women have the sacred responsibility to study God's word and learn it by the Spirit so they may open the scriptures to others—especially to their children. Women should not leave this duty to anyone else, even to good Primary or Sunday School teachers.

Every Latter-day Saint woman is called "to exhort the church." To exhort is to advise, warn, or caution. No woman should hold back her counsel in her family or Church calling "because I'm just a woman." On the contrary, she has a duty to seek inspiration and share it.

The best teacher I ever had in the Church was Sister Stapley, who taught Sunday School when I was a teenager. She made every lesson a conversation about important things and treated us like adults, talking straight with us about the things that were on our minds. She knew the gospel well and seemed to pull insights out of the air. She "expounded and exhorted," but in a loving way (unlike so many men who, in those days, were pretty awkward teachers—although they meant well).

God has obviously gifted women with the power to teach in nurturing ways. The sister missionaries I worked with long ago had a loving, spiritual influence over people that I couldn't match. I can still picture them and feel the Spirit they carried with them. In one case, a series of elders had taught a prominent French businessman over several years; although intellectually intrigued, he was resistant. But when a pair of sisters met with him, he melted. We elders baptized the man, but the sisters had taken the gospel into his heart.

BE A COMFORT UNTO THY HUSBAND

The media thrive on conflict between women and men. Celebrity divorces are huge news items. TV shows depict husbands as boorish dolts, their wives as schemers, and marriage as a frivolous battleground. Reality shows let us eavesdrop on men and women plotting against each other. Women are seen as cold calculators of what they can "get out of the relationship."

Again, there's a stark gap between this picture and the unity and holy beauty of a couple holding hands in the temple. When I take my Valerie's hand in the celestial room, I'm flooded with a sense of gratitude for her. I'm no prize husband, and the love she has bestowed on me for so many years helps me understand what divine mercy must be. She has invariably lived by the commandment the Lord gave to wives:

Doctrine and Covenants 25:5. Thy calling shall be for a comfort unto . . . thy husband, in his afflictions, with consoling words, in the spirit of meekness.

Some husbands are afflicted more than others, but a sensitive wife knows about those afflictions—his responsibility of providing for the family, his uncertainty about fatherhood, his insecurity in carrying often-heavy church callings, his awkwardness in relating to her. A woman's roles can be overwhelming, *and so can a man's.*

Too many marriages turn into contests about who is sacrificing more for the partnership. Of course, imbalances of commitment can cause serious heartache. A woman who is neglected or abused needs the help of her bishop and of professional counselors *now*, not later. But most couples at least sometimes sense that one might be giving more to the marriage than the other.

The Lord wants us to stop measuring out what we're willing to give. He's told us what to give. A wife who wants a close, vibrant marital relationship heeds the Lord's simple counsel: Give comfort to your husband. Use consoling words in a spirit of meekness.

A soothing word from Valerie calms my troubles and gives me perspective. She reminds me with her touch what I live for and why. She strengthens my mind enfeebled over the confusing problems I face at work. She lifts my chin and looks into my eyes, and everything is immediately better—just because she's there.

BE EQUAL IN HEAVENLY AND EARTHLY THINGS

I've worked with professional women all my adult life, in both education and business; so for me, women are colleagues, my equals (or superiors) in every sense, independent in their judgment and capable in every role they take. Some men, however, look at women in the workplace a little like children, wondering if they can really do the job or why they're not home with the kids. In leadership roles, such men often downplay the contribution of women or oppose their promotions—"they'll just get all emotional and pregnant and leave." Some men resist working with, not to mention *for*, a woman.

Unfortunately, these are often the attitudes of Mormon men.

When confronted with these retrograde attitudes, women should remember not to buy into them. These beliefs are based on folk doctrine specifically contradicted by prophets: "Eve became God's final creation, the grand summation of all of the marvelous work that had gone before," President Hinckley taught.

> Notwithstanding this preeminence given the creation of woman, she has so frequently through the ages been relegated to a secondary position. She has been put down. She has been denigrated. She has been enslaved. She has been abused. . . . Every woman is a daughter of God. You cannot offend her without offending Him.[11]

The true doctrine is that the potential of a daughter of God is unlimited, and she should feel free to pursue her heart's desire in any area. Elder Dallin H. Oaks comments, "Women especially may receive negative feedback when they aspire to professional occupations. A young sister entering her late twenties and faced with supporting herself wrote for advice. Apparently, men she looked up to had tried to discourage her from going to law school." Elder Oaks responded differently. "Her determination could be felt through the pages of her letter, and it was clear that she should be advised to reach the full level of her potential."[12]

Doctrine and Covenants 78:5. Be equal in the bonds of heavenly things, yea, and earthly things also, for the obtaining of heavenly things.

A basic principle of the gospel is the equality of all in the eyes of God. Women and men are to be equals in all their relations, in both heaven and earth. Women do not have secondary status in the kingdom of God. They are not chattels of their husbands. Ideas about "submission" to male authority or "obedience" owed by wives to their husbands are folk doctrines that can do great damage.

The New Testament does say to wives, "Submit yourselves unto your own husbands." But in the previous verses, the Apostle says, "Be filled with the Spirit . . . *submitting yourselves one to another* in the fear of God" (Ephesians 5:18, 21–22).[13] The New Testament Greek word translated as "submit" is *hypotasso,* which means something like "put beneath." The sense of these verses is "to put your partner first and yourself second." They certainly do not mean that the wife is somehow inferior to the husband.

Nor are women inferior because they are not called to the priesthood. They have a different calling.

Typically, "priesthood" means professional clergy, employed as officers of a religious organization. But in the Church of Jesus Christ, the priesthood is an organized body of men who have received a license from the Lord to serve others in certain ways. These servants are not professional priests or employees but volunteers. The instant a priesthood holder tries to serve his own ends, the Spirit withdraws and the man loses priesthood power (see Doctrine and Covenants 121:37).

In the Church, the Relief Society is an organized body of women who have also received a license from the Lord to serve others in certain ways. In the Relief Society, women preside, counsel, teach, and minister. They officiate in the temples of the Lord. The standing of women should not be secondary to the priesthood but in every way complementary.

The late Elder Bruce R. McConkie shared this insight at the dedication of a monument to the women of the Church at Nauvoo in 1978: "Where spiritual things are concerned, as pertaining to all of the gifts of the Spirit, with reference to the receipt of revelation, the gaining of testimonies and the seeing of visions, in all matters that pertain to godliness and holiness and which are brought to pass as a result of personal righteousness—in all these things men and women stand in a position of *absolute equality before the Lord.*"[14]

Nor are single women somehow less valuable than married women.

There are probably as many or more single women in the Church than married women. Yet, as one single woman wrote, "Within the Church, there are traces of the idea that women who have not married are still, somehow, immature. They are only half-formed. Their development has been arrested. There is something wrong with them."[15] Some singles are even misled into believing these things about themselves.

Again, these are folk doctrines, hurtful and destructive to many sensitive women.

I work every day with delightful and accomplished professional women who are single and LDS. For one reason or another, marriage opportunities haven't arisen for them. Wise women, they succeed in their lives in every way that matters. They are faithful to covenants, they are self-reliant and hard workers, and they are cherished friends. In my view, their lives are not a loss but a gain—a great gain.

LIFT UP YOUR HEART AND REJOICE

Just before the Prophet Joseph's death, Emma Smith asked Joseph for a priesthood blessing. He suggested she write the blessing she wanted, and he would give it to her. We have that document today. She asked the Lord to bless her with self-understanding; a fruitful, active mind; prudence; a cheerful countenance; and the wisdom to honor and respect her husband.

This was her final request: "I desire to see that I may rejoice with [the daughters of Eve] in the blessings which God has in store for all who are willing to be obedient to his requirements."[16]

The Lord's revealed word to Emma and to all women encourages them to see themselves as meek women of God rather than as prideful women of the world:

> *Doctrine and Covenants 25:13–14. Lift up thy heart and rejoice, and cleave unto the covenants which thou hast made. Continue in the spirit of meekness, and beware of pride. Let thy soul delight in thy husband. Keep my commandments continually, and a crown of righteousness thou shalt receive.*

NOTES

1. Cited in *Daughters in My Kingdom: The History and Work of Relief Society*, 2012, http://www.lds.org/relief-society/daughters-in-my-kingdom /manual/.

2. M. Russell Ballard, "Mothers and Daughters," *Ensign*, May 2010.

3. Richard G. Scott, "The Sanctity of Womanhood," *Ensign*, November 2008.

4. Ibid.

5. Dieter F. Uchtdorf, "Forget Me Not," *Ensign*, November 2011.

6. Gordon B. Hinckley, "Words of the Prophet: Daughters of the Almighty," *New Era*, November 2003.

7. Sarah Hogan, "Like Eve, All Women Make Choices," *Exponent II*, Fall 2010, 4, emphasis added.

8. Gordon B. Hinckley, *Cornerstones of a Happy Home*, pamphlet, January 29, 1984, 6. http://www.lds.org/bc/content/shared/content/english/pdf/ language-materials/33108_eng.pdf?lang=eng.

9. Hinckley, "Words of the Prophet."

10. *Webster's 1828 Dictionary*, "Expound."

11. Gordon B. Hinckley, "The Women in Our Lives," *Ensign*, November 2004.

12. Dallin H. Oaks, "Learning and the Latter-day Saints," *Ensign*, April 2009.

13. Emphasis added.

14. Bruce R. McConkie, "Our Sisters from the Beginning," *Ensign*, June 1978.

15. Natalie Prado, "I Am My Own Wife," *Exponent II*, Summer 2011, 21.

16. Cited in Janet Gaunt, Larene Peterson, *Faith, Hope, and Charity: Inspiration from the Lives of General Relief Society Presidents* (Covenant Communication, 2008), 18–19.

TEN

HEALTH

My life is so busy I have a hard time finding time to eat right and exercise. I just can't get my weight under control. And I feel tired so much of the time. What's happening to me? What can I do?

Experts always point to the Mormon people as some of the healthiest in the world. The statistics are old news: 35 percent less heart disease, 20 percent less cancer, 40 percent less chance of dying in a given year. Mormon men live ten years longer and Mormon women five years longer than their non-Mormon counterparts.

Scientists now say the average American Latter-day Saint can expect to live nearly ninety-two years. (Of course, some of us don't want to live that long; still, if we stay healthy we might enjoy it: "Healthy behaviors don't just increase your life expectancy. They are also going to decrease your incapacity," one authority points out.)[1]

A prominent researcher concludes that the Mormon way of life produces these results: "Active . . . Mormons practice a healthy lifestyle advocated by their religion, which emphasizes a strong family life, education and abstention from tobacco and alcohol."[2] Faithful Saints also know they receive additional blessings of spiritual enlightenment and direction by keeping the commandments.

At the same time, the Saints live in a larger culture, and we suffer increasingly from many of the afflictions of that culture. The pressures of work, heavy schedules, poor diet, lack of sleep and exercise— these everyday stresses can add up to serious health problems, such as a "growing obesity and diabetes epidemic."[3] Like others in our over-achieving culture, many Mormons take false pride in being "crazy busy" and taking no time for themselves.

Add to these problems our growing dependence on technology. For many of us, work consists of sitting all day in front of a computer screen, and recent studies show that "excessive sitting is a lethal activity" because it promotes heart disease.[4] On top of this, many of us have become near addicts to the Internet, unable to put down our smart phones or iPads or laptops because we love the constant stimulus of being online.

Although the Saints as a group are blessed with good health, these cultural behaviors will inevitably take an unwelcome toll on us if we don't change. The Doctrine and Covenants gives divine guidance that can help us make the needed changes.

KEEP THE WORD OF WISDOM AS A COVENANT WITH A PROMISE

Doctrine and Covenants 89:5, 8–9. Inasmuch as any man drinketh wine or strong drink among you, behold it is not good, neither meet in the sight of your Father. . . . And again, tobacco is not for the body, neither for the belly, and is not good for man. . . . And again, hot drinks are not for the body or belly.

The health benefits of these few verses are now undisputed. Although it's not true that in Joseph Smith's time these substances were universally accepted and used (many people in the Popular Health Reform movement of the 1830s protested their use), the value of this revelation has been proven beyond question. The cost of alcohol abuse and tobacco-related disease is in the hundreds of billions of dollars, far less staggering than the cost in terms of broken lives and physical pain. Even in small amounts, alcohol and tobacco smoke can cause brain-cell death in unborn children and harm them for life.

Still, over the years I've been asked why Mormons practice total prohibition of these things. "Isn't it unreasonable to give up wine totally? A glass of red wine has proven health effects (although grape juice seems to do the same thing—without the alcohol). A cigar now and then doesn't hurt you, does it? And the jury is out on coffee and tea—some studies show benefits, others don't—but I couldn't live without them."

Of course, many people use these products in moderation and suffer few ill effects. My answer to this is simple: God has commanded me not to use them. For me, the Word of Wisdom is a token of a covenant I've made with my Heavenly Father. I believe He intended to help me protect my health; but more than that, He intended to test my faith and remind me that I belong to Him.

Anciently, God commanded the children of Israel to abstain from certain foods. People have different theories about this—some argue that some meats were unsafe, and others maintain that those foods were often used in pagan worship. Personally, I think the Mosaic dietary laws were intended as tokens to remind the people of their covenant with their Redeemer.

Like the ancient Mosaic covenant, the Word of Wisdom is a covenant with a promise:

> *Doctrine and Covenants 89:18–21. All saints who remember to keep and do these sayings, walking in obedience to the commandments, shall receive health in their navel and marrow to their bones; and shall find wisdom and great treasures of knowledge, even hidden treasures; and shall run and not be weary, and shall walk and not faint. And I, the Lord, give unto them a promise, that the destroying angel shall pass by them, as the children of Israel, and not slay them. Amen.*

These are stunning promises, for which bypassing a cup of coffee or a smelly cigarette hardly seems a sacrifice at all.

Of course, to qualify for these promises, we must follow not only the *proscriptions* but also the *prescriptions*.

> *Doctrine and Covenants 89:10–12. All wholesome herbs God hath ordained for the constitution, nature, and use of man—every herb in the season thereof, and every fruit in the season thereof; all these to be used with prudence and thanksgiving. Yea, flesh also of beasts and of the fowls of the air, I, the Lord, have ordained for the use of man with thanksgiving; nevertheless they are to be used sparingly.*

I have heard nutritionists say that it would be tough to summarize what we now know about nutritional science in fewer words than these. Every nutritional guide published today is simply a variation on these same themes: eat seasonal vegetables and fruits in moderation, along with small portions of meat to provide essential proteins.

Since the time of the Prophet Joseph Smith, the Saints have known this prescription. Today, however, we are less likely than ever to live by it. Utah, where Mormons dominate, has seen an alarming increase in obesity and diabetes.[5]

Doctrine and Covenants 89:16–17. All grain is good for the food of man; as also the fruit of the vine; that which yieldeth fruit, whether in the ground or above the ground—nevertheless, wheat for man.

Researchers know that whole grains like wheat make you healthier. They provide fiber, protein, B vitamins, and minerals such as iron and zinc, which in combination reduce the risk of heart disease, obesity, diabetes, and cancer. "Yet the average American eats less than one serving per day, and over 40% never eat whole grains at all."[6] This is somewhat less true in Mormon populations, but still too true.

Also, I've wondered if the words in Doctrine and Covenants 89:20, "[they] shall run and not be weary and shall walk and not faint," are meant to describe a result—or an admonition. (Or both.) In any case, the health benefits of moderate exercise are well established. A brisk walk in the morning helps you control your weight, combat disease, improve your mood, and boost your energy.[7] Dr. John Ratey of Harvard Medical School says, "Nothing helps the growth of new brain cells more than aerobic exercise" like walking or running.[8]

RETIRE EARLY AND ARISE EARLY

Doctrine and Covenants 88:124. Cease to sleep longer than is needful; retire to thy bed early, that ye may not be weary; arise early, that your bodies and your minds may be invigorated.

Our culture suffers from a chronic sleep deficit. Our neurotic pace of life and our obsession with social media, along with the mounting stresses of work and family, mean that adults are getting 27 percent less sleep than they did in the middle of the last century.[9]

The commandment to stop sleeping longer than is needful of course implies that a certain amount of sleep *is* needful. We are to retire early and get up early—but in between there must be an adequate amount of sleep. The stereotype of the Mormon mom who stays up late to sew and gets up before dawn to cook is *not* a virtuous stereotype but a dysfunctional one. Like all of us, she needs her seven to nine hours of sleep every night—self-martyrdom will not overcome the consequences of failing to abide by this commandment.

Brain scientists now know that the brain does not simply relax at night—it is doing a very important kind of work and requires time to do it. During sleep, the brain consolidates, analyzes, stores, and discards memories, a process essential to learning. We literally cannot learn without adequate sleep.[10]

CONTINUE IN PRAYER AND FASTING

Doctrine and Covenants 88:76. Also, I give unto you a commandment that ye shall continue in prayer and fasting from this time forth.

The commandment to continue in fasting brings many benefits to the faithful—it humbles us and brings us closer to the Spirit, and the fast offering relieves suffering. But then, in a major study including LDS people, scientists discovered that fasting has an additional, unsuspected benefit: It measurably improves heart health. To their surprise, the scientists found that "fasting was the strongest predictor of lower heart disease risk" and that occasional fasting seems to protect the heart against coronary artery disease.[11]

Obviously, we can't claim the Lord's healing promises if we don't follow His prescriptions. God has set His laws of good health before us, and it's up to us to choose whether to live by them.

The obstacles are clear enough. It's not that we don't want to live up to the Lord's standard, but we're too busy to deal with preparing healthy meals, which takes work. We love fresh vegetables, but who has time for gardening? We're too busy to exercise. The kids, pressured by advertising, in turn pressure us to feed them high-carb, low-nutrition fast food.

Many of these obstacles come down to a lack of time. Those who choose to live the Word of Wisdom need to recognize that *it will require an investment of time*—to learn how to cook, to garden, to shop, to slow down and eat right, and to educate the family. It will require the discipline to exercise and to set aside the time to get enough sleep.

EXPRESS GRATITUDE FOR THE GOOD GIFTS OF GOD

It might also help to cultivate a sense of gratitude for the good gifts of God that come from the earth:

Doctrine and Covenants 59:18–19. All things which come of the earth, in the season thereof, are made for the benefit and the use of man, both to please the eye and to gladden the heart; yea, for food and for raiment, for taste and for smell, to strengthen the body and to enliven the soul.

Like any good parent, our Father in Heaven delights in providing good things for us—tender vegetables, delicious fruits, and succulent meats—"to please the eye, to gladden the heart, to strengthen the body, to enliven the soul." Too many of us rush through meals of bland, processed foods, considering dinnertime wasted time. "Let's just get this over with," we say, so we can go on to do something "worthwhile." Our eyes are unpleased, our bodies overstuffed and under-nourished, and our souls deadened instead of enlivened.

Doctrine and Covenants 59:20. It pleaseth God that he hath given all these things unto man; for unto this end were they made to be used, with judgment, not to excess, neither by extortion.

If we are too busy to enjoy the gifts of God as He intended, then we are *too* busy—and very ungrateful.

On the other hand, it is possible to use these things "to excess." Prudence and thanksgiving are the watchwords.

In this connection, another dangerous obstacle lies before those who choose to live the Word of Wisdom—it is a *lack* of prudence and a tendency to excess. For example, exercise is essential, but it can be taken to an extreme. People who make a cult of exercise risk neglecting other important priorities, such as family, work, and church. Besides, researchers now think that "moderate exercise, such as walking 30 minutes a day, may offer better protection against diabetes and heart disease than a more rigorous workout regimen."[12]

BEWARE OF THE DESIGNS OF CONSPIRING MEN

Some become fanatics about the Word of Wisdom and lose sight of what it actually says. For example, some people prefer vegetarian meals—which is fine—but it's extreme to teach others that the Word of Wisdom is a vegetarian doctrine:

Doctrine and Covenants 49:18. Whoso forbiddeth to abstain from meats, that man should not eat the same, is not ordained of God.

Some extremists maintain that the commandment to eat "every herb in the season thereof" means that we should take in mega-doses of herbal supplements. This folk doctrine is popular among some Mormons, but they don't realize that in Joseph Smith's day, the term "herb" was used differently. It defined any edible plant, primarily what we now call vegetables.[13]

Often, extremists maintain that the Lord requires reliance on herbs rather than medicines to treat illness. They find justification in this verse:

Doctrine and Covenants 42:43. Whosoever among you are sick, and have no faith to be healed, but believe, shall be nourished with all tenderness, with herbs and mild food, and that not by the hand of the enemy.

Again, this verse advises nourishing the sick with vegetables and foods that are not pungent or sharp, which is still good advice. Of course, herbal remedies were popular in Joseph's time. Some were moderately effective. Joseph is also on record advising the Saints to treat sickness with herbs and avoid physicians with their medicines:

> I preached to a large congregation at the Stand, on the Science and practice of Medicine, desiring to persuade the Saints to trust in God when sick, and not in an arm of flesh, and live by faith and not by medicine, or poison; and when they were sick, and had called the Elders to pray for them, and they were not healed, to use herbs and mild food.[14]

In historical perspective, Joseph was right. It was a pre-scientific era, and medicines of the time *were* likely to be poisonous. Doctors prescribed toxic doses of calomel, producing severe digestive problems, and laudanum, a combination of opium and alcohol that made drug addicts out of their patients. They bled their patients and knew nothing about infectious bacteria and viruses. Some even advised people against bathing for fear of "washing off one's protective substances."

Some Church members still quote statements and scriptures like these to argue that herbs are "God's medicine as opposed to man's medicine," promoting, instead of competent medical care, unorthodox herbal therapies that can be useless or even dangerous (although highly profitable for the promoters).

Historically, however, Church leaders changed their views with the spread of scientific medicine. The Church sponsored the training of doctors in the late nineteenth century, and President Joseph F. Smith eventually taught: "Let a reputable and faithful physician be consulted. By all means, let the quack, the traveling fakir, the cure-all nostrum and the indiscriminating dosing with patent medicine be abolished."[15]

Today's sellers of high-priced, unproven herbal remedies could easily be counted among "the conspiring men" the Lord warns against:

> *Doctrine and Covenants 89:4. In consequence of evils and designs which do and will exist in the hearts of conspiring men in the last days, I have warned you, and forewarn you, by giving unto you this word of wisdom by revelation.*

The Lord warned us that certain designing men would, in our day, conspire against our physical and spiritual health for the sake of their own profits. The enormous illicit drug trade wrecks lives and health worldwide (I have friends—good, solid Latter-day Saints—who have fallen into addiction and even suicide, victims of these despicable combinations).

Legislators meet behind closed doors with the leaders of tobacco, alcohol, and drug companies to strategize how to extend their influence—vast sums of money are at stake in these meetings. Mammoth advertising campaigns program children to choose less nutritious processed foods over fresh fruits and vegetables. The profitable propaganda for illicit, unhealthy behaviors is like a rising tide of muck.

The influence of the muck-merchants can stop with us, at the doors of our homes. It is up to us to choose the promises of the Lord—health, wisdom, hidden treasures of knowledge, the vigor to walk and run, and protection against the destroyer.

It is not a burden but a blessing to live by the Lord's revealed laws of health. These laws spare us from the curses of addiction, the ruin of our bodies, and early death. They also teach us how to enjoy life. A refreshing walk in the early morning, a healthy breakfast, a well-prepared dinner with the family, a rejuvenating night's sleep—the Lord wants us not just to avoid the pitfalls of life, but also to enjoy these good things of life that He delights to provide for us.

NOTES

1. Deborah Bulkeley, "LDS Standards Contribute to Life Expectancy," *Deseret News*, August 4, 2008.

2. Mark W. Cannon, Danielle Stockton, "UCLA Study Proves Mormons Live Longer," *Deseret News*, April 13, 2010.

3. Bulkeley, "LDS Standards Contribute to Life Expectancy."

4. James Vlahos, "Is Sitting a Lethal Activity?" *New York Times Magazine*, April 14, 2011. http://www.nytimes.com/2011/04/17/magazine/mag-17sitting-t.html.

5. "New Report: Utah Is Sixth Least Obese State in the Nation," *Trust for America's Health*, July 7, 2011. http://healthyamericans.org/reports/obesity2011/release.php?stateid=UT.

6. Kathleen M. Zelman, "Tips for Reaping the Benefits of Whole Grains," WebMD.com. http://www.webmd.com/food-recipes/features/=reap-the-benefits-of-whole-grains.

7. "Exercise: 7 Benefits of Regular Physical Activity," Mayoclinic.com. http://www.mayoclinic.com/health/exercise/HQ01676.

8. Cited in *The 5 Choices to Extraordinary Productivity*, monograph (Salt Lake City: FranklinCovey, 2011).

9. "Americans Don't Get Enough Sleep," mercola.com March 25, 2010. http://articles.mercola.com/sites/articles/archive/2010/03/25/americans-don't-get-enough-sleep.aspx.

10. I. Wilhelm, S. Diekelmann, et al. "Sleep Selectively Enhances Memory Expected to Be of Future Relevance," *Journal of Neuroscience*, January 18, 2012. http://www.jneurosci.org/content/31/5/1563.short.

11. "Occasional Fasting Associated with Lower Heart Disease Rates," *Science Daily*, November 6, 2007. http://www.sciencedaily.com/releases/2007/11/071106092013.htm.

12. Robert Preidt, "Moderate Exercise Might Be Healthier than Intense Exercise," July 2007. ABCNews.com. http://abcnews.go.com/Health/Healthday/story?id=4508248&page=1.

13. *Webster's 1828 Dictionary*: "Herb, any plant or vegetable with a soft or succulent stalk or stem."

14. *History of the Church* 4:14.

15. Norman Lee Smith, "Why Are Mormons So Susceptible to Medical & Nutritional Quackery?" *Journal of the Collegium Aesculapium* 1 (1983):30-34.

16. http://www.collegiumaesculapium.org/Journal%20Archives/Dec83_3_Why%20Are%20Mormons%20So%20Susceptible.pdf.

ELEVEN

MONEY

I worry constantly about money. With mortgage, credit card debt, kids—there's never enough. How do I solve my financial problems?

There's no shortage in the Church of counsel to help us with our financial problems. But let's see what the Doctrine and Covenants has to say on the subject.

CEASE TO BE COVETOUS

As a group, the Latter-day Saints are a generous people. The Church's humanitarian efforts are legendary. When someone needs help, the Church and its members are often first on the scene and highly effective when they get there. Mormon families are notably openhanded with each other. "They take care of their own," people often say of the Mormons.

Ironically, though, we often have a problem with being covetous—jealous, greedy, envious, avaricious, acquisitive, and materialistic. The result is high levels of debt, financial distress, and bankruptcy among Mormons.

"Utah bankruptcy rate third highest in U.S.," says the headline of an article that points to a troubling trend in the American state with the most Latter-day Saints.[1] The respected *Economist* magazine calls Utah "the state thought to have the most affinity fraud per head." In one year, the FBI investigated cases involving 4,400 victims and perhaps $1.4 billion in fraud. Stories of Mormons bilking other Mormons are too common. One ward member swindled an eighty-one-year-old widow out of more than a million dollars: "When I sold my farm, he came and said the bishop had asked him to help me invest the proceeds." She never saw another penny.[2]

Elder Dallin H. Oaks says:

> Modern Latter-day Saints are peculiarly susceptible to the gospel of success and the theology of prosperity. According to this gospel, success in this world . . . is an essential ingredient of progress toward the celestial kingdom. . . . Whether inherently too trusting or just naively overeager for a shortcut to the material prosperity some see as the badge of righteousness, some Latter-day Saints are apparently too vulnerable to the lure of sudden wealth.
>
> Men and women who have heard and taken to heart the scriptural warnings against materialism should not be vulnerable to the deceitfulness of riches.[3]

How can a people who are so generous also be so covetous? It's hard to explain this paradox, but the Lord has warned us about it from the earliest days of the Church.

Doctrine and Covenants 88:123. Cease to be covetous; learn to impart one to another as the gospel requires.

This scripture ought to be mounted on the refrigerator in every LDS home. Most of our money problems derive from covetousness. In fact, except for justifiably going into debt for an education or a home, there's rarely a *need* to spend money we don't have.

Buying things we can't afford is the result of covetousness, "the sin nobody talks about." Somehow it's not polite or politic to discuss among ourselves what Elder Oaks calls "the deceitfulness of riches."

As a boy growing up in Utah, I lived on the side of a mountain. Our status in life had a lot to do with the elevation of the house we lived in. We spoke in terms of living "down here" or "up there." I remember envying the kids who had more money and a bigger house "up there" on the mountain, and I imagine I was envied by kids who lived "down there." Maybe the mountains are to blame for our class-consciousness. "Upward mobility" for us had more than just symbolic meaning. The measure of success and happiness in life was "moving on up" to a house in the foothills—preferably one with a view.

As a young father, I worried a lot about money, of which we had very little. Our house was a small one—"down there." What would become of my children? Could I ever afford to give them any advantages in life? What if something happened to me? I looked at the folks "up there" with some resentment, envying their apparent comfort, their vacations to the Cayman Islands, their big houses, their nice cars, their stylish clothes, and most of all their security. I felt very vulnerable.

Meanwhile, my splendid wife, Valerie, made our little house a wonderful home. With her eye for bargains, she kept our kids inexpensively but nicely dressed. She made the girls' Sunday dresses and summer play clothes. We lived on her home-fresh cooking, mostly from our family garden—one summer she canned one hundred quarts of tomatoes. We had an apple tree, a sandbox, a tire swing, one broken-down car, and a happy family.

In hindsight, I realize how wonderful those years were; without my covetousness, I would have enjoyed them more.

One day, I was talking with a friend of mine who was the bishop of a ward "high up on the hill," as we said, and I half-jokingly asked him what it was like to oversee a ward where people had no problems. He looked at me with sudden soberness. "You have no idea, do you?" he asked and changed the subject.

As the years went by, we gradually built up enough resources as a family to be able to move into a neighborhood higher "up there" on the mountain—into that bishop's ward. I soon found out that my wealthy fellow ward members carried burdens that in many cases were far heavier than I had ever imagined: chronic illnesses, broken hearts, suicides, ruptured families, crushing debts. That's when I discovered that "wealth" is relative.

PAY ALL YOUR DEBTS

Over the years, I've been stunned by how many people I know have serious debts. In most cases, they've overextended themselves gradually, taking on more and more obligations with credit cards, loans, and mortgages. I've never been that brave; I've always been scared of getting in over my head.

The Lord gives unmistakably plain commandments about debt in the Doctrine and Covenants:

> *Doctrine and Covenants 104:78. Verily I say unto you, concerning your debts—behold it is my will that you shall pay all your debts.*

> *Doctrine and Covenants 19:35. Pay the debt thou hast contracted. . . . Release thyself from bondage.*

Some debts are justifiable. Businesspeople often use debt to increase their production power. A person might borrow to get an education that will pay great dividends over time. But debt is a kind of bondage, as President Gordon B. Hinckley taught:

> So many of our people are heavily in debt for things that are not entirely necessary. When I was a young man, my father counseled me to build a modest home, sufficient for the needs of my family, and make it beautiful and attractive and pleasant and secure. He counseled me to pay off the mortgage as quickly as I could so that, come what may, there would be a roof over the heads of my wife and children. I was reared on that kind of doctrine. I urge you as members of this Church to get free of debt where possible and to have a little laid aside against a rainy day.
>
> We cannot provide against every contingency. But we can provide against many contingencies.[4]

President Hinckley's prophetic advice came some years before a major economic downturn that left many people bankrupt. I personally know people who measured their wealth in terms of the big house, the fancy cars, and the cool clothes. But they weren't wealthy at all. It was an illusion; they owed far more than they owned.

SEEK EARNESTLY THE RICHES OF ETERNITY

How do you measure your wealth?

There are many kinds of wealth. A trove of money is only one kind. Some think only of the net worth on a balance sheet, but there's also talent, intelligence, wisdom, a capacity for hard work, and physical health and energy. A man with a wife like mine—who embodies all of those virtues—is wealthy indeed. A joyful heart is a form of wealth that pays endless dividends. A house full of loving, faithful children and giggling grandchildren, I've found, is a true treasure house.

Above all, there is the immeasurable wealth of the gospel of Jesus Christ. The Doctrine and Covenants speaks many times of gaining riches, but always and only in one sense: the "riches of eternity."

> *Doctrine and Covenants 38:39. And if ye seek the riches which it is the will of the Father to give unto you, ye shall be the richest of all people, for ye shall have the riches of eternity.*

> *Doctrine and Covenants 68:31. Now, I, the Lord, am not well pleased with the inhabitants of Zion, for . . . they . . . seek not earnestly the riches of eternity, but their eyes are full of greediness.*

Too much of the time our eyes are "full of greediness." Zion represents the riches of eternity; Babylon represents the riches that "moth and rust corrupt." Which way are we looking? It's impossible to focus on both Zion and Babylon at the same time—which vision "fills our eyes"?

Brigham Young once asked the Saints, "Have we not brought Babylon with us? Are we not promoting Babylon here in our midst? . . . Yes, yes, to some extent and there is not a Latter-day Saint but what feels that we have too much of Babylon in our midst. The spirit of Babylon is too prevalent here."[5]

The spirit of Babylon pervades our culture, and the Latter-day Saints are just as susceptible as others. We feel that somehow we "deserve" more than we can afford, and so we end up deep in debt. "The effects of greed and entitlement are evident in the multimillion-dollar bonuses of some corporate executives," says Elder Oaks. "But the examples are more widespread than that. Greed and ideas of entitlement have also fueled the careless and widespread borrowing and excessive consumerism behind the financial crises that threaten to engulf the world."[6]

Doctrine and Covenants 11:7. Seek not for riches but for wisdom; and, behold, the mysteries of God shall be unfolded unto you, and then shall you be made rich. Behold, he that hath eternal life is rich.

This commandment could not be clearer. The riches we are to seek are found "in the mysteries of God," which are the temple covenants that qualify us for eternal life.

And instead of riches, we are to seek wisdom, a quest that is generally pretty far from our hearts. Ask college students why they're in school and most will answer, "To get a job." If you ask them about "seeking wisdom," they'll look at you strangely; yet, as the scriptures say, "Wisdom is the principal thing; therefore get wisdom" (Proverbs 4:7). In a culture for which getting rich is the principle thing, this sounds like nonsense. We have our priorities exactly backwards.

According to the Doctrine and Covenants, we gain wisdom in two ways:

Doctrine and Covenants 136:32. Let him that is ignorant learn wisdom by humbling himself and calling upon the Lord his God, that his eyes may be opened that he may see, and his ears opened that he may hear.

The wisdom we need to handle our financial problems (or any other problem) comes in part from humbling ourselves and calling on the Lord through prayer. The Lord promises to open our eyes and ears so that we can discern the way forward.

The other way to gain wisdom is through study and faith:

Doctrine and Covenants 109:7. Seek ye out of the best books words of wisdom, seek learning even by study and also by faith.

If we would solve our financial problems, we need to become financially literate. The Lord expects us to "hit the books"—to educate ourselves from the most trustworthy sources about managing money. When we make educated choices about money and seek the Lord's guidance in how we use money, we gain wisdom and the Lord will bless us. And the Lord *has* blessed us. Latter-day Saints who keep the commandments are often blessed financially even beyond their expectations. Personally, I am probably paid way too much for what I do—not that I'm complaining. But I am grateful to the Lord for providing for my family and me "enough and to spare," as He always has.

If the Lord does bless us with wealth, He gives it with a warning:

Doctrine and Covenants 38:39. It must needs be that the riches of the earth are mine to give; but beware of pride, lest ye become as the Nephites of old.

With wealth too often comes pride. After two hundred years of living the gospel in peace and harmony, the Nephites became wealthy, then proud, then destructive. It all started with the pearls: "There began to be among them those who were lifted up in pride, such as the wearing of costly apparel, and all manner of fine pearls" (4 Nephi 1:24). It's hard to believe that the utter downfall of the most blessed people under heaven was due to fancy clothes and jewels, but that's apparently what happened.

As Professors Dean Garrett and Stephen E. Robinson point out, "Wealthy Saints must be aware of the natural effect wealth has on people. . . . The natural progression, whether in one generation or the next, is to pride, then to unfaithfulness, and thence to wickedness and destruction."[7]

PAY YOUR TITHES AND OFFERINGS

A final key to handling financial difficulties is to pay tithing:

Doctrine and Covenants 119:3–4. This shall be the beginning of the tithing of my people. . . . Those who have thus been tithed shall pay one-tenth of all their interest annually; and this shall be a standing law unto them forever, for my holy priesthood, saith the Lord.

It's obvious that the Lord doesn't need our money to carry out his purposes. Why then this "standing law" to pay tithing? In the Doctrine and Covenants, the Lord explained the purposes of tithing:

Doctrine and Covenants 119:2. For the building of mine house, and for the laying of the foundation of Zion and for the priesthood, and for the debts of the Presidency of my Church.

The first purpose of the law of tithing then is "for the building of mine house"—the temple—so that we may come into the presence of our Heavenly Father and His Son, Jesus Christ. All other uses for tithing are secondary to building temples. "Laying the foundation of Zion" refers to the great work of gathering and building the infrastructure of a Zion people—once again—so they can construct temples. And last, to repay what we have to borrow to make all this happen. But the temple comes first.

> *Doctrine and Covenants 97:12, 16. Behold, this is the tithing and the sacrifice which I, the Lord, require at their hands, that there may be a house built unto me for the salvation of Zion. . . . Yea, and my presence shall be there, for I will come into it, and all the pure in heart that shall come into it shall see God.*

In the temples, we make covenants that ensure our exaltation in His kingdom if we are faithful; the tithing we pay is a *token* of our willingness to abide by the covenant of sacrifice that helps to qualify us for exaltation.

Because the ordinances of the temple are so essential to our exaltation, the Lord has always required a temple of his people, his "holy house, which my people are always commanded to build unto my holy name" (Doctrine and Covenants 124:39).

That's why we are always commanded to live the law of tithing. Brigham Young explained: "The law of tithing is an eternal law. The Lord Almighty never had his Kingdom on the earth without the law of tithing being in the midst of his people and he never will. It is an eternal law that God has instituted for the benefit of the human family, for their salvation and exaltation."[8] The token sacrifice of the tithing, which all equally contribute, enables the building of the temple, which we all enter on an equal footing to receive the blessings of eternal life and exaltation.

In a way, our tithing is a token that we accept the sacrifice that was made for us on Calvary. It is a sign of our belonging to the Son of God—that as He consecrated Himself for us, we are willing to consecrate ourselves to Him. As Brigham Young taught: "We are not our own, we are bought with a price, we are the Lord's; our time, our talents, our gold and silver . . . and all there is on this earth that we have in our possession is the Lord's, and he requires one-tenth of this for the building up of his Kingdom."[9]

Building Zion is our primary responsibility on this earth, and we contribute in many ways. Parents who work hard to provide for their families are doing the consecrated work of building Zion. When we give our time to the Lord in our callings, we are building Zion. And when we donate generously to the various missions of the Church—humanitarian service, missionary work, temple building, the Perpetual Education Fund—we are building Zion.

It's easy to let our own covetousness divert us from this grand mission. When money was needed to print the first edition of the Book of Mormon, the Lord spoke to Martin Harris in words that remain vital counsel to us all:

Doctrine and Covenants 19:26. I command thee that thou shalt not covet thine own property, but impart it freely to the printing of the Book of Mormon, which contains the truth and the word of God.

We still have the privilege of contributing to the work of the Lord just as Martin Harris did.

But how do tithes and offerings help us with our own financial difficulties? In simple terms, the Lord pours out blessings on tithe payers from the "windows of heaven" (see Malachi 3:10). (The actual Hebrew word for "windows" is probably better translated "sluice gates"—which implies a veritable flood!)

When Valerie and I were a young couple with little money, our bishop asked us to donate a certain amount to the building of the Jordan River Temple. We calculated that if we paid this offering, we would be completely broke. (That's the problem with mathematics—it just doesn't work well for some people.) But we had made a covenant to pay the Lord first; we held our breath and did it. I took a temporary job teaching night school, which helped us break even.

Within a few days, a creditor to whom we owed a considerable debt came to see us. He wondered if it would be all right with us if he were to cancel our debt because it would give him certain tax advantages. Well, we were happy to help him out.

After he left, Valerie and I looked at each other in surprise. We did the math and realized that the canceled debt was worth forty times what we had given to the temple fund. And because we didn't have to pay our creditor, we had money left over. We thanked the Lord.

As Elder Robert D. Hales has said, "Would any of us intentionally reject an outpouring of blessings from the Lord? Sadly, this is what we do when we fail to pay our tithing. We say no to the very blessings we are seeking and praying to receive. If you are one who has doubted the blessings of tithing, I encourage you to accept the Lord's invitation to 'prove [Him] now herewith.' Pay your tithing. Unlock the windows of heaven."[10]

NOTES

1. Dave Anderton, "Utah Bankruptcy Rate Is 3rd Highest in the U.S.," *Deseret News*, December 18, 2004.

2. "Fleecing the Flock," *The Economist*, January 28, 2012. http://www.economist.com/node/21543526.

3. Dallin H. Oaks, *Pure in Heart* (Salt Lake City: Bookcraft, 1988), 83–84.

4. Gordon B. Hinckley, "The Times in Which We Live," *Ensign*, November 2001.

5. Brigham Young, *Journal of Discourses* 17:41.

6. Dallin H. Oaks, "Unselfish Service," *Ensign*, May 2009.

7. H. Dean Garrett, Stephen E. Robinson, *A Commentary on the Doctrine and Covenants* (Salt Lake City: Deseret Book, 2005), 1:267.

8. *Teachings of Brigham Young*, 155.

9. Ibid., 156.

10. Robert D. Hales, "Tithing: A Test of Faith With Eternal Blessings," *Ensign*, October 2002.

TWELVE

EDUCATION

I know I should be "forever learning," but I don't even have time to pick up a book. Why does the Lord put so much emphasis on learning and education?

For a Latter-day Saint, education is the purpose of life.

Elder David A. Bednar observes, "The overarching purpose of Heavenly Father's great plan of happiness is to provide His spirit children with opportunities to learn."[1] We are in this mortal world not just to be tested but to go through a course of study, intricately tailored to the needs of each one of us.

We have always existed as independent intelligences, and so we will always exist (see Doctrine and Covenants 93:29). It is apparently in the nature of intelligence to seek more intelligence, wisdom, light, and truth:

> *Doctrine and Covenants 88:40. Intelligence cleaveth unto intelligence; wisdom receiveth wisdom; truth embraceth truth; virtue loveth virtue; light cleaveth unto light.*

Brigham Young asked, "When shall we cease to learn? I will give you my opinion about it; never, never."[2]

We are not equal to each other in intelligence; the Lord revealed to Abraham that "where there are two spirits, one being more intelligent than the other; there shall be another more intelligent than they." The Lord is "more intelligent than they all" (Abraham 3:19). Our purpose in this mortal existence is to gain in intelligence:

Doctrine and Covenants 130:18–19. Whatever principle of intelligence we attain unto in this life, it will rise with us in the resurrection. And if a person gains more knowledge and intelligence in this life through his diligence and obedience than another, he will have so much the advantage in the world to come.

Clearly, the word *intelligence* has two meanings in the scripture. We *are* intelligences, as eternal as God is, but we are also capable of *growing* in intelligence in this life through "diligence and obedience."

The Prophet Joseph Smith was foremost a seeker of knowledge. His mission as the prophet of the Restoration began with a question, and he never stopped asking questions. "Which church is true? Why must we be baptized? What is the gift of the Holy Ghost? What is heaven like?" These and many, many other questions led to great revelations, in part because the Prophet was willing to ask God for the answers. In one respect he was like a small child forever asking "Why?" Perhaps the quality of insatiable curiosity is one reason Jesus said, "Become as a little child, or ye can in nowise inherit the kingdom of God" (3 Nephi 11:38).

The intelligences born into this world are brimming with childlike curiosity. Over time, most tend to lose it under mortal pressures. But, although Joseph Smith had little formal education, he never stopped taking delight in learning. In Kirtland, even while the Saints were struggling to build shelter and hack out roads in the forest, Joseph was holding schools for the elders. They would spend hours studying mostly the gospel, but also science, law, medicine, foreign languages, city planning, and architecture. He was excited to obtain "an old edition of the New Testament in the Latin, Hebrew, German and Greek languages. I have been reading the German, and find it to be the most [nearly] correct translation."[3]

Joseph Smith exulted in the idea that he could go on learning forever. "I want to come up into the presence of God, and learn all things." "When things that are of the greatest importance are passed over by weak-minded men without even a thought, I want to see truth in all its bearings and hug it to my bosom."[4]

Few people have ever been so voraciously thirsty for learning, which could be one reason why the Lord selected Joseph Smith as His instrument in revealing the great truths of the Restoration. He knew Joseph would value the tremendous intellectual and spiritual adventure that was in store for him.

By contrast, a great frustration for Joseph was the low value so many of his associates put on education, "weak-minded men" who pass over the most important truths "without even a thought." "How vain and trifling have been our spirits," he observed, "our conferences, our councils, our meetings, our private as well as public conversations— too low, too mean, too vulgar, too condescending for the dignified characters of the called and chosen of God."[5]

I wonder what Joseph Smith would say about our neglect of learning. Too many Latter-day Saints are more obsessed with sports, mindless entertainment, and endless games than with learning. Even in church you see not only youth but adults openly playing games on their phones and tablets. As a larger culture, we seem magnetically attracted to the "low, mean, and vulgar" at the expense of things that are virtuous, lovely, and of good report (see Articles of Faith 1:13).

We hear a lot in the Church about the evils of pornography, which truly is vicious, ugly, and of bad report. Pornography turns that which is most beautiful in life into something shameful and repulsive. But pornography is actually part of a much larger problem.

The problem is what we *seek* after.

ESTABLISH A HOUSE OF LEARNING

Doctrine and Covenants 88:119. Establish a house . . . a house of learning, a house of glory, a house of order, a house of God.

What are we seeking after in our homes? Are we "establishing a house of learning, a house of God," centered on the Savior and the things He would delight in?

Or have we become so accustomed to the "low, mean, and vulgar" that we've forgotten—or more tragically, never known—what is truly virtuous, lovely, of good report, and praiseworthy? For many of our families, great music, great films, great books, great art are no part of our lives. Instead we live on a steady diet of trash.

When I taught high school years ago, I assigned my students to read a story by Willa Cather entitled "A Wagner Matinée." It's about a woman who grew old on a farm in the middle of nowhere. Her life was hard, backbreaking, dirty, and dusty.

Then she had a chance to visit a relative in Boston, who took her to a concert of the music of Richard Wagner given by a great symphony orchestra. The music was so beautiful and so majestic that she began to cry and sob uncontrollably. When it was over, she pleaded, "Oh I don't want to go! I don't want to go!" Having tasted what true beauty is, she couldn't face returning to the gray dirt that made up her normal life.

Now, none of my students had ever heard of Wagner. "Who is this Wagner?" they asked me. So I said, "Let's go find out." So next day I had my students meet me in a classroom that was set up with a big quadraphonic stereo system and I played a CD of Wagner's music.

It was glorious. The music filled the room, so indescribably rich and beautiful, and you could see that the students were stunned. Several began to cry. When it was over they said, "That was the most beautiful thing I've ever heard in my life. Whose music was that? Wagner? Why haven't we heard of this before?" One student seemed almost angry. "Why have I been denied this?"

Well, they had never tasted exquisite beauty in their lives. They had grown up on cultural fast food and were undernourished. And all of a sudden this glorious banquet was spread out for them. It was totally new to them.

If we have a pornography problem, it's because we have been violating the thirteenth Article of Faith in nearly every aspect of our lives. We don't seek out the truly virtuous and lovely. We don't value the praiseworthy.

> We'd rather watch a stupefyingly boring reality show on MTV instead of a Shakespeare play on PBS.

> We'd rather read cheap romances about vampires than a great romance by Jane Austen.

> We'd rather go to a shock-rock concert blasting filth than a symphony or an opera.

We feed off a dirty floor and then wonder why our families and our children and our whole society get sick.

Parents in the Church should establish "a house of learning, a house of glory," raising their children on greatness, not on the cheap and shoddy and the filthy. Families need to be nourished by the fine things in life and not just live on dirt. They need *good* music, not trashy, cheap music. They need to see the highest-quality films, theater, dance, and entertainment, not the lowest quality. They need to read the best books, not the worst.

SEEK YE DILIGENTLY

Doctrine and Covenants 109:7. Seek ye diligently and teach one another words of wisdom; yea, seek ye out of the best books words of wisdom; seek learning even by study and also by faith.

The people of God are learners and teachers. We invest a vast amount of effort and time into teaching in the Church, and we have the best of the best books—the scriptures and the teachings of latter-day prophets—to work from. So often, however, the teaching we do is mediocre. Lessons are poorly prepared, attendees are bored, and people don't change.

We are commanded to "seek diligently," both those who teach and those who are taught, the "words of wisdom" our Father in Heaven wants so much to communicate to us. Diligence is not a burst of energy, but a cultivated habit. The dictionary of Joseph's time defined *diligent* as "steady in application . . . constant in effort or exertion to accomplish what is undertaken."[6]

A diligent seeker doesn't flip open the study guide a few minutes before the lesson; on the other extreme, a diligent seeker doesn't waste time extensively gathering extraneous materials so he can impress the class with his mastery of the subject.

A diligent seeker is a close reader. A close reader is attentive to the words on the assigned page, always asking him- or herself the question Joseph Smith asked: "Why?" When I study for a lesson, I am constantly intrigued by the Prophet's choice of stories, phrases, and even individual words. What principle is he trying to teach us? Why is he emphasizing this point at this time? How should I change my life based on what I have just read?

Pondering "why" is the mark of the diligent seeker. President Dieter F. Uchtdorf says, "When we focus on the 'why' of the gospel, much of the confusion fades away. Why are we here? Why are we asked to obey the commandments? Why is the Atonement of Jesus Christ of such value to us?"[7]

A diligent seeker does research. If I am teaching a difficult passage in Isaiah, for example, I at least want to be able to explain briefly the obscure references to kings, cities, and ancient battlefields. This does not mean I have to be a historian; it *does* mean I look things up so I can understand what I'm reading and help others to understand.

Finally, a diligent seeker prays for inspiration. As a teacher, my prayers are simple: "Please help us to be edified and rejoice together."

Doctrine and Covenants 50:22. He that preacheth and he that receiveth, understand one another, and both are edified and rejoice together.

One of the energy sources of my testimony is the fresh inspiration I get while teaching. If I'm prepared, a new, precious insight will come like a light to my mind, along with a whisper in my ear, "Now you see, don't you?" I've come to anticipate that whisper, and it's exciting to me. It really is a source of rejoicing. I can testify of the real truth in this verse:

Doctrine and Covenants 100:6. It shall be given you in the very hour, yea, in the very moment, what ye shall say.

I believe that blessing is available to any diligent seeker—and not just the teacher.

"He or she that receiveth" also must be a diligent seeker. My good friend Elder A. Roger Merrill asks, "What is your role in creating the environment in which the Spirit can teach you the things you need to know? If you find a Church class or a sacrament meeting boring, does that say more about the teacher—or about you?"[8] Seek at least one new insight from each learning opportunity; and when you discover it, thank the teacher for helping you.

Assuming you are interested in gaining knowledge, the Lord promises to give you answers to all of your most searching questions:

> *Doctrine and Covenants 121:26, 28. God shall give unto you knowledge by his Holy Spirit, yea, by the unspeakable gift of the Holy Ghost, that has not been revealed since the world was until now. . . [in] a time to come in which nothing shall be withheld.*

Those answers might not come in this mortal world, but they will come if we pay the price of diligent seeking and obedience to the principles that bring us knowledge. Often, we face serious questions that disturb us. We might have a problem with a doctrine that we can't understand. We might encounter what looks like a contradiction in scripture or teaching in the Church. We might be unsettled by the behavior of other people in the Church.

I've had many of these problems myself, but I've learned a little bit about how to deal with them. I've learned that whenever I pay the price of patient, hard study; when I invest time in prayer; and when I truly seek to understand (especially *why* other people behave as they do), my concerns evaporate. I don't pretend to have answers to everything that baffles or upsets me, and I can't always articulate why I feel comforted, but I *do know* what that "unspeakable gift of the Holy Ghost" feels like and sounds like.

BE INSTRUCTED MORE PERFECTLY

If we want that unspeakable gift of God in our lives, we must be diligent teachers and learners:

> *Doctrine and Covenants 88:78–79. Teach ye diligently and my grace shall attend you, that you may be instructed more perfectly in theory, in principle, in doctrine, in the law of the gospel, in all things that pertain unto the kingdom of God, that are expedient for you to understand; Of things both in heaven and in the earth, and under the earth; things which have been, things which are, things which must shortly come to pass; things which are at home, things which are abroad; the wars and the perplexities of the*

nations, and the judgments which are on the land; and a knowledge also of countries and of kingdoms.

What should we study? Clearly, the Lord gives priority to the principles and doctrines of the gospel. Secondarily, but also vitally important, are sciences such as astronomy and geology; the disciplines of history, geography, politics, economics, and law are also mentioned.

The Lord expects us to "be instructed more perfectly" in both sacred and secular knowledge. I've always wondered if the Lord distinguishes between those two categories of knowledge as we do. I'm not sure how to classify knowledge because I know the Spirit can enlighten us in all areas of study—this has happened in my life.

Doctrine and Covenants 93:30. All truth is independent in that sphere in which God has placed it, to act for itself, as all intelligence also.

Truth can't be neatly organized into sacred and secular truth. I believe all truth is somehow sacred, and that God is the source of our knowledge of the truth. Seeking truth in any field is perhaps our highest calling in life, if our purpose here is truly to become like our Father, who is "more intelligent than they all" (Abraham 3:19).

Brigham Young said, "The religion embraced by the Latter-day Saints, if only slightly understood, prompts them to search diligently after knowledge. There is no other people in existence more eager to see, hear, learn and understand truth."[9]

Brigham saw an endless banquet of knowledge before him, and his very purpose for living to indulge himself in the banquet:

> The object of this existence is to learn. . . . How gladly would we understand every principle pertaining to science and art, and become thoroughly acquainted with every intricate operation of nature, and with all the chemical changes that are constantly going on around us! How delightful this would be, and what a boundless field of truth and power is open for us to explore! We are only just approaching the shores of the vast ocean of information that pertains to this physical world, to say nothing of that which pertains to the heavens.[10]

Unfortunately, Brigham's eagerness to learn is often missing among us. We live under the thumb of our culture and its material obsessions:

"The reason to go to school is to get a good job."

Of course, we need to provide for our families. But the purpose of education is not primarily economic—the overarching purpose of education, whether sacred or secular, is literally to enable us to fulfill our divine potential. If money is what motivates our learning, we will never experience the "boundless delight" Brigham Young spoke of—and we will fall short of our calling from God.

I have worked with professional people all over the world for decades now. In every instance, the most delightful people I have met are deeply invested in their work because they love growing in knowledge. I've asked, "What do you love about your work?" Invariably, it's some variation of learning and sharing what they learn.

By contrast, the ones who obviously don't enjoy their work are the time-servers, the ones who have long since stopped learning anything or making any contribution beyond what's written in the job description.

Doctrine and Covenants 93:36. The glory of God is intelligence, or, in other words, light and truth.

There is no glory in a mind shut down and a body simply collecting a paycheck. The glory of God is not "a good job"; it is *intelligence*, a word that is formed from "inter," between, and the Latin *legere,* to read. Intelligence is the ability to discern truth—to "read between the lines," so to speak—and thereby to understand what is deep beneath the surface of things.

If we are to grow to be like God, we must grow in intelligence, in profound knowledge and the skill to apply it. But there is a price to be paid. Brigham Young said, "While the inhabitants of the earth are bestowing all their ability, both mental and physical, upon perishable objects, those who profess to be Latter-day Saints . . . are duty bound to study and find out, and put in practice in their lives, those principles that are calculated to endure, and that tend to a continual increase . . . in the world to come."[11]

NOTES

1. David A. Bednar, "Learning to Love Learning," *BYU Speeches*, April 24, 2008. http://speeches.byu.edu/reader/reader.php?id=12272.

2. Brigham Young, *Journal of Discourses*, 3:28.

3. *Teachings of the Prophet Joseph Smith* (Salt Lake City: Deseret Book, 1977), 349. Joseph Smith, "The King Follet Sermon," *Ensign*, April 1971.

4. *Teachings of the Prophet Joseph Smith*, 262.

5. Ibid., 263.

6. *Webster's 1828 Dictionary*, "Diligent."

7. Jason Swensen, "President Dieter F. Uchtdorf: Acting on the Truths of the Gospel of Jesus Christ," *Church News*, February 11, 2012.

8. A. Roger Merrill, "To Be Edified and Rejoice Together," *Ensign*, January 2007.

9. *Teachings of Brigham Young*, 194.

10. Ibid., 85.

11. Ibid., 193.

THIRTEEN

POLITICS

As a Latter-day Saint, what should I think about politics? I know I should get involved in the community, but there are so many other things to do; and frankly, it's such a contentious subject.

President Spencer W. Kimball taught, "Early in this dispensation the Lord made clear the position his restored church should take with respect to civil government:

> *Doctrine and Covenants 98:4–6. And now, verily I say unto you concerning the . . . law of the land which is constitutional, supporting that principle of freedom in maintaining rights and privileges, [that it] belongs to all mankind, and is justifiable before me. Therefore, I, the Lord, justify you . . . in befriending that law which is the constitutional law of the land.*[1]

BEFRIEND THE CONSTITUTIONAL LAW OF THE LAND

The responsibility of the Saints is clear: we are commanded to "befriend" constitutional laws and support the principle of freedom.

Since the "principle of freedom" can be interpreted in many ways, the Lord explains that this principle refers to "maintaining rights and privileges." In other sections of the Doctrine and Covenants, the Lord clarifies the concept of "rights":

Doctrine and Covenants 101:77–78. The laws and constitution of the people . . . I have suffered to be established, and should be maintained for the rights and protection of all flesh, according to just and holy principles; that every man may act in doctrine and principle pertaining to futurity, according to the moral agency which I have given unto him, that every man may be accountable for his own sins in the day of judgment.

In the Lord's view, human rights are the powers He gives us to act according to our moral agency. Without these powers, we could not be held accountable for our actions, and the Lord's plan for our eternal progression would be frustrated. We have the right to choose how we will act "pertaining to futurity"—in other words, we have the power to direct the future course of our lives. Constitutional laws that ensure that right are to be maintained.

Different constitutional systems in many countries have evolved to protect those rights—more or less. The French "Declaration of the Rights of Man and of the Citizen" is a respected model: "Men are born and remain free and equal in rights." The aim of politics is "the preservation of the natural and imprescriptible rights of man. . . . Liberty consists in the freedom to do everything which injures no one else."

Of course, the American Declaration of Independence asserts the same rights: "We hold these truths to be self-evident, that all men are created equal, that they are endowed by their Creator with certain unalienable rights, that among these are Life, Liberty, and the pursuit of Happiness—That to secure these rights, Governments are instituted among Men."

PROTECT AND SECURE INDIVIDUAL CONSCIENCE AND FREEDOM OF ACTION

The purpose of these and many other charters like them is to protect and secure the right to free action. That's why the American Constitution and others are explicit about what the state can and cannot do to restrict freedom of action (for example, arrest warrants, trial by jury, prohibitions on certain types of searches and seizures).

The protection of individual freedom of action is for the Saints a basic principle:

Doctrine and Covenants 134:5. We believe that all men are bound to sustain and uphold the respective governments in which they reside, while protected in their inherent and inalienable rights by the laws of such governments; and that sedition and rebellion are unbecoming every citizen thus protected.

Furthermore, we also believe that protection of individual conscience is a basic principle:

Doctrine and Covenants 134:4. We believe that religion is instituted of God; and that men are amenable to him, and to him only, for the exercise of it, unless their religious opinions prompt them to infringe upon the rights and liberties of others; but we do not believe that human law has a right to interfere in prescribing rules of worship to bind the consciences of men . . . that the civil magistrate should restrain crime, but never control conscience; should punish guilt, but never suppress the freedom of the soul.

Because government is an instrument for protecting our "inherent and inalienable rights," we see government as a benefit, not an enemy; and we are responsible for sustaining and upholding governments that protect our rights of action.

Doctrine and Covenants 134:1. We believe that governments were instituted of God for the benefit of man; and that he holds men accountable for their acts in relation to them, both in making laws and administering them, for the good and safety of society.

Government is a divine, not entirely human, institution; but He has made us responsible for using the instrument of government "for the good and safety of society."

Doctrine and Covenants 134:5. All governments have a right to enact such laws as in their own judgments are best calculated to secure the public interest; at the same time, however, holding sacred the freedom of conscience.

As long as the freedom of conscience is held sacred, this revelation allows governments considerable freedom of action in determining what is in the "public interest." That interest is expressed in terms of "the good and safety of society," which are of course large areas for discussion. Working through governments toward the good and safety of society is part of our duty and our training here on earth.

Insofar as the law protects and secures the right to free action, the Saints are commanded to "befriend" and "maintain" it. Presumably, therefore, we need to get involved in changing laws that endanger the right to free action. But this is not to be done by any or all means; it's to be done "according to just and holy principles."

Latter-day Saints are not to be politically contentious. That would be contrary to "just and holy principles." The Lord has said that "sedition and rebellion are unbecoming every citizen." While rebellion is war against the government, sedition, according to *Webster's 1828 Dictionary*, is "a factious commotion of the people, a tumultuous assembly of men rising in opposition to law or the administration of justice, and in disturbance of the public peace."

True Saints are not seditious. We have no part in "factious commotion" or "tumultuous assemblies" or disturbing the public peace. Much of what we hear in the political arena today borders on sedition—it is not only angry and childish but dangerous to the peace. President Dieter F. Uchtdorf warns the Saints against those who "vilify and demonize their rivals. They look for any flaw and magnify it. They justify their hatred with broad generalizations. . . . When ill fortune afflicts their rival, they rejoice. . . . My beloved fellow disciples of the gentle Christ, should we not hold ourselves to a higher standard?"[2]

That higher standard is the spirit of Christ, which is the spirit of pure love and charity and unity. President Stephen L Richards said, "A threat to our unity derives from unseemly personal antagonisms developed in partisan political controversy."[3] Elder Russell M. Nelson decries "the burden of bickering in election campaigns. Contention is all about us. . . . Serious separation results when offensive labels are utilized with the intent to demean. Even worse, such terms camouflage our true identity as sons and daughters of God."[4]

Another violation of that "higher standard" is to identify our personal political views with the gospel. Hugh Nibley wrote, "Nothing is easier than to identify one's own favorite political, economic, historical, and moral convictions with the gospel. That gives one a neat, convenient, but altogether too easy advantage over one's fellows. If my ideas are the true ones—and I certainly will not entertain them if I suspect for a moment that they are false!—then, all truth being one, they are also the gospel, and to oppose them is to play the role of Satan. This is simply insisting that our way is God's way, and therefore the only way. It is the height of impertinence."[5]

This behavior is common in the religious world, where people wrest the scriptures to "prove" that their political views are also God's views. I heard a bizarre example on the radio one day when a religious leader used Jesus's parable of the laborers in the vineyard (Matthew 20:1–16) to "prove" that God is against labor unions.

In my own experience, there's no shortage of our own church members who will virtually bear testimony of the gospel and their party in the same breath, or insist that no one can be "a good member of the Church" who belongs to this or that political party. Yet prophets and apostles counsel that "principles compatible with the gospel may be found in the platforms of the various political parties"[6] and hold the Church itself strictly neutral among political partisans.

DO NOT MINGLE RELIGIOUS INFLUENCE WITH CIVIL GOVERNMENT

Doctrine and Covenants 134:9. We do not believe it just to mingle religious influence with civil government, whereby one religious society is fostered and another proscribed in its spiritual privileges, and the individual rights of its members, as citizens, denied.

The Church disapproves of those who would impose their religious beliefs on others through the force of law, in defiance of the principle of freedom. Unfortunately, some religious organizations around the world seek to do just that. Even among Latter-day Saints, there's a tendency to blur the line between "religious influence" and "civil government," mingling their political party with the Church in their minds. We must be especially careful about the "mingling" reflex. "We regret that more than anything—that there would become a church party and a non-church party. That would be the last thing that we would want to have happen," according to Elder Marlin K. Jensen of the First Quorum of the Seventy.[7]

As a young missionary in France, I came to know quite well the district president in a certain region of that country. He had been a devoted Latter-day Saint for decades, raised his family in the Church, and was the first on the spot if a member or a missionary needed help. A short, fiery individual with a strong testimony, he told me one day that, politically, he was a "socialist." I was startled. In my upbringing, socialism was identified with the menacing, godless communist empire that then dominated much of the world. I couldn't believe a devout Church member could possibly be a socialist. It didn't take long for me to learn, however, that French Church members held a wide range of political opinions, that this was traditional in France, and that the members didn't think much about it. The Church members there were deep in their affection for one another.

In the years since, I have attended wards and branches around the world and learned that Latter-day Saints are as diverse in their political convictions as any group could be. I have a dear friend from Australia who is unabashedly liberal and another dear friend from South Africa who is just as firmly conservative. In our Paris ward, our Sunday School teacher was a socialist activist from the Comoros Islands, a branch counselor a left-wing art student from San Francisco, and our branch president a banker and a Gaullist—a member of President Charles DeGaulle's staunchly conservative party. Each Sunday morning, they embraced each other warmly like only French Saints can.

CHOOSE THE WISE, THE GOOD, AND THE HONEST TO GOVERN

Of course, ideology is important; we each have our own political perspectives and our reasons for them. However, the Lord seems to be less concerned with political perspective than with the character of those who participate in politics:

> *Doctrine and Covenants 98:8–10. I, the Lord God, make you free, therefore ye are free indeed; and the law also maketh you free. Nevertheless, when the wicked rule the people mourn. Wherefore, honest men and wise men should be sought for diligently, and good men and wise men ye should observe to uphold; otherwise whatsoever is less than these cometh of evil.*

Latter-day Saints who live in a republic have the duty to inform themselves and choose the "wise, good, and honest" as public servants. As Elder Neal A. Maxwell taught,

> In the Doctrine and Covenants . . . we read that we should seek out men who are wise, good, and honest. When I first read these criteria years ago, they seemed quite general to me; they don't now. Too often leaders can lead men astray because they lack one or more of these qualities. A leader can be bright but dishonest, and a leader can be honest and conceptually inadequate. A man may be a good man yet lack the wisdom to cope with complex circumstances that can come upon him. This triad of virtues, for me, is a significant guide to selecting future leaders in any representative government.[8]

Therefore, when we vote for a candidate, we should ask these questions of ourselves: (1) *Is this person wise?* Does he or she have the background, understanding, and judgment to deal effectively with complicated governmental issues? (2) *Is this person good?* Does he or she seem generous, compassionate, and selfless? (3) *Is this person honest?* Is there a track record of integrity? Will this person put the public interest ahead of private gain?

Notice what is missing from this list: the party or ideology of the person. The Lord seems to be more concerned that we choose leaders of competence and character than that they uphold every point of a political manifesto.

The prophets have always taught that the Saints should participate in politics, but with a difference. We have something to bring to the world of politics.

COUNSEL TOGETHER; DO NOT CONTEND

We bring a rich tradition of counseling together, a tradition that is grounded in revealed principles. We don't look to one leader to know or do everything. At our best, we have long experience in presidencies and councils, listening to and weighing different views.

Elder M. Russell Ballard says this of his experience as a member of his priesthood quorum:

> We come from different backgrounds, and we bring to the Council of

the Twelve Apostles a diverse assortment of experiences in the Church and in the world. In our meetings, we do not just sit around and wait for [the President of the Church] to tell us what to do. We counsel openly with each other, and we listen to each other with profound respect for the abilities and experiences our brethren bring to the council. We discuss a wide variety of issues, from Church administration to world events, and we do so frankly and openly. Sometimes we discuss issues for weeks before reaching a decision.[9]

This ability to counsel together, to discuss and weigh issues frankly but with empathy and respect for one another, is precisely what is lacking in the world of politics. The Doctrine and Covenants speaks fifty-five times of councils and of the importance of taking stock of the collective wisdom of the group, as these few examples illustrate:

> Doctrine and Covenants 50:10. Come, saith the Lord, by the Spirit, unto the elders of his church, and let us reason together.

> Doctrine and Covenants 58:56. Let the work of the gathering be . . . done as it shall be counseled by the elders.

> Doctrine and Covenants 96:3. Let it [the land] be divided into lots, according to wisdom . . . as it shall be determined in council among you.

> Doctrine and Covenants 104:21. Let all things be done according to the counsel of the order.

But what about political discussion? Shouldn't we debate and try to persuade others of our points of view?

Yes, but there is a difference between discussion and contention. Hugh Nibley said, "Contention is not discussion, but the opposite; contention puts an end to all discussion, as does war."[10]

In our councils, the Saints have a tradition of discussion—dialogue, examination, and analysis. We are told of a council of spirits in heaven, where various plans (or at least two) for our mortal sojourn were discussed and examined, weighed, and finally resolved. The plan of salvation was not imposed on us but presented to us for our consideration. The majority chose the Father's plan. This tradition of thinking together continues in the Church in such forums as priesthood quorums, auxiliary presidencies, ward councils, and the basic family council.

USE PERSUASION, LONG SUFFERING, GENTLENESS, MEEKNESS, AND LOVE UNFEIGNED

What we Latter-day Saints should bring to political discourse is straight out of the Doctrine and Covenants. We are to exert our influence only . . .

Doctrine and Covenants 121:41–42. . . . by persuasion, by long-suffering, by gentleness and meekness, and by love unfeigned; by kindness, and pure knowledge, which shall greatly enlarge the soul without hypocrisy, and without guile.

This kind of political dialogue would be revolutionary indeed and would, I believe, readily lead to far better political solutions. Imagine a political body—a congress, a local council, a parliament—without the adversarial tone, the partisan posturing, and the outright lies and misrepresentations about one another. Imagine no more childish hypocrisy, accusing the other side of the same sins you're guilty of yourself. Imagine no more guile, with hidden agendas that undermine trust. Imagine governance by "pure knowledge" gained from careful study of the objective facts, untainted by partisan or personal advantage.

Imagine liberals and conservatives who are gentle and meek with one another, valuing their different perspectives and learning from each other. Imagine combining the compassion and concern for social justice among liberals with the self-starting energy and fiscal discipline of conservatives—what could they not accomplish together if they stopped disdaining each other and governed themselves by the correct principles of "gentleness, meekness, and love unfeigned"?

Note that total agreement is not required. We don't expect to see things the same way—in fact, what would be the use of councils if everyone held the same opinions all the time? But Latter-day Saints have a tradition of moving forward together to accomplish great things despite our diversity. This is a great paradox of the gospel: the more we can capitalize on the differing strengths we bring, valuing each one, the more unified we become.

If we were to bring the gospel mind-set to politics, even as individual "disciples of the gentle Christ," we might create a political as well as a spiritual revolution.

NOTES

1. "Guidelines to Carry Forth," *Ensign*, May 1974, 4.

2. Dieter F. Uchtdorf, "Pride and the Priesthood," *Ensign*, November 2010.

3. Cited in Spencer W. Kimball, "Guidelines to Carry Forth the Work of God in Cleanliness," *Ensign*, April 1974.

4. Russell M. Nelson, "A More Excellent Hope," *Ensign*, February 1997.

5. Hugh Nibley, "Beyond Politics," Maxwell Institute. http://maxwellinstitute.byu.edu/publications/transcripts/?id=162.

6. "First Presidency Issues Letter on Utah Precinct Caucus Meetings," February 13, 2012. http://www.mormonnewsroom.org/article/first-presidency-issues-letter-utah-precinct-caucus-meetings.

7. Cited in Lee Davidson, "Mormon View on Role of Governing Is Distinct," *Salt Lake Tribune*, January 3, 2012. http://www.sltrib.com/sltrib/home2/53225419-183/church-lds-mormon-leaders.html.csp.

8. Neal A. Maxwell, "The Lonely Sentinels of Democracy," *New Era*, July 1972.

9. M. Russell Ballard, "Counseling With Our Councils," *Ensign*, May 1994.

10. Nibley, "Beyond Politics."

FOURTEEN

SCIENCE

There's a lot of noise about the conflict between science and religion. People worry about the contradictions. What should I think about this?

The Doctrine and Covenants breaks through the artificial barriers people raise between science and religion to the point that believing Latter-day Saints have no interest in this so-called "conflict."

> *Doctrine and Covenants 93:24. And truth is knowledge of things as they are, and as they were, and as they are to come.*

This expansive statement releases us from believing anything that isn't true. The Lord does not say, "Truth is what the government says it is" or "Truth is what your teacher says it is" or even, to be honest, "Truth is what this or that Church authority says it is."

No, the book says that truth is knowledge of what *actually* is—what is real, verifiable, and complete. To know the truth is to know things *as they really are* now, as they really used to be, and as they really will be.

Intriguingly, the revelation does not say that "truth is things as they are," but that "truth is *knowledge* of things as they are." Only when we know a thing as it really is, do we know the truth of it.

When you think about it, knowing the truth about anything is quite a challenge. Look at any object—say, a pencil or a stone on the ground or even your own finger—and ask yourself if you know it as it really is. You see it only in part at any given moment, so you can't really say you know the truth about it. Before space travel, people could see

147

only one side of the moon—seeing nothing of the other side meant that for centuries *we didn't know it as it really is.*

And then we've had to invent instruments to explore what's underneath the moon's surface, but the conclusions of scientists are quite speculative (although we're reasonably sure it isn't cheese). Now we "know" more about the moon, but we still don't know it as it really is.

How much less do we know a person as he or she really is. Although we live so close to people, we often know amazingly little about their deepest dreams, doubts, and hurts. We don't even know ourselves very well. The Prophet Joseph Smith put it well when speaking to the Saints: "All things with you are so uncertain."[1]

But for a Latter-day Saint, and for a real scientist, the vastness of our uncertainty is not a depressing but an enlivening realization. Both of us, scientist and Saint, are excited by the prospect of no end of things to learn, no shortage of truths to be uncovered. Joseph Smith was excited for:

> *Doctrine and Covenants 121:28–31. A time to come in the which nothing shall be withheld, whether there be one God or many gods, they shall be manifest. All thrones, dominions, principalities and powers, shall be revealed . . . And also, if there be bounds set to the heavens or to the seas, or to the dry land, or to the sun, moon, or stars—all the times of their revolutions, all the appointed days, months, and years, and all the days of their days, months, and years, and all their glories, laws, and set times, shall be revealed.*

In other words, the Lord promises to reveal the truths about the mysteries that intrigue *scientists:* the truths of astronomy, geology, mathematics, physics, sociology, and politics. The origin of the universe, the nature of time and space—all "shall be manifest" and "nothing shall be withheld."

SEEK DILIGENTLY TO LEARN WISDOM AND TO FIND TRUTH

In the meantime, we are all commanded to be scientists of a sort in the quest for truth:

Doctrine and Covenants 88:118. Seek learning, even by study and also by faith.

Doctrine and Covenants 97:1. I speak unto you with my voice . . . concerning your brethren in the land of Zion, many of whom are truly humble and are seeking diligently to learn wisdom and to find truth.

We are never relieved of the obligation and opportunity to seek the truth by careful study and the exercise of faith. In the quest for truth we are to "go search in the depths where it glittering lies or ascend in pursuit to the loftiest skies"[2]—studying astronomy and marine biology and everything in between! The Lord commends those who are "truly humble and are seeking diligently to learn wisdom and to find truth." These are the principles all genuine scientists live by, regardless of their discipline: humility, diligent study, and faith.

Humility is required because of our mortal limitations. The fact that mortals can never completely know "things as they are, were, and are to come" should make us humble. Scientists are right to say that no law or theory or formulation of science is ever complete or established beyond all doubt. All it takes is one exception to throw everything into question.

Intellectual pride is the chief source of the so-called conflicts between science and religion. On the one side are those known as fundamentalists, for whom religion is all answers and no questions. Those who are taught not to question tend to close themselves off from new knowledge. For them, science is a threat to be countered. Latter-day Saints, by contrast, are taught that all knowledge, whether scientific or spiritual, begins with questions. Brigham Young taught, "In these respects we differ from the Christian world, for our religion will not clash with or contradict the facts of science in any particular."[3]

On the other side from the fundamentalists are those who ridicule religion and categorically refuse to consider the possibility of arriving at spiritual as well as material truth. In doing so, they actually violate one of the basic principles of science by reasoning *a priori,* or coming to a conclusion about a proposition before the experiment is done.

BE ADMONISHED IN ALL YOUR
HIGH-MINDEDNESS AND PRIDE

An authentic truth-seeker avoids intellectual pride or what the Doctrine and Covenants calls "high-mindedness":

Doctrine and Covenants 90:17: Be admonished in all your high-mindedness and pride, for it bringeth a snare upon your souls.

The term "high-minded" appears in Romans 11:20 and comes from the Greek word *hypselophroneo*, "to have a lofty brain." When the ego gets connected to learning, the soul is easily snared or trapped into error. The history of science is littered with people who have fallen into such traps; fortunately, there have also been many humble ones who avoided the traps and helped along the advancement of science.

The intellectual arrogance of medieval scholars was overthrown by men like Galileo, Copernicus, and Francis Bacon, who dared to ask questions. Then Isaac Newton's description of the laws of mechanics and gravitation appeared to be the last word on the subject.

Newtonian science was so persuasive that it help give rise to the Enlightenment, an era in which science overturned superstition and, for many, took the place of religion. Much of the scholarly world took a position known as "positivism," the view that there is no truth at all in religion. To the positivist, religious questions are simply meaningless. The positivists defended themselves as totally objective truth seekers, utterly neutral and untouched by "blind faith."

Thoughtful scientists abandoned the "high-mindedness" of positivism as it became clear that they were likely to mistake their provisional opinions for settled truths. A landmark 1960 book by Dr. Thomas Kuhn, *The Structure of Scientific Revolutions,* introduced the notion that scientists are influenced by the values and assumptions of the times they live in. Two scientists living in different periods of history might look at the same evidence and arrive at totally different conclusions about it.

For example, for more than two hundred years scientists were baffled by an obscure problem with Isaac Newton's laws of gravity and planetary motion. By using Newton's laws, they could predict precisely the orbits of the planets—except for one, the planet Mercury. Mercury was just not where it was supposed to be according to Newton's laws.

The positivists of the time insisted that the universe was like a great clock, that everything always and forever worked according to exact mathematical models described by Newton. The nasty little secret was that Mercury would not cooperate.

Then along came a young patent-office clerk named Albert Einstein, who suggested that Mercury's orbit was erratic because it was close to the sun, and that the space around the sun was "bent." To the scientific world, the idea of "bent space" was too preposterous for words. The great physicist Ernst Mach called it "paradoxical nonsense." How can you "bend" empty space? But in 1919, astronomers observed that light from a distant star did indeed bend around the sun. Einstein was right. Astounded, the scientific world went through a fundamental and radical change. The universe was not at all the giant clock the positivists had assumed it was; it was far stranger than they had ever imagined.

When one famous philosopher was asked about the problems that had arisen with the positivistic outlook, he responded, "I suppose the most important of the defects was that nearly all of it was false."[4]

As Kuhn pointed out, science only takes place within what are called "grand narratives," overall stories of how the universe works. Before Copernicus, the "grand narrative" of the universe was Ptolemaic—that is, the earth was the center of the universe, as taught by the Greco-Roman philosopher Ptolemy. When Copernicus demonstrated that the earth moved around the sun, the Copernican grand narrative replaced the Ptolemaic. Then the Copernican grand narrative was replaced by the Newtonian grand narrative, which in turn was displaced by the Einsteinian grand narrative, and so it goes. In each case, the grand narrative is incomplete. The values and assumptions behind it are always tentative, which is also true of the science based on the grand narrative.

AVOID COVETOUSNESS AND FEIGNED WORDS

In addition to the incomplete assumptions of the grand narrative, other biases can also interfere with the objectivity of science. A good deal of the science done these days is paid for by special interests, and the conclusions often reflect that. A classic example is the study commissioned by a large manufacturer of disposable diapers, which "proved" that the diapers didn't harm the environment. A year or so later, a manufacturer of cloth diapers published a study "proving" that disposables *are* harmful. This kind of science has become commonplace:

> "Chocolate may inhibit cavities" according to one university research center—funded by a candy company.

> "White bread will not make you gain weight" according to a private research institution—funded by a bakery company.

> "Milk is the number one health hazard facing young children" according to a committee of physicians—funded by a "pressure group of mostly vegetarians who oppose animal research."[5]

The search for truth is too often biased, either consciously or unconsciously, by greed. As one researcher writes, "Behind the explosion of corrupted information is money. . . . Truth has come to belong to those who commission it."[6] The Doctrine and Covenants calls this sort of corruption "feigned words" rooted in "covetousness" (104:4, 52).

Latter-day Saints should be on their guard about feigned words, covetousness, and high-mindedness masquerading as science—particularly if it seems to confirm our own cherished biases.

Of course, honest scientists are well aware that their conclusions are always unsettled. Also, they know that despite the best intentions, science is never neutral. Science writer Richard Dawkins puts it well:

> Science thrives on its inability—so far—to explain everything, and uses that as the spur to go on asking questions, creating possible models and testing them, so that we make our way, inch by inch, closer to the truth. If something were to happen that went against our current understanding of reality, scientists would see that as a challenge to our present model, requiring us to abandon or at least change it. It is through such adjustments and subsequent testing that we approach closer and closer to what is true.

Then Dawkins sets up a conflict between the scientific method and the "religious" method of seeking truth. For Dawkins, faith is a "great excuse to evade the need to think and evaluate evidence. Faith is belief in spite of, even perhaps because of, the lack of evidence."[7] This view of faith might well fit a good many people, but it is certainly not the Latter-day Saint view of faith—quite the contrary.

In fact, the Lord teaches us to follow Dawkins's own formula closely when seeking truth. The Doctrine and Covenants repeatedly enjoins us to do exactly as Dawkins prescribes—ask questions, study the best books, reason things through, test our models of truth, and be ready to adjust our understanding when endowed with further light and knowledge. We have a *duty* to "think and evaluate evidence" of our religion.

Doctrine and Covenants 9:8. You must study it out in your mind.

What Dawkins attacks is the easy assertions of fundamentalist religion that rest on unexamined faith and pseudoscientific readings of scripture. Unfortunately, some Latter-day Saints fall into that way of thinking, but the Doctrine and Covenants takes us beyond it. We "study it out in the mind," which means we work very hard at getting to the truth. To "study something out" requires "time, experience, and careful and ponderous and solemn thought," as Joseph Smith put it. "Thy mind, O man," he said, "must stretch as high as the utmost heavens, and search into and contemplate the darkest abyss, and the broad expanse of eternity."[8] Diligent, careful stretching of the mind and study and contemplation are required. There is no shortcut to truth.

Just as a scientist forms a hypothesis and takes it to the laboratory to test it, so do we exercise faith and test the principles of the gospel to see if they hold up under scrutiny. Only then can we expect the spiritual confirmation of truth that comes from God.

STUDY IT OUT IN YOUR MIND, THEN ASK GOD

Doctrine and Covenants 9:8. You must study it out in your mind; then you must ask me if it be right, and if it is right I will cause that your bosom shall burn within you; therefore, you shall feel that it is right.

Of course, for Richard Dawkins, this kind of spiritual confirmation probably doesn't fit his criteria for acceptable evidence, but that just reveals the narrowness of his definition of evidence. The positivist view of evidence is at best too conditioned to be sufficient. Additionally, those who exercise faith and do the experiment described in Alma 32 will be blessed with the evidence they need: "Your understanding doth begin to be enlightened, and your mind doth begin to expand. O then, is not this real? I say unto you, Yea" (32:34–35).

The blessings that come from testing the Lord's word are immediate and unmistakable. I can personally vouch for this, as can many other Latter-day Saints. It is a repeatable, verifiable fact.

Doctrine and Covenants 132:5. All who will have a blessing at my hands shall abide the law which was appointed for that blessing, and the conditions thereof.

The fruits of the Spirit—love, joy, peace, long-suffering, gentleness, goodness, faith, meekness, and temperance—are as real to the soul as are the fruits of patient experimentation in the laboratory to the mind (see Galatians 5:22–23). The results are sure and immediate, as King Benjamin taught: "He doth require that ye should do as he hath commanded you, for which if ye do, he doth immediately bless you" (Mosiah 2:24). I can testify that the fruits of the Spirit come without delay into the lives of people who "do as he commands." The revelations and blessings poured out on the lives of the faithful are evidence of the reality of spiritual laws—just as the new insights that come from the laboratory are evidence of the reality of physical laws.

Another approach to verifying the scientific truth is the test of "falsifiability." For example, if you find one albino crow in the world, then you earn the right to smile when someone says, "Everybody knows all crows are black." Look closely and thoughtfully at the counter examples: examine the lives of those who choose not to carry out the experiment of faith. Many of them will encounter varying degrees of avoidable tragedy in their lives, while others might lead good, honorable lives and enjoy a modicum of happiness. But the outcome will not be the same as for those who do the experiment. The spiritual blessings will be lacking, and it will be evident to you.

We learn through this process of divine experimentation that the gospel is true. As the eminent Mormon scientist Henry Eyring put it: "This religion we have is *only* truth. It is not anything else. . . . Every Mormon and every Gentile can see that, by golly, the thing works. And that was the test the Savior gave for it. Try the thing; see if it works."[9]

To conduct any experiment, whether it be scientific or spiritual, we must have the humility to ask the question in the first place—this is where the high-minded fail because for them the question is meaningless or beneath them or already answered. Then we must obey the conditions governing the experiment. We must have faith in the process, at least until the process proves itself helpful or unhelpful. Finally, we must be open and honest about our findings, doing our best to put away our biases. Gradually, our knowledge of truth will expand.

Brigham Young taught that the gospel "embraces all truth, wherever found, in all the works of God and man that are visible or invisible to mortal eye. . . . It embraces every fact there is in the heavens and in the heaven of heavens—every fact there is upon the surface of the earth, in the bowels of the earth, and in the starry heavens."[10]

No careful student of the Doctrine and Covenants will be bothered by the supposed contradiction between true science and revealed religion.

NOTES

1. "The Prophet's Remarks at the Funeral of Judge Higbee," August 13, 1843, *History of the Church* 5:530.

2. "O Say What Is Truth?" *Hymns of the Church of Jesus Christ of Latter-day Saints*, 272.

3. Brigham Young, *Journal of Discourses* 14:116.

4. Michael D. Aeschlimann, *The Restitution of Man* (Wm B. Eerdmans Publishing, 1998), 60.

5. Cynthia Crossen, *Tainted Truth: The Manipulation of Fact in America* (New York: Simon & Schuster, 1994), 41–42, 130, 140.

6. Ibid., 19.

7. Richard Dawkins, *The Magic of Reality: How We Know What's Really True* (New York: Simon & Schuster, 2011), 24. See also Dawkins, "The Know-Nothings, the Know-Alls, and the No-Contests," *The Nullifidian*, December 1994. http://www.thirdworldtraveler.com/Dawkins_Richard/NoNothings_Dawkins.html.

8. *Teachings of the Prophet Joseph Smith* (Salt Lake City: Deseret Book, 1977), 137.

9. Henry J. Eyring, *Mormon Scientist: The Life and Faith of Henry Eyring* (Deseret Book, 2007), 230–31, emphasis added.

10. *Teachings of Presidents of the Church: Brigham Young*, 15.

FIFTEEN

CALLINGS

When I get a church calling I'm excited but also anxious. I want to "magnify my calling," but I'm not sure how to do that. How can I make a difference in my calling?

In a less-than-reverent moment I once asked a new Sunday School president, a good friend of mine, this question: "So, how will the Sunday School in our ward be different when you're released?"

As soon as I asked the question, I was embarrassed. It was presumptuous and inappropriate. However, he did look thoughtful and said, "That's a terrific question. I'm going to have to think about that one." I too have thought about that one—a lot. I've held a few callings, and I wonder to this day if I've fulfilled them.

BRING SOULS TO CHRIST

When Joseph Smith left the Sacred Grove, he had received his calling, a commission that would consume the rest of his life: to return to the presence of the Father and the Son, and to prepare as many as were willing to come with him.

That is the difference we too are called upon to make as disciples of Jesus Christ.

In that sense, we are all called with the same calling, whether it's to teach Primary, serve as bishop, lead the music, collect the fast offerings, visit a homebound sister, or "master the Scouts" (a truly daunting challenge). That calling is to bring ourselves and our brothers and sisters to Christ. The Doctrine and Covenants teaches us how to carry out that calling.

Doctrine and Covenants 104:59. Prepare my people for the time when I shall dwell with them, which is nigh at hand.

This verse sums up every calling in the Church. If our eyes are not fixed on preparing those for whom we have stewardship for the coming of the Savior, we are not fulfilling our callings.

A bishop I know came to the end of his assignment and confided to me that he wondered if he had made a difference. Sacrament meeting attendance was about where it had been when he was called. Tithe-paying and temple attendance had not changed. He had held hundreds of meetings, but to what end?

I did not consider him a failure and assured him that he had made a tremendous difference in the lives of ward members, including mine. But he still felt that too often he had gotten lost in the minutiae of administration at the expense of his essential calling: to bring the ward closer to the Savior.

Doctrine and Covenants 88:84. Labor diligently, that you may be perfected in your ministry . . . to prepare the saints for the hour of judgment which is to come.

Are bishoprics, stake presidencies, and auxiliary leaders preparing the Saints for that hour? Are meetings held without that clear purpose in view? Do Gospel Doctrine lessons have the objective of bringing souls to Christ, or are they too often wandering discussions? Do priesthood interviews and home teaching visits focus on a loving Savior, or are they just to pass the time of day? Do fathers and mothers clearly teach their families about the goal of family exaltation in the Lord's kingdom?

Unless the mission of bringing souls to Christ is constantly before us, the classes, Scout troops, auxiliaries, wards, and quorums we lead will substitute their own purposes. We can become busy doing things that do not fulfill that mission. These purposes might be worthy—fun ward activities, a pleasant crafts night, a well-prepared lesson on tithing, advancements in Scouting—but unless they clearly and overtly focus on bringing souls to Christ, they are not the callings we are called to.

Scouting advancements in themselves are worthwhile; but a wise youth leader is asking himself, "How do I bring the boys to the Savior through Scouting?" A Gospel Doctrine teacher is fulfilling her calling if she prepares a lesson that explicitly brings her class members closer to the Savior, even if the topic is emergency preparedness. A Primary teacher fulfills his calling by telling the stories of Jesus that, in the words of Elder Neil L. Andersen, are "like a rushing wind across the embers of faith in the hearts of our children."[1]

Doctrine and Covenants 82:19. [Do] all things with an eye single to the glory of God.

Joseph Smith was unfailingly clear about his purpose: He often spoke of having an "eye single to the glory of God," which is "to bring to pass the immortality and eternal life of man" (Moses 1:39). The "eye single" is totally focused. Obviously, an eye afflicted with double or triple vision can never be focused. Joseph's own eye was fixed on what Alma called "the one thing of more importance than all [else]" (Alma 7:7)—preparing the Saints for the Savior and His coming.

Regardless of our specific role, we should have our eyes "single" to this goal, which is "to bring to pass the immortality and eternal life of man" (Moses 1:39). Elder Dallin H. Oaks has called this the "ultimate Latter-day Saint priority": "First, we seek to understand our relationship to God the Eternal Father and His Son, Jesus Christ, and to secure that relationship by obtaining their saving ordinances and by keeping our personal covenants."[2] Everything we do in our callings should measurably advance this goal.

LEAD THE WAY TO THE TEMPLE

Our mission is clear; but how do we achieve it?

Joseph Smith had the benefit of revelation to show him the way forward, and anyone who properly seeks the guidance of the Holy Ghost can enjoy similar direction.

That path clearly leads to the temple.

In the temple, every step along the path, every covenant necessary for exaltation is clearly spelled out. In 1843 Joseph sent the elders to gather the Saints, and the purpose of the gathering was in turn to build the House of the Lord:

> What was the object of gathering the . . . people of God in any age of the world? . . . The main object was to build unto the Lord a house whereby He could reveal unto His people the ordinances of His house and the glories of His kingdom, and teach the people the way of salvation. . . . It is for the same purpose that God gathers together His people in the last days, to build unto the Lord a house to prepare them for the ordinances and endowments.[3]

Thus, the temple was Joseph's primary concern. All of his business dealings, his locating of cities, his establishment of stakes—everything he did was aimed at providing a sacred place for the Saints to meet the Savior. Every calling he extended was to help gather people to the temple so they could be prepared to meet the Lord at the opening of the veil:

> *Doctrine and Covenants 101:23. Prepare for the revelation which is to come, when the veil of the covering of my temple . . . shall be taken off, and all flesh shall see me together.*

But you say, "I'm the ward clerk/preparedness chairman/visiting teaching coordinator. What does my calling have to do with the temple?"

No matter what our callings may be, helping each other move toward the temple is our first priority. So far from being just one priority among many, the temple is the "main object," as Joseph Smith said. Everything we do in the Church should focus on helping the Saints to make and keep temple covenants. Youth conferences, Sunday School classes, Primary programs, family activities—unless they clearly lead to the temple, their purposes might be questioned.

Of course, we get to the temple in stages. Every calling in the Church is designed to help members make the next logical covenant. The Primary prepares children for baptism and for the priesthood; the Aaronic Priesthood and Young Women prepare youth for the covenants of the temple and the Melchizedek Priesthood; clerks assist the priesthood and the bishopric in advancing people towards their endowments and sealings. Everyone has a role to play in helping everyone else advance to the temple.

AVOID DISTRACTIONS

Once we understand the goal of our callings and the ordinances and covenants of the temple as the means to achieving the goal, we face the most challenging time of all: letting less important things distract us from our discipleship.

The *ultimate* important goal might seem far off. It lacks the feeling of urgency, so it is always at the mercy of "fatal distractions"—priorities that seem good in the moment but in the end rob time and energy from the most important thing.

No one accepts a calling to fail in it. We want to do our best, but we might lose sight of our purpose and get distracted from it by a whirlwind of worldly demands.

> *Doctrine and Covenants 30:2. Your mind has been on the things of the earth more than on the things of me, your Maker, and the ministry whereunto you have been called; and you have not given heed unto my Spirit, and to those who were set over you.*

With distracted minds, we miss hearing the direction of the Spirit and inspired leaders. As a result, children might miss a baptismal date; youth fail to advance in the priesthood or Young Women; young men fall short of receiving the Melchizedek Priesthood and a mission call. The lonely go unvisited, the sick unblessed, and the needy unfed.

How can we deal successfully with the fatal distractions?

As Heidi Swinton observes in her biography of the Prophet, "Joseph understood distractions and did not squander 'the time . . . to prepare to meet God' (Alma 34:32)."[4] In carrying out the mission, Joseph had more than his share of trouble to deal with: illness, persecution, forced removals, mob attacks, imprisonment, faithless friends. The setbacks were many and cruel. But by applying a few simple principles, Joseph found ways to transcend anxieties and carry out his calling.

"Sometimes," says Elder Jeffrey R. Holland, "we come to Christ too obliquely."⁵ As a boy, Joseph learned to take no indirect paths. He went straight to God for answers to his burning questions. The Book of Mormon taught him, "Behold, the way for man is narrow, but it lieth in a straight course before him, and the keeper of the gate is the Holy One of Israel" (2 Nephi 9:41). Joseph followed an undeviating course and led the Saints—those who would follow—along that course.

Additionally, Joseph was wary of the "much business" that kept people from attending to truly important priorities. "Men may preach and practice everything except those things which God commands us to do, and will be damned at last. We may tithe mint and rue, and all manner of herbs, and still not obey the commandments of God."⁶ In other words, we may be very busy doing apparently good things and still deviate from the straight path toward our goal.

On this point, Elder Dallin H. Oaks admonishes the Saints to avoid immersing themselves in merely good things and to focus on the "best things":

> Just because something is *good* is not a sufficient reason for doing it.
> . . . Remember that it is not enough that something is good. Other
> choices are better, and still others are best. . . Be careful not to exhaust
> our available time on things that are merely good and leave little time
> for that which is better or best. . . Stake presidencies and bishoprics
> need to exercise their authority to weed out the excessive and ineffec-
> tive busyness that is sometimes required of the members of their stakes
> or wards.⁷

Joseph Smith did not allow "excessive and ineffective busyness" to distract him from his calling. He focused his efforts on the straight and single path that would lead to the Savior.

MAGNIFY YOUR CALLING

Doctrine and Covenants 88:80. Be prepared in all things . . . to magnify the calling whereunto I have called you, and the mission with which I have commissioned you.

The Lord spoke of this focused effort as "magnifying a calling," and Joseph used that expression frequently.⁸ He was once asked about it. "Brother Joseph, you frequently urge that we magnify our callings. What does this mean?"

He is said to have replied, "To magnify a calling is to hold it up in dignity and importance, so that the light of heaven may shine through one's performance to the gaze of other men. An elder magnifies his calling when he learns what his duties as an elder are and then performs them."[9]

For Joseph, to magnify a calling was like viewing it through a microscope. In his time, the term *magnify* would have been associated with a magnifying glass, as *Webster's 1828 Dictionary* defines the word: "To make great or greater; to increase the apparent dimensions of a body. A convex lens magnifies the bulk of a body to the eye."[10] A magnifying lens does not scatter light; it focuses light. It brings the rays of the sun to a bright, hard, clear point. Magnifying a calling allows the "light of heaven to shine through."

Therefore, we magnify our callings by diminishing the distractions. We focus on what we *must* achieve and avoid the scattering and dissipating effect of trying to do everything. Elder M. Russell Ballard has said:

> Occasionally we find some who become so energetic in their Church service that their lives become unbalanced. They start believing that the programs they administer are more important than the people they serve. They complicate their service with needless frills and embellishments that occupy too much time, cost too much money, and sap too much energy. . . . The instruction to magnify our callings is not a command to embellish and complicate them.[11]

We need to burn through the "frills and embellishments" and focus on the hard, diamond core of what *must* be achieved in our callings. Elder Oaks has said: "The instruction to magnify our callings . . . does not necessarily mean to expand; very often it means to simplify."[12]

LET EVERYONE LEARN HIS DUTY

Doctrine and Covenants 107:99. Wherefore, now let every man learn his duty, and to act in the office in which he is appointed, in all diligence.

In simplifying our callings, we learn our essential duties. We ask the Lord what *we* must do in *our* callings, and then we go forward "in all diligence."

Then we let others learn their duties too. We do little in the Church by ourselves; we have quorums, companions, counselors, and leaders to work with so that no one person has to "do it all." Everyone knows dedicated brothers or sisters who jump in and try to do everything, to take the whole burden on themselves.

In doing so, they burn themselves out and deprive others of the opportunity to serve and grow. As I look back on the callings I've held, I regret not involving other people more. Often it seemed easier to just "do it myself" instead of delegating or asking for help.

Throughout the Doctrine and Covenants, the Lord calls us "my friends." He calls us to work with Him, and He works with us. He not only dictates what we must do but also counsels, sustains, and travels alongside us. I have felt His presence and His whispering influence when carrying out a calling.

We should follow His example in working with our brothers and sisters. Elder Ballard tells about a ward council he observed where that principle was misunderstood. As the meeting began, "The bishop took charge of the situation immediately and said, 'Here's the problem, and here's what I think we should do to solve it.' Then he made assignments to the various ward council members. This was a good exercise in delegation, I suppose, but it did not even begin to use the experience and wisdom of council members to address the problem."

After some instruction, this bishop did things differently. He asked for ideas and recommendations from council members. When they counseled together, they opened "a reservoir of insight and inspiration."[13]

RENDER AN ACCOUNT

To help us stay focused on the cause of Christ, to ward off distractions, the Lord asks for frequent and regular accountability sessions.

Doctrine and Covenants 104:11–12. A commandment I give unto you, that ye shall organize yourselves and appoint every man his stewardship;

that every man may give an account unto me of the stewardship which is appointed unto him.

Doctrine and Covenants 72:3. It is required of the Lord, at the hand of every steward, to render an account of his stewardship, both in time and in eternity.

In the Church, we have frequent and regular opportunities to "render an account of our stewardship," such as priesthood councils, ward councils, presidency meetings, and personal interviews. These opportunities are a blessing—we get the chance to counsel together about our challenges and thank the Lord for our successes.

But too often, these are perfunctory meetings where goals are not advanced and progress is not tracked. No record is kept and no accounting required. Elder Ballard asks, "Are you using the ward and stake councils effectively as they were intended? Don't let them become meaningless exercises in organizational bureaucracy."[14]

In one stake I know of, the presidency presented to the members an ambitious goal at the stake conference. This goal was to involve all members of the stake, who were asked to make this goal a priority in their lives for the coming year. Weeks and months went by. When semiannual stake conference rolled around again, the goal was barely mentioned. By the end of the year, the goal had been virtually forgotten.

What had gone wrong? The presidency had prayerfully selected the goal and put great emphasis on it. A strategy was designed. The goal was communicated very effectively. But no one in particular was accountable for the goal. No one was called upon to "render an account of his stewardship." No one tracked progress. Because of the lack of accountability, virtually nothing was done.

When people know they are going to report on their assignments, when they know that someone cares if those assignments are carried out, they simply perform better.

The Prophet Joseph insisted that Church councils record and follow up on their decisions, which "will forever remain upon record, and appear an item of covenant or doctrine."[15] Commitments made in a Church council might well have the weight of a covenant and should be honored and accounted for.

The temple provides a pattern of precise, frequent, and regular accountability for assignments. In the house of the Lord, no one receives an assignment or makes a covenant without the requirement of a formal accounting. The reason for this is simple: the goal of exaltation in the celestial kingdom is simply too big and too ambitious to attain all at once. The Lord divides the goal into manageable tasks and steps suited to our capacity—"here a little and there a little" (2 Nephi 28:30)—but then requires that we report our progress *regularly* and *frequently* so He can qualify us for the next step and give us further direction.

For this reason, we take the sacrament not once in a lifetime or twice a year, but every week. President Gordon B. Hinckley said, "I am confident the Savior trusts us, and yet he asks that we renew our covenants with him frequently and before one another by partaking of the sacrament, the emblems of his suffering in our behalf."[16] This system of frequent and regular accounting for our lives and our callings prevents us from deviating too far from the straight path to the Savior. It also helps us move forward along that path toward His loving embrace rather than languishing in place.

The Prophet Joseph was called to help us return to the glorious presence of our Savior. He gathered thousands of Saints with their eyes fixed on that goal. He built temples to open the way. No distraction could deter him from his single-minded pursuit of that goal. He didn't try to do it all himself but relied on all members to do their part and to account to each other for their callings. He was a model disciple of the Savior.

President Thomas S. Monson sums up the goal of every calling in the Church: "Our goal is the celestial kingdom of God. Our purpose is to steer an undeviating course in that direction."[17]

NOTES

1. Neil L. Anderson, "Tell Me the Stories of Jesus," *Ensign*, May 2012.

2. Dallin H. Oaks, "'Focus and Priorities," *Ensign*, May 2001.

3. *History of the Church*, 5:423–25.

4. Heidi Swinton, "Joseph Smith: Lover of the Cause of Christ," *BYU Speeches*, November 2, 2004. http://speeches.byu.edu/reader.php?id=8794.

5. Jeffrey R. Holland, "Come unto Me." *BYU Speeches*, March 2, 1997. http://speeches.byu.edu/reader.php?id=2912 .

6. *History of the Church*, 6:223; *Teachings of Joseph Smith*, 159.

7. Oaks, "Good, Better, Best," *Ensign*, November 2007.

8. See for example Doctrine and Covenants 24:3, 9; 66:11; 84:33; 88:80; *History of the Church* 4:603, 606.

9. Thomas S. Monson, "All That the Father Has," *Ensign*, July 1989.

10. *Webster's 1828 Dictionary*, "Magnify."

11. M. Russell Ballard, "O Be Wise," *Ensign*, November 2006.

12. Oaks, "Good, Better, Best."

13. M. Russell Ballard, "Counseling with Our Councils," *Ensign*, May 1994.

14. M. Russell Ballard, "Members are the Key," *Ensign*, September 2000.

15. Kirtland High Council Minutes, January 18, 1835, cited in Richard L. Bushman, *Joseph Smith: Rough Stone Rolling* (New York: Vintage, 2007), 257.

16. Gordon B. Hinckley, "Trust and Accountability," *BYU Speeches*, October 13, 1992. http://speeches.byu.edu/reader.php?id=7095. Accessed March 8, 2008.

17. Monson, "True to the Faith."

SIXTEEN

MISSIONS

I know every member is supposed to be a missionary, but the idea scares me, and I don't know how to do it.

The purpose of missionary work is to bring souls to Jesus Christ. We are all "on a mission" in this world by virtue of being baptized. Every soul who takes the name of Christ is clearly under the obligation to share the gospel. The Lord has said:

> *Doctrine and Covenants 1:4. The voice of warning shall be unto all people, by the mouths of my disciples, whom I have chosen in these last days.*

Every disciple of Christ has this obligation. What we often forget, however, is the second half of the Lord's exhortation:

> *Doctrine and Covenants 1:5. And they shall go forth and none shall stay them, for I the Lord have commanded them.*

Too often we allow ourselves to be "stayed" instead of "going forth" to do the work of bringing souls to Christ. We are fatally distracted from our missionary responsibility by our fears and by the cares of the world. We are lax in our study of the gospel and in the cultivation of our own testimonies. We think ourselves weak. We fail to exercise the great power that the Lord gives to those who follow his commandments: the power to bring our brothers and sisters out of darkness and into his marvelous light and warm embrace.

Doctrine and Covenants 1:30. Those to whom these commandments [are] given . . . have power to lay the foundation of this church, and to bring it forth out of obscurity and out of darkness.

BRING SOULS TO JESUS CHRIST

When we tell people that they have a Savior who loves them, the Spirit invests that testimony with power. When they hear that the Prophet Joseph was sent by God to bring them this message, they feel the force of that witness. When they can tell that we in our turn love them, what a powerful influence it has on them.

As a ward missionary, I taught one family for quite a few years. I thought highly of them, but they were not interested in changing their habits at all. They were nice people but seemed impervious to the Spirit.

A son of the family suffered from a neurological disorder; he kept to himself and rarely left his room. Knowing he was there alone all the time made me sad. Once I asked his mother if it would be all right to visit with him and teach him. She shook her head firmly; we were not to disturb him. Then I asked her, "Do you think he knows that he has a Heavenly Father who loves him?"

The look on her face startled me. She seemed unable to speak. For just a moment, I believe, the Spirit touched her heart. It was a slight victory, but I believe that family will someday be gathered. It may take many more years.

I believe the message we share with people is that they have a Heavenly Father and a Savior who love them. Bringing them to Him, what we know as the gathering of Israel, is the Lord's greatest priority. Because He loves us, He yearns to gather us, to encircle us in the "arms of His love" (Doctrine and Covenants 6:20). Through the Prophet Joseph he calls to each of us:

Doctrine and Covenants 29:1–2. Listen to the voice of Jesus Christ, your Redeemer, the Great I Am, whose arm of mercy hath atoned for your sins; who will gather his people even as a hen gathereth her chickens under her wings, even as many as will hearken to my voice and humble themselves before me, and call upon me in mighty prayer.

This tender image—the hen gathering her chicks—represents Jesus Christ seeking out scattered Israel. Under His "healing wings" (Malachi 4:2) we find not only salvation but also the embrace of a loving Savior. In this one symbol is the gospel of Christ.

In the many dispensations that have come before, the Savior has grieved at the unwillingness of Israel to gather to Him. "O Jerusalem, Jerusalem, thou that killest the prophets, and stonest them which are sent unto thee, how often would I have gathered thy children together, even as a hen gathereth her chickens under her wings, and ye would not!" (Matthew 23:37). Because they would not, they were scattered. As Jeremiah prophesied, "Therefore will I scatter them as the stubble that passeth away by the wind of the wilderness" (Jeremiah 13:24). Their lost, wandering, ignorant condition was symbolized by the desolate image of the wilderness.

In this last dispensation, however, a remnant of Israel *will* gather willingly under His wings, "even as many as will hearken unto my voice and humble themselves before me, and call upon me in mighty prayer." What a great privilege if we are counted among them! Now we have the calling to gather others, the opportunity to tell them about a loving Savior and what He has done for us.

Doctrine and Covenants 65:1, 3. Hearken, and lo, a voice as of one sent down from on high . . . Prepare ye the way of the Lord, make his paths straight. . . . Yea, a voice crying—Prepare ye the way of the Lord, prepare ye the supper of the Lamb, make ready for the Bridegroom.

These commandments are the very essence of missionary work. We are to "prepare the way" by helping others to come to the "supper of the Lamb," or the sacrament table. How do we do this? By "making His paths straight." We cannot go at this work in a roundabout fashion. What people need is the straightforward teaching of the plain gospel of Christ and the straightforward testimony of the love of our Savior.

One night my ward mission companion and I visited a family in which the wife belonged to the Church but the husband did not. When we went to the door, we met a muscular young man who looked like he could throw us both off his front porch and was about to do so. His wife intervened, and although he resisted, we were invited in.

We made a few introductions and asked about the family. The wife, a less-active member, was happy to show us her new baby but not really interested in returning to church. The husband visibly scowled at us, obviously willing us to leave.

After a few minutes, we prepared to go. But we didn't leave without telling the little family straightforwardly that they had a Heavenly Father who loved them, and we asked if we could pray with them. The mother agreed and the father acquiesced.

I don't remember which of us offered the prayer, but we were soon on our way.

A few days later, the woman telephoned and asked if we could come back. We were glad to, and on entering the house, we found an entirely different situation. Her husband jumped from the couch, shook our hands, and invited us to sit. It was as if he had a different face—it was alight, humble, almost childlike.

There was a remarkable change in the spirit in the room. Instead of tension, I felt an abundant peace that was almost tangible. The young man, whose name was Mike, sat down and eagerly asked us to teach him. His voice, his manner, everything about him was the reverse of what we had experienced before.

At length he explained that before our visit he had never experienced prayer. No one had ever told him that he had a Heavenly Father who loved him. These things had worked on Mike's heart in the intervening days.

Doctrine and Covenants 112:13. I, the Lord, will feel after them, and if they harden not their hearts, and stiffen not their necks against me, they shall be converted, and I will heal them.

The Lord had been "feeling after" Mike and found a man whose heart was actually soft instead of hard, whose great muscled neck was not stiff after all. The Spirit of the Lord had gathered Mike under a healing wing without our even being aware of it.

Teaching Mike was pure delight after that. He accepted everything as a child would, unquestioning and full of faith. His wife was touched too; and when he was baptized, the tears softened every heart in the room. I had rarely seen anyone so thoroughly converted and so fully healed in his spirit.

GO WITH THE SPIRIT IN YOUR HEART

In carrying out our missionary responsibility, we should remember we have a quiet Companion who always goes with us. The Lord Himself "feels after" the people we meet, pursuing them, testing their hearts for readiness to accommodate the Spirit. Knowing that Companion is there should give us the confidence we need in our efforts. His promise is clear:

> *Doctrine and Covenants 84:88. Whoso receiveth you, there I will be also, for I will go before your face. I will be on your right hand and on your left, and my Spirit shall be in your hearts, and mine angels round about you, to bear you up.*

Every missionary has an army of unseen supporters working alongside him or her. Many times in my life I have had the privilege of meeting and teaching people like Mike, and each time I felt the powerful influence of the emissaries of God.

I remember as a missionary going door to door in the suburbs of Bordeaux, France, one hot August afternoon. Literally no one was home; it was not only working hours but the time of the year the French call *les vacances*—nearly everyone leaves town to take a vacation. The heat turned everything white—houses, dusty streets, even plants. It was so quiet; the only sounds we encountered were the occasional yelp of a dog home alone behind a locked door.

At one home, we were both startled when a woman opened the door. She was a young woman in a summer dress, with upswept auburn hair and an equally startled look on her face. We told her that we had an important message for her.

She invited us to return that evening when her husband would be home, and we made an appointment.

I couldn't get that startled feeling out of my mind. It was like a shock of recognition, like a nudge from an unseen arm waking me out of sleep.

When we returned, the woman and her husband invited us in. He was a young military doctor, slender and dark and extremely intelligent. We told him the story of Joseph Smith and the Restoration, and he laughed at us. We didn't really believe that nonsense, did we? But they were polite people and let us finish our discussion. At the end, we explained about family prayer and asked if the doctor would be willing to offer such a prayer. He said, *"Je veux bien"* ("I guess it's okay with me"). We knelt, and he prayed.

As we left, he seemed a bit more subdued and was willing to have us come back.

On our return visit, night had turned to day. The doctor was a changed man, and his wife close to tears. There was no more laughter. "It was the family prayer," he said. They had been having family prayer with their two small sons every day since our visit, and the effect of the Spirit in those intervening days had nearly overpowered them. The doctor seemed almost exhausted by it. From that moment, they accepted everything we taught them as pure truth, and within a couple of months, they were baptized.

At one point, I asked the wife why she had invited us into her home in the first place. "You said you had an important message for me, and something told me that it really *was* important." She also talked about the curious spark of recognition she had felt when she opened the door to us. "It was meant to be."

After that, I began to understand how the Lord works with his missionaries. Our task: to persevere in finding and teaching people who will respond. His task: to change their hearts. Over time, I came to expect these miracles—they were rare, but they happened. A humble working-class sister, a college student, a widow and her teenage son, a young couple who had been living together, a former nun, a prominent businessman, a refugee from communist Eastern Europe—these were some of the "miracle people" I had the privilege to work with in France.

DO ALL THINGS THAT LIE IN YOUR POWER

Doctrine and Covenants 123:17. Dearly beloved brethren, let us cheerfully do all things that lie in our power; and then may we stand still, with the utmost assurance, to see the salvation of God, and for his arm to be revealed.

I have seen this promise fulfilled numerous times in my own missionary efforts over the years. The Lord reveals His arm when He will. He extends salvation where He will. Our role is to "cheerfully do all things that lie in our power" while He does His work. My own experiences have given me "utmost assurance" that He is there and working miracles in the hearts of His children.

So what "lies in our power" to do? What specifically must we do to qualify for our role in these miracles?

First, we must recognize that gathering people to the Lord is the most worthwhile work we can do in this life. The Doctrine and Covenants makes that point clear. People who asked the Prophet Joseph Smith what they could do that would be of most worth in the kingdom all received the same revealed answer:

Doctrine and Covenants 15:6. The thing which will be of the most worth unto you will be to declare repentance unto this people, that you may bring souls unto me, that you may rest with them in the kingdom of my Father.

By far the most important work anyone can do is to serve as an agent of the Atonement of Christ to enable as many as will come to gather under His healing wings. Anyone who wants to do this important work is called to it:

Doctrine and Covenants 4:3. If ye have desires to serve God ye are called to the work.

Whether we receive a formal call as a full-time missionary or not, we are "called to the work."

REMEMBER FAITH, HOPE, AND CHARITY

To qualify for that work, we must cultivate certain virtues in our lives:

Doctrine and Covenants 4:5. Faith, hope, charity and love, with an eye single to the glory of God, qualify him for the work.

The formula of "faith, hope, and charity" is a familiar one, but we can see how essential it is to missionary work if we consider the opposite formula: "doubt, despair, and contempt for others."

That unholy trinity destroys the work. Doubt is natural, but faith is simply the action we must take to prove that God will fulfill His promises. When I began my mission years ago, I was filled with doubt—in myself, mostly—but thankfully I had enough faith to get up in the morning on time and do the work.

A missionary's chief enemy is despair—after knocking on a thousand doors with nothing to show for it, it's understandable to feel hopeless. Also, the devil perseveres in trying to make your day as hard as he can. In my experience, however, the Lord provides hope to those who are cast down. One rainy afternoon in France, I was out on the street, feeling discouraged and miserable, wondering why we even bothered to ring the next doorbell. Just then, the storm stopped, and I looked up and saw a brilliant cloud turned silver by the sun. For a moment, I couldn't breathe; it was so beautiful. "The Lord's light," I thought. And my spirit quietly turned a corner.

Another danger to missionaries is quiet, growing contempt for the many people who reject them. Only a few of my companions genuinely disliked the French, but most of us got just plain fed up from time to time. Some days I almost wished no one would answer the door when I rang.

But deep down, I felt a curious connection to those people and that country. From the time I was a small boy, when people would ask me where I wanted to serve a mission, I would point to a purple patch on the world globe and say, "There." It was France. I studied French all through school. I visited France on a student tour in high school. Other students hated it; I loved it. When I was called to the Paris Mission, I thought, "Of course. Where else?"

I still love that country and those people. Their music, their food, their history, their art—all of it appeals to me. They are reputed to be sharp with foreigners, but overall I found them endearing and sometimes unusually helpful. It became like home to me, and the people like family. It's not hard for me to feel charity for them because, after all, so many of them showed charity to me.

To be missionaries we don't have to be perfect—but we do have to face and overcome our natural tendencies to shrink back, become discouraged, and feel defensive. Faith, hope, and charity never fail to produce fruit in missionary work.

Doctrine and Covenants 4:6. Remember faith, virtue, knowledge, temperance, patience, brotherly kindness, godliness, charity, humility, diligence.

Like all missionaries in my day, I memorized this catalogue of virtues, but in my case I forgot them too easily. I was impatient. I had a hard time concentrating on the work because I like to talk too much (my first companion had to tell me to quiet down). Diligence was a problem for me, and I've never been particularly humble.

But my mission did teach me the value of faith, the necessity of virtue, and the delights of gaining knowledge through study and the Spirit. I learned a lot about controlling my temper; thousands of rejections taught me patience. When it came to brotherly kindness, I can honestly say I loved my brother missionaries, some of the best people I've ever known. To be godly gradually came to me; at least I did not have the same glib mouth at the end as I had at the beginning. "Charity, humility, and diligence"—to learn them cost me some of the hardest moments I've ever gone through.

KNOCK AND IT SHALL BE OPENED UNTO YOU

So I grew in the gospel and in the work, as most missionaries do. But the most important lesson I learned about effective missionary work is summed up in the last verse of Section 4:

Doctrine and Covenants 4:7. Ask, and ye shall receive; knock, and it shall be opened unto you.

In my mission, where we knocked on doors all day, this verse gave rise to more than a little ironic humor. Doors were rarely opened to us.

However, I learned something about the Lord that I had not known before—that His door and His ear are always open. In hindsight, I see exactly how He responded to my prayers for help, sometimes later rather than sooner, but always in quietly miraculous ways.

The Lord makes clear that if we pray with real intent, He will guide us so that the people we meet will receive Him and His kingdom will move forward:

> *Doctrine and Covenants 65:5. Call upon the Lord, that his kingdom may go forth upon the earth, that the inhabitants thereof may receive it, and be prepared for the days to come, in the which the Son of Man shall come down in heaven, clothed in the brightness of his glory, to meet the kingdom of God which is set up on the earth.*

If we do so, we can have the confidence of a true disciple of Christ. We can have confidence that He will grant us the power we need to do His work.

> *Doctrine and Covenants 123:12. There are many yet on the earth among all sects, parties, and denominations, who are blinded by the subtle craftiness of men, whereby they lie in wait to deceive, and who are only kept from the truth because they know not where to find it.*

Our task is to show them where to find the truth.

The day will come when the Lord will unveil the heavens and invite each of his disciples to come forward—one by one—and greet and embrace Him (see Doctrine and Covenants 109:72–74). On that day, we will want to be surrounded by as many as possible of our brothers and sisters, by those we have influenced in some way to come unto Him—our children, our family members, our ward or branch members, our friends, our neighbors—as many as we have touched with the power of our testimonies.

If we do so, He will take us into his loving embrace and whisper to us, "Well done, thou good and faithful servant."

SEVENTEEN

PRIESTHOOD

I'm not sure I'm doing what I should as a priesthood holder. How do I magnify my calling in the priesthood?

In the Sacred Grove, Jesus Christ informed the young Joseph Smith that the power of godliness had been taken from the earth. Joseph was told that the religious organizations of the day had "a form of godliness, but they deny the power thereof" (Joseph Smith–History 1:19).

The "power of godliness" was restored to the earth in 1829 when Joseph Smith and Oliver Cowdery received the priesthood by the hands of heavenly messengers. John the Baptist, who held the keys of the Aaronic, or lesser priesthood, conferred it on Joseph and Oliver on May 15, 1829, on the banks of the Susquehanna River in upper Pennsylvania. Later, the two men received the Melchizedek, or higher priesthood, by ordination from Peter, James, and John, the holders of the keys of that priesthood. In this way, the "power of godliness," or the power to come back into the presence of God, was restored to the earth.

To most people in the world, "priesthood" is "the order of men set apart for sacred offices; an order composed of priests."[1] This is how *Webster's Dictionary* of Joseph Smith's time defined *priesthood*.

Latter-day Saints also use the word priesthood to refer to a body of men ("the priesthood will put up chairs for the ward dinner"). But the priesthood is actual power given by God to men to act in His name.

Elder Robert D. Hales asks, "Brothers and sisters, can you imagine how dark and empty mortality would be if there were no priesthood?"

You and I would never have been baptized or received the gift of the Holy Ghost. Valerie and I would never have been sealed in the temple, and we would be lost to each other and our children at death. I would never have been able to bless my children when they were sick and suffering. "Without the power of the priesthood," says Elder Hales, "the whole earth would be utterly wasted. There would be no light, no hope—only darkness."[2]

OPEN THE GATES OF THE CELESTIAL KINGDOM

The purpose of the Aaronic Priesthood, named for Aaron, the brother of Moses, is to open to us the gates of the celestial kingdom of God. Encompassed in the Aaronic Priesthood is the authority to baptize and to administer the sacrament, which is a renewal of the baptismal covenant.

When I turned twelve, I was ordained a deacon. I was anxious but pleased. The first time I passed the sacrament, I got confused and ended up in all the wrong places. This has been a pattern with me every time I advanced in the priesthood. How many times as a priest did I misspeak the sacrament prayer? I don't know.

Doctrine and Covenants 84:26. The lesser priesthood . . . holdeth the key of the ministering of angels and the preparatory gospel.

Once called on in ward conference to talk about my new position as president of the deacons quorum, I said, "I'm grateful for the Aaronic Priesthood because it holds the keys of the ministering of angels." My bishop stood up and congratulated me for understanding my role. Actually, I didn't understand what I had said at all—I didn't know what "keys" meant or what the ministering of angels was.

When I was seventeen, a close friend from school decided to join the Church and asked me if I would baptize him. I well remember the white clothes, the warm water, and the embrace and a few tears I had never experienced before. I remember how much I loved my friend and how he thanked me again and again for helping him cross that threshold into the celestial kingdom of God.

It was then I understood something about the ministering of

angels. An angel is an authorized messenger of the Savior who brings salvation and peace to wounded people.

OPEN THE GATES OF EXALTATION IN THE CELESTIAL KINGDOM

Doctrine and Covenants 107:18. The power and authority of the higher, or Melchizedek Priesthood, is to hold the keys of all the spiritual blessings of the church.

The purpose of the priesthood named for Melchizedek, the great high priest who conferred the priesthood on Abraham, is to bestow the gift of the Holy Ghost and to open to us the gates of exaltation, or the highest heaven of the celestial kingdom of God:

Doctrine and Covenants 131:1–3. In the celestial glory there are three heavens or degrees; and in order to obtain the highest, a man must enter into this order of the priesthood [meaning the new and everlasting covenant of marriage]; and if he does not, he cannot obtain it.

Only by the authority of the Melchizedek Priesthood can the ordinance of eternal marriage be performed.

Thus, the task of these two priesthoods is to prepare us to enter and to dwell in the presence of our Father in Heaven. His authorized servants are sent into the world to bring our Father's children to the temple, so that they may be ready for eternal life and exaltation. No work is more significant than this—it is truly "a marvelous work and a wonder."

Adam received both the Melchizedek and Aaronic Priesthoods, which were passed from father to son through Enoch and Noah to Melchizedek, and from Melchizedek to Abraham to Moses. The Lord wanted to confer both priesthoods on the children of Israel at the time of Moses, but because of their hardened hearts, they declined to receive the blessings and responsibilities of the Melchizedek Priesthood. So the Lord in his mercy gave them the Aaronic Priesthood so they could continue to qualify themselves for his kingdom and prepare for even greater blessings (Doctrine and Covenants 84:6–28).

The priesthood ceased with the cancer of pride and contention in the Church after the time of Christ. Thus, to reopen the gates of salvation and exaltation, the priesthood had to be restored. Duly authorized administrators were sent from the presence of God to confer the priesthood once again on living men. God has promised that it will "never be taken again from the earth" (Doctrine and Covenants 13:1).

Before my mission, I was ordained an elder. For two years, I wore a suit and white shirt and tie and a nameplate that said "Elder England." I understood intellectually that I had been given the authority of the higher priesthood to do "many wonderful works" (Doctrine and Covenants 84:66), but when I was asked to confirm a just-baptized member, I honestly didn't know what to say.

I put my hands on the wet, blonde hair of the young housewife we had taught for many weeks. She was an emigrant from Yugoslavia with little education and lots of children living in a very humble apartment. Her husband was pretty much absent both physically and emotionally, and she did housework to make ends meet. A nonentity in this world, I suppose—but I will never forget her.

I started the ordinance slowly, halting and hesitating between sentences for something to happen. Then something did happen. I began to speak more quickly. The words flowed stronger and faster as if someone had taken over my mouth. This powerful voice that I was no longer in control of promised that inconsequential young mother amazingly consequential blessings. When it was over, I was trembling and had to sit down.

The priesthood is power. It made my body shake with its power.

Since then, I have been privileged to lay hands on many people and give them blessings. I've learned a little more about how the priesthood works, how to wait for the Spirit to nudge my mind, and how clearly the Spirit can speak. I've also learned how much love pours from the Spirit of God through the hands and the voice, and the intense light and peace that fills everyone around.

OBTAIN THE PRIESTHOOD AND MAGNIFY YOUR PRIESTHOOD CALLING

In Doctrine and Covenants 84, the Lord makes an oath to those who receive the priesthood and magnify their callings, that He will grant them the following blessings if they fulfill certain conditions:

- **They are sanctified by the Spirit unto the renewing of their bodies (v. 33).**

Those faithful to the priesthood will be resurrected first and with glorified, sanctified bodies. "These are they who shall have part in the first resurrection" (Doctrine and Covenants 76:64).

- **They become the sons of Moses and of Aaron (v. 34).**

As sons of Moses, they are rightful administrators in the Melchizedek Priesthood and are heirs of the privileges of that great prophet—to commune with God, to receive revelation in their callings, and to act in the higher ordinances under God's direction.

As sons of Aaron, they are rightful administrators in the Aaronic Priesthood, and partake of the privileges of Aaron—to teach the gospel and to administer the saving ordinances of baptism and the sacrament.

- **They become the seed of Abraham (v. 34).**

As the seed of Abraham, they are entitled to the blessing of Abraham: "Exaltation and glory in all things, as hath been sealed upon their heads, which glory shall be a fulness and a continuation of the seeds [posterity] for ever and ever" (Doctrine and Covenants 132:19)—in other words, the joy of the eternal family belongs to them.

- **They become the church and kingdom, and the elect of God (v. 34).**

To be elect is to be an heir, as Isaiah prophesied: "I will bring forth a seed out of Jacob, and out of Judah an inheritor of my mountains: and mine elect shall inherit it" (Isaiah 65:9). The faithful priesthood holder and his family are those seeds of Jacob who will inherit the "mountains" of the Lord—the promised land, kingdom, and temples of the Lord.

- **They receive Jesus Christ (v. 35).**

To receive the priesthood is to receive Jesus Christ; and to receive Him is to be "encircled about eternally in the arms of his love," as Nephi taught (2 Nephi 1:15). Those who receive Christ are ensured of their exaltation: "If ye receive me in the world, then shall ye know me, and shall receive your exaltation; that where I am ye shall be also" (Doctrine and Covenants 132:23). Furthermore, we are commanded in 3 Nephi 27:27 to be like Christ ("even as I am"); to be like Him a man is required to hold the priesthood, for His priesthood is His power. All men who seek to be like Jesus Christ must be faithful in their priesthood callings.

- **They receive the Father and all that the Father hath (v. 36-38).**

Of course, this is the greatest blessing God can bestow, for He cannot bestow more than all that He has. "The priests of the Most High, after the order of Melchizedek," are the legitimate heirs of God's kingdom. "They are they into whose hands the Father has given all things—they are they who are priests and kings, who have received of his fulness, and of his glory" (Doctrine and Covenants 76:55–57).

These high blessings are promised to those who "are faithful unto the obtaining these two priesthoods . . . and the magnifying their calling" (Doctrine and Covenants 84:33). To obtain the priesthood, one must qualify for it. This requires keeping the commandments of God. Also, the faithful priesthood holder "magnifies" his calling. In an inspired address, President Gordon B. Hinckley explained what it means to magnify one's priesthood calling:

> All of you, of course, are familiar with binoculars. When you put the lenses to your eyes and focus them, you magnify and in effect bring closer all within your field of vision. But if you turn them around and look through the other end, you diminish and make more distant that which you see.
>
> So it is with our actions as holders of the priesthood. When we live up to our high and holy calling, when we show love for God through service to fellowmen, when we use our strength and talents to build faith and spread truth, we magnify our priesthood. When, on the other hand, we live lives of selfishness, when we indulge in sin, when we set

our sights only on the things of the world rather than on the things of God, we diminish our priesthood. . . .

How do *we* do this? How do *we* enlarge the power of the priesthood with which we have been endowed? We do it when we teach true and sound doctrine. The Lord has said: "And I give unto you a commandment that you shall teach one another the doctrine of the kingdom" (Doctrine and Covenants 88:77).

We diminish that calling, we shrink that mission when we spend our time speculating about or advocating that which is not set forth in the scripture or that which is not espoused by the prophet of the Lord. Rather, ours is the responsibility, as set forth in revelation, "to bind up the law and seal up the testimony, and to prepare the saints for the hour of judgment which is to come; that their souls may escape the wrath of God, the desolation of abomination which awaits the wicked, both in this world and in the world to come" (Doctrine and Covenants 88:84–85).

We magnify our priesthood and enlarge our calling when we serve with diligence and enthusiasm in those responsibilities to which we are called by proper authority. I emphasize the words, "diligence" and "enthusiasm." This work has not reached its present stature through indifference on the part of those who have labored in its behalf. The Lord needs men, both young and old, who will carry the banners of His kingdom with positive strength and determined purpose.[3]

In summary, President Hinckley has taught that to magnify our calling in the priesthood is to:

Live up to our high and holy calling.

Show love to God through service to fellowmen.

Use our strength and talents to build faith and spread truth.

Teach true and sound doctrine to one another.

Serve with diligence and enthusiasm in those responsibilities to which we are called by proper authority.

USE THE PRIESTHOOD ONLY UPON THE PRINCIPLES OF RIGHTEOUSNESS

By contrast, he has indicated that we diminish our calling in the priesthood by living selfishly, indulging in sin, and setting our sights only on the world. The Lord has said that the power of the priesthood will not continue with such men:

Doctrine and Covenants 121:34–36. There are many called, but few are chosen. And why are they not chosen? Because their hearts are set so much upon the things of this world, and aspire to the honors of men, that they do not learn this one lesson—that the rights of the priesthood are inseparably connected with the powers of heaven, and that the powers of heaven cannot be controlled nor handled only upon the principles of righteousness.

The power of godliness *cannot* be exercised through the use of force or compulsion. This is one of the reasons the priesthood was taken from the earth in ancient times.

In the world, the priesthood of a religious organization often holds political sway in the community. The priesthoods of the earth have often amassed wealth, reigned over nations, and compelled obedience from people. In our culture, the concept of priesthood then is distorted by a long history of usurpation of power.

This mistaken view of priesthood leads to complaints: "Why do only men hold priesthood? Why are others shut out of Church government?"

Ironically, any priesthood holder who attempts to "govern" his stewardship as if he were some secular potentate immediately loses his power:

Doctrine and Covenants 121:37. When we undertake to cover our sins, or to gratify our pride, our vain ambition, or to exercise control or dominion or compulsion upon the souls of the children in any degree of unrighteousness, behold, the heavens withdraw themselves; the Spirit of the Lord is grieved; and when it is withdrawn, Amen to the priesthood or the authority of that man.

No one can succeed for one instant in using the priesthood for his own gain or for lording it over people. Jesus Christ never used the priesthood except to heal, bless, and serve others. The authorities who condemned Jesus probably would have had no interest in Him except that He was said to be a king—the priests and governors could tolerate no threat to their power. But, as He said, His kingdom was not of this world (see John 18:36).

Particularly destructive is the idea some men have that their priesthood gives them the right to dictate to others, particularly to their wives and children. There couldn't be more contrast between the gentle firmness shown by the Savior in correcting others and the abusive, swaggering behavior of some men. "No man who abuses his wife or children is worthy to hold the priesthood of God," President Hinckley has said.[4]

There is no government on earth like the priesthood of God. In one sense, it is not a government at all but an organization of servants. President Stephen L Richards, once a counselor in the First Presidency, taught this principle:

> The Priesthood is simply defined as "the power of God delegated to man." This definition, I think, is accurate. But for practical purposes I like to define the Priesthood in terms of service and I frequently call it "the perfect plan of service" . . . It is an instrument of service, and the man who fails to use it is apt to lose it, for we are plainly told by revelation that he who neglects it "shall not be counted worthy to stand."[5]

Holders of the priesthood lose the power of godliness if they fail to learn their duties and do them.

LET EVERY MAN LEARN HIS PRIESTHOOD DUTY

Doctrine and Covenants 107:99–100. Wherefore, now let every man learn his duty, and to act in the office in which he is appointed, in all diligence. He that is slothful shall not be counted worthy to stand, and he that learns not his duty and shows himself not approved shall not be counted worthy to stand.

The work of the priesthood is not easy. It requires deep prayer, thought, and courage, because we are dealing with the progression of souls. It requires getting up on your hind legs and teaching a class. It requires the worthiness and willingness to bless others. It requires answering a prophet's call to serve anywhere in the world at any time.

No wonder some men hesitate, feeling inadequate to the task.

President Thomas S. Monson says, "Now, some of you may be shy by nature or consider yourselves inadequate to respond affirmatively to a calling. Remember that this work is not yours and mine alone. It is the Lord's work, and when we are on the Lord's errand, we are entitled to the Lord's help. Remember that the Lord will shape the back to bear the burden placed upon it."[6]

I am not a particularly courageous soul. Several times I've been a quorum leader, which requires reaching out to people who often don't want you around, and teaching groups of men who are sometimes a little intimidating. Over the years, I've been assigned as a home teacher to numerous people who would rather I go away.

But I'm sincerely thankful that I could stand with my son and bless tiny twin granddaughters who were born prematurely. I'm so grateful for the power that enabled me to bless and calm the convulsions of my own two-year-old daughter when she became seriously ill. I treasure the opportunity to give an annual blessing to my children, a custom we began when they started school each year.

In all of these moments, in the challenges or the delights, I have felt the powerful governing hand of the Lord take my hand and help me.

NOTES

1. *Webster's 1828 Dictionary*, "Priesthood."

2. Robert D. Hales, "Blessings of the Priesthood," *Ensign*, November 1995.

3. Gordon B. Hinckley, "Magnify Your Calling," *Ensign*, May 1989, 46.

4. Gordon B. Hinckley, "What Are People Asking About Us?" *Ensign*, November 1998, 72.

5. Cited in Thomas S. Monson, "To Learn, to Do, to Be," *Ensign*, November 2008.

6. Monson, "To Learn, to Do, to Be."

EIGHTEEN

SCRIPTURES

Finding the motivation to study the scriptures is a problem for me. There's so much emphasis on it, but it's hard to understand them. The family resists. And there's no good time . . .

The year 1918 was a sad year for the world. The "Great War," as it was then called, seemed unending in blood and brutality. The war had stopped nearly all missionary work, as young men had been drafted in huge numbers. A flu epidemic raged around the globe, killing tens of millions of mostly young victims. Death was all around.

It was a particularly sad year for Joseph F. Smith, the aged President of the Church. In his eightieth year, he had to face the early death of his oldest son. Hyrum Mack Smith, forty-five and a vigorous member of the Quorum of the Twelve, died suddenly of a ruptured appendix. His father was devastated: "My soul is rent asunder. My heart is broken, and flutters for life! O my sweet son, my joy, my hope!"[1]

After this, President Smith suffered "a siege of very serious illness." For many months, he lingered over the scriptures and his prayers. In October conference, he said, "I have not lived alone these five months. I have dwelt in the spirit of prayer, of supplication, of faith and of determination; and I have had my communication with the Spirit of the Lord continuously."[2]

OPEN THE SCRIPTURES AND HEAR
THE VOICE OF THE LORD

The loss of his son and of so many millions of others to war and plague must have weighed heavily on his mind:

> *Doctrine and Covenants 138:1–2. On the third of October, in the year nineteen hundred and eighteen, I sat in my room pondering over the scriptures; and reflecting upon the great atoning sacrifice that was made by the Son of God, for the redemption of the world.*

> *Doctrine and Covenants 138:6–8. I opened the Bible and read the third and fourth chapters of the first epistle of Peter, and as I read I was greatly impressed, more than I had ever been before, with the following passages: "For Christ also hath once suffered for sins, the just for the unjust, that he might bring us to God, being put to death in the flesh, but quickened by the Spirit: by which also he went and preached unto the spirits in prison."*

There followed one of the great prophetic revelations of all time, the Vision of the Redemption of the Dead, in which President Smith was shown the grand sweep of saving work done for those who passed into the spirit world without the opportunity to respond to the call of Jesus Christ. The vision is now incorporated into the Doctrine and Covenants as Section 138.

President Smith's experience teaches us to go to the scriptures with our deepest problems. Of course, we should make scripture study a habit, but I've found my own study to be most meaningful when I have real problems to solve—which is all the time.

The text of President Smith's vision was published a few weeks after the close of World War I, in the deathly silence following the bombardments that had killed millions. The cruel influenza was taking young lives everywhere, including my wife's great-grandfather. Few families were untouched. The Lord gave this revelation to comfort not only the grieving prophet, but also a world stunned by mass death.

As Professor George S. Tate has written, "The vision came at a time of great, worldwide need. Such a panoply of dying; such universal and unresolved grief . . . such pervasive hunger to know the fate of the dead—all these things give a special resonance to Doctrine and Covenants 138, with its great concourses of the dead, its assurance of divine love and of the unspeakable comfort of the Atonement."[3]

In the aftermath of the war, there was a great outpouring of literature of anguish in the works of the Lost Generation, articulate voices despairing over the futility of life and suffering. But there was another voice as well, the still voice of reassurance that came from God through His prophet Joseph F. Smith.

The Lord knows what we need when we need it, and in His mercy He provides counsel through His Spirit and through the voices of prophets ancient and modern. If we go to the scriptures in prayer, seeking His guidance, we will find it. I know that because it has happened to me countless times.

Doctrine and Covenants 33:16. The holy scriptures are given of me for your instruction; and the power of my Spirit quickeneth all things.

In his wisdom, President Smith knew where to turn in his need for comfort, counsel, and guidance. The scriptures are not only for our instruction but also as a means to be "quickened" by the Spirit. He said, "There is a peculiarity which I have found accompanies the reading of the word of God, that whenever read it is calculated to refresh the soul, to revive the spirit of man, and to draw him nearer to the fountain of light."[4]

Opening the books has become more and more instructive to me over the years, and I'm grateful that I feel more quickened as well. A feeling settles over me when I open the scriptures, no matter where or what page, that I have come to recognize as the Spirit of the Lord. It's a spirit of quietness, of anticipation, and of perspective—it lifts me away from my concerns and helps me see them "in a different light," so to speak.

"Scriptures are like packets of light that illuminate our minds and give place to guidance and inspiration from on high," says Elder Richard G. Scott. "They can become the key to open the channel to communion with our Father in Heaven and His Beloved Son, Jesus Christ."[5]

Usually, that light is soft. It's a soothing light that communicates peace as well as knowledge. It's a light by which I can see into meanings hidden from me until I need them.

That light can also be powerful and beautiful. All I have to do is open the Book of Mormon and the light from that book nearly blinds me.

One of my missionary companions told me of his life before he found the Church. He had grown up abused and battered by his father, a military man. At eighteen, he ran away and joined the drug culture around San Francisco. One day, lost, broke, dirty, and miserable, with no home and nowhere to go, he slunk into a public building in Berkeley to get out of the rain.

Here was a quiet, clean place, with soft chairs, carpet on the floor, and a soft light coming from a reading lamp. No one was around, so he took a chance—hoping he wouldn't be thrown out—and found welcome rest in an armchair. Picking up the book on the small table next to him, he opened it to a random page:

> Behold, I am Jesus Christ, whom the prophets testified shall come into the world.
>
> And behold, I am the light and the life of the world; and I have drunk out of that bitter cup which the Father hath given me, and have glorified the Father in taking upon me the sins of the world, in the which I have suffered the will of the Father in all things from the beginning (3 Nephi 11:10–11).

"I felt like Jesus Christ was introducing Himself to me personally," my friend told me. The voice he heard lit up a darkened heart, and he read on and on. For hours, he sat there alone, nurtured as never before in his life by the Book of Mormon and the Spirit of the Lord.

The building he sat in was the LDS Institute of Religion near the University of California. The scriptures transformed his life, and he joined the Church and eventually joined me on a mission in Paris, France. We were companions only for a short time, but I will always love him and his remarkable story.

SEEK YE DILIGENTLY OUT OF THE BEST BOOKS WORDS OF WISDOM

Joseph F. Smith said, "The greatest achievement mankind can make in this world is to familiarize themselves with divine truth. . . . 'In the footsteps of the Master,' the greatest of all the teachers that this world has ever received, is the safest and surest course to pursue. . . . We can absorb the precepts, the doctrines and the divine word of the Master."[6]

Doctrine and Covenants 88:118. Seek ye diligently . . . seek ye out of the best books words of wisdom.

When I study the scriptures (which are the best of the best books), I tend to focus on individual words and phrases and ask myself, "Why does the Lord say this in this particular way?"

In my graduate work, I learned about the art of "close reading," sometimes called "explication." Close readers are interested in word choice and literary formulas and their history (an example would be Jack Welch's famous discovery of chiasm in the Book of Mormon). They "unpack" metaphors as if they were suitcases, pulling out various meanings and applications of a verse like "Ye are the light of the world" (in how many ways is that true?).

Scholars of scripture become intense "close readers"; their tools are called exegesis (the science of interpretation) and hermeneutics (the science of evaluating an interpretation to see if it's any good).

Although I'm not a biblical scholar (my training is in English literature), I have personally found these tools very helpful in understanding the scriptures. As you read this book, you'll probably notice that I often use the *1828 Webster's Dictionary* to throw light on what a word or phrase might have meant to Joseph Smith when he first recorded it. Because language changes over time, it helps to know how a word might have been used differently in Joseph's time.

I also turn to the ancient Latin, Greek, and Hebrew scriptures that are often cited in the Doctrine and Covenants in order to capture insights that would otherwise be lost. For example, in Section 76 we are introduced to a word no one ever heard before in English: *telestial.*

Doctrine and Covenants 76:81. We saw the glory of the telestial, which glory is that of the lesser, even as the glory of the stars differs from that of the glory of the moon in the firmament.

Anciently, the Greek-speaking Paul wrote of "bodies celestial and bodies terrestrial" when explaining the degrees of glory of the sun and moon, but he never labeled the "glory of the stars" (See 1 Corinthians 15:40–42.) Does it help to know that "telestial" might be derived from the Greek word *telos*, which meant "farthest, uttermost, final"? Might Paul have used *telos* to describe that kingdom farthest from the throne of God? We know he used the word in other places (see for example 1 Thessalonians 2:16).

Of course, I don't know the answer, but it's an interesting possibility. The tools of close reading can't be used to establish doctrine, but they can enrich our understanding. "We value scholarship that enhances understanding," says Elder D. Todd Christofferson. "But in the Church today, just as anciently, establishing the doctrine of Christ . . . is a matter of divine revelation to those the Lord endows with apostolic authority."[7]

Obviously, no one needs formal training to find what they need from the scriptures. It does help, however, to become a "diligent seeker," a student of scripture, to learn something of the cultural background, the history, and the techniques that prophets have used over the ages to communicate their revealed insights.

When I was twenty years old, I had Asian flu and was trapped for ten days in the dormitory of the France Paris Mission headquarters. I was really sick, but here was an opportunity to get deeply into the Book of Mormon. For a long time I had wanted the time to really study the book.

I got as far as 2 Nephi 18. It was a quotation from Isaiah: "Forasmuch as this people refuseth the waters of Shiloah that go softly, and rejoice in Rezin and Remaliah's son; now therefore, behold, the Lord bringeth up upon them the waters of the river, strong and many, even the king of Assyria and all his glory; and he shall come up over all his channels, and go over all his banks."

At that point I stopped "studying" and just "skimmed" the rest. I don't know if it was the fever or the headache, but I couldn't take Shiloah and Rezin and Remaliah's son and the king of Assyria all in one verse. Who were all these people, and why was the water rising, and who cares? I remember having delirious dreams about soldiers drowning in Cecil B. DeMille costumes.

Years later, a wise teacher explained to me that the words of Isaiah are "eternal words," as are all the words of scripture. I learned about the power of figurative language and parable to apply to everyone where in all ages of the world. I learned how Isaiah illustrated the fate of the wicked in all generations by reference to the depraved kings of his own time, who were in every sense "in over their heads." I learned about their rejection of the "waters of Shiloah that go softly"—these are the waters of baptism, and Shiloah is the Savior (see 1 Nephi 20:1). I learned that Isaiah was an eternal writer, and that his warning voice is just as applicable to our time as to his.[8]

For me, diligent seeking means more than the casual skimming I did when I had the flu in Paris. In the *1828 Webster's Dictionary*, *diligence* meant "steady application, constant effort, and exertion."

PONDER OVER THE THINGS WHICH ARE WRITTEN

Joseph F. Smith knew from long experience that he could count on receiving more light and knowledge only if he carefully studied and pondered the light and knowledge already given.

Doctrine and Covenants 138:11. As I pondered over these things which are written, the eyes of my understanding were opened, and the Spirit of the Lord rested upon me, and I saw the hosts of the dead, both small and great.

I think there's a subtle difference between "studying" and "pondering," although they're closely related activities. Perhaps study is more active than pondering and meditation. *Webster's 1828 Dictionary* defines *to ponder* as "to weigh in the mind; to consider and compare circumstances and consequences." The word comes from Latin *pondo*, "weight," the same root as the English word "pound."

To ponder is to give great weight to what is on the page—to consider the scriptures seriously in terms of their implications for our lives. When studying the scriptures, ask yourself these two "pondering" questions:

How does a passage of scripture relate to your own circumstances?

What are the consequences of heeding or disregarding the counsel on the page before you?

The Lord commands us to ponder the scriptures:

Doctrine and Covenants 88:62–63. Verily I say unto you, my friends, I leave these sayings with you to ponder in your hearts, with this commandment which I give unto you, that ye shall call upon me while I am near— Draw near unto me and I will draw near unto you.

By pondering on the scriptures and praying about them, we draw near to the Lord. When we open the scriptures, we invite Him to sit with us and teach us. He draws near to us, but that's possible only if we are willing to ponder and not just dismiss Him.

Pondering and prayer go together. When I was struggling with a problem once, a friend said to me, "Joseph Smith never got any answers to questions he didn't ask." Then I realized that Joseph was a questioner—the Restoration began because a young boy was pondering the scriptures and asking the Lord about them. Inquiring of the Lord became habitual for Joseph, and he was answered liberally.

Skimming the scriptures is like eating skimpy food. We need the solid nourishment that comes from pondering the scriptures and giving the Spirit the chance to guide us, as Joseph F. Smith was guided, to new understanding. President Gordon B. Hinckley observed, "There is hunger in the land, and a genuine thirst—a great hunger for the word of the Lord and an unsatisfied thirst for things of the Spirit. . . . the world is starved for spiritual food."[9]

One sister writes that she felt distant from God and so asked to meet with a Church leader for guidance. She told him that she read her scriptures, paid tithing, went to church, and served in the temple. "Despite my efforts," she said, "I felt little comfort and few answers for my growing doctrinal questions.

What followed was advice that I will never forget. He said, "Your spirit is bigger than it once was and it is hungry. You are not feeding it enough." He explained that because my spirit had grown over the years, it would not suffice to feed it the same "seminary food." He encouraged me to dig deep into the scriptures to look for answers and to focus on feeding my spirit, emphasizing that I could not continue with the same amount of study and expect deeper understanding.

I chose to take his advice.[10]

Many people wonder, "Why read the same stories over and over again? David still kills Goliath. Noah gets through the flood. Nephi makes it to the Promised Land. We've heard it all before."

I've been puzzled by these questions because I feel that I've never read the same scripture twice. It's like stepping into a river—every time you do it, you're in different waters. Elder Scott observes, "Scriptures can communicate different meanings at different times in our life, according to our needs. A scripture that we may have read many times can take on nuances of meaning that are refreshing and insightful when we face a new challenge in life."[11]

KEEP ALL MY WORDS THAT I HAVE GIVEN YOU

Doctrine and Covenants 136:37. Ye are not yet pure; ye can not yet bear my glory; but ye shall behold it if ye are faithful in keeping all my words that I have given you, from the days of Adam to Abraham, from Abraham to Moses, from Moses to Jesus and his apostles, and from Jesus and his apostles to Joseph Smith.

Of course we can't be faithful in keeping all of God's words unless we study them and know them. "The glory of God is intelligence," and we can't bear that glory if we don't faithfully obtain intelligence ourselves (Doctrine and Covenants 93:36). This verse implies that careful obedience to "all my words" has a purifying effect, perhaps because God's word is also God's law.

Doctrine and Covenants 132:12. No man shall come unto the Father but by me or by my word, which is my law, saith the Lord.

From Adam to the latest revelation in the Doctrine and Covenants, we have in the scriptures ready access to the lessons of those who have exercised faith and those who have not. We have the commandments and principles that lead to peace in this life and eternal life in the world to come. With such a rich treasure of guidance, we are blessed far beyond any previous generation:

"Every man, woman, and child may possess and study his or her own personal copy of these sacred texts," notes Elder Christofferson. "How incredible such a thing would have seemed to . . . the Saints of earlier dispensations! Surely with this blessing the Lord is telling us that our need for constant recourse to the scriptures is greater than in any previous time."[12]

When I had teenagers, I often found them in some corner of the house, struggling with a school assignment. The textbook lay open, music pounded through the earphones, often the TV was on in the background, and the scratch paper was truly scratched up. A kind of open-mouthed despair shows up on a teenage face in those circumstances that every parent recognizes.

When I was wise about it, I would turn off the TV, gently pull off the earphones, and after absorbing some protests, I would sit with my son or daughter and work through the problems with them. I often took the opportunity, in my pedantic way, of teaching a few new things to them myself—if I knew anything about the subject, that is. Sometimes their despair became so great my children would actually seek *me* out, the textbook flapping in hand, and ask for my help. (That usually happened late the night before the assignment was due.)

Our Father in Heaven watches for us to open our scriptures. I'm convinced He is delighted when we do, and He draws near, hoping we will invite Him to linger with us and help us understand and work through our problems. He will gladly teach us a few new things. The invitation is also open to take the textbook and go to Him in our moments of discouragement.

If we are wise, we will accept the invitation. We will shut off the smartphones, the TVs, the text messages, the tablets, and the laptops (unless that's where we keep our scriptures!). We will draw near unto Him, and He will draw near unto us and teach us from the best of the best books.

NOTES

1. *Teachings of Presidents of the Church: Joseph F. Smith* (Salt Lake City: Intellectual Reserve, 1999), 407.

2. *Teachings of Joseph F. Smith*, 362.

3. George S. Tate, "'The Great World of the Spirits of the Dead': Death, the Great War, and the 1918 Influenza Pandemic as Context for Doctrine and Covenants 138," *BYU Studies* 46 (2007), 1:40.

4. *Teachings of Joseph F. Smith*, 44.

5. Richard G. Scott, "The Power of Scripture," *Ensign*, November 2011.

6. *Teachings of Joseph F. Smith*, 42.

7. D. Todd Christofferson, "The Doctrine of Christ," *Ensign*, May 2012.

8. See also Ezra Taft Benson, "A Message from Judah to Joseph," *Ensign*, December 1976.

9. Gordon B. Hinckley, "Feed the Spirit, Nourish the Soul," *Ensign*, November 1998.

10. Suzette Smith, "My Faith's Journey," *Exponent II*, Fall 2010, 8.

11. Scott, "The Power of Scripture."

12. Christofferson, "The Blessing of Scripture," *Ensign*, May 2010.

NINETEEN

TEMPLE

*I know I should go to the temple more often, but I'm so busy.
I wish I knew how to get more out of temple worship. And of
course I'd love to get into family history, but with everything
else to do, who has time?*

The gospel teaches that our whole purpose in life is to experience
joy: "Men are that they might have joy." (2 Nephi 2:25). People
look for joy in many places. A certain measure of joy can be found in
many things, such as winning a game or doing a job well. A counterfeit
joy can be found in the pursuit of pleasure—what the scriptures call
"riotous living."

But in only one place in this world can we experience anything like
a full measure of joy, and that is the holy temple.

In the temple, we unite our precious families for eternity. In the
temple, we receive the promise of exaltation. In the temple, we feel the
presence of our Father in Heaven. And in the temple, we encounter our
Savior. "We come unto Christ through the ordinances of the temple."[1]

FIND THE FULNESS OF JOY IN THE TEMPLE

The scriptures always couple the temple with finding the most
superlative joys of life.

*Doctrine and Covenants 124:39. The beginning of the revelations and
foundation of Zion, and . . . the glory, honor, and endowment of all her*

municipals, are ordained by the ordinance of my holy house, which my
people are always commanded to build unto my holy name.

I divide my life into two parts—before and after my first day in the
temple. Before that, I was a snarky, uncommitted teenager. The experience of the endowment humbled me. I came out of the temple not
only a different person newly committed, but also more of a man with
a hugely expanded view of the joys of life. As I rejoined my mother in
the celestial room, I saw her smiling, glorious in white—and for the
first time I caught the vision of a glorious being exalted by pure love.

after

Doctrine and Covenants 132:46. Whatsoever you seal on earth shall be
sealed in heaven; and whatsoever you bind on earth, in my name and by
my word, saith the Lord, it shall be eternally bound in the heavens.

My own wedding day in the Salt Lake Temple was the mountaintop experience of my life. Picture beautiful Valerie at the altar with me;
our loved ones encircling us in a small, crystalline sealing room; Valerie's grandfather beaming, white hair, white suit; his gentle words as
by the power of the holy priesthood he sealed us for time and eternity.
What would I trade for the joy of that moment? Nothing. *Herace*

I've witnessed the temple sealings of all five of my children. Like
any father in my position, I can't describe the intense joy I felt, sitting
with my beloved Valerie and watching beloved sons and daughters, all
in white, sealed for eternity to their beautiful companions. There is
simply no earthly equivalent to that feeling. *I was there*

STAND IN THE PRESENCE OF THE LORD

Doctrine and Covenants 97:15–16. Inasmuch as my people build a house
unto me in the name of the Lord, and do not suffer any unclean thing to
come into it, that it be not defiled, my glory shall rest upon it; yea, and my
presence shall be there, for I will come into it, and all the pure in heart that
shall come into it shall see God.

Just to stand in the presence of our Lord is the greatest joy we
can experience. By entering the temple we enter into His presence.

The Psalms teach us, "In thy presence is the fulness of joy" (Psalm 16:11). "I will go unto the altar of God, unto God my exceeding joy" (Psalm 43:4). The Apostle Paul equates the presence of the Lord with our hope and joy: "For what is our hope, or joy, or crown of rejoicing? . . . the presence of our Lord Jesus Christ" (1 Thessalonians 2:19).

The Savior promises that the day will come when we are "encircled about eternally in the arms of his love" (2 Nephi 1:15). Imagine that moment. What will it mean to you? What wouldn't you sacrifice to experience it? What would you give in exchange for it? In the temple, we can enjoy a foretaste of that supreme joy.

> *Doctrine and Covenants 124:40–41. Let this house be built unto my name, that I may reveal mine ordinances therein unto my people; for I deign to reveal unto my church things which have been kept hid from before the foundation of the world, things that pertain to the dispensation of the fulness of times.*

In the ordinances of the temple, we find joy. It is a house of prayer, blessings, sacrifices, and covenants, all of which bring the Spirit into our lives, and the fruit of the Spirit is joy (Galatians 5:22). The Lord said to Isaiah, "Them will I bring to my holy mountain [the temple], and make them joyful in my house of prayer: their burnt offerings and their sacrifices shall be accepted upon mine altar" (Isaiah 56:7).

The ordinance of the endowment brings joy to our lives not only by teaching us the Father's plan of happiness but also by providing us the means to return to His presence. Isaiah attributes the joy in his life to endowment blessings: "My soul shall be joyful in my God; for he hath clothed me with the garments of salvation, he hath covered me with the robe of righteousness" (Isaiah 61:10).

In his dedication prayer at the Kirtland Temple, the Prophet Joseph Smith taught that joy is the grand outcome of the temple ordinances. He prayed . . .

> *Doctrine and Covenants 109:76. That our garments may be pure, that we may be clothed upon with robes of righteousness, with palms in our hands, and crowns of glory upon our heads, and reap eternal joy.*

Of course, the crowning joy of the House of the Lord is the sealing ordinance that unites husband and wife for eternity. Elder Russell M. Nelson teaches that "the noblest yearning of the human heart is for a marriage that can endure beyond death. Fidelity to a temple marriage does that. It allows families to be together forever. This goal is glorious. All Church activities . . . are means to the end of an exalted family."[2] Why? Because in the exalted family we experience the fulness of joy.

The prophet Jeremiah foresaw that the very definition of human joy would be the sealing of the eternal family in the temple of God. "The voice of joy, and the voice of gladness, the voice of the bridegroom, and the voice of the bride, the voice of them that shall say, Praise the Lord of hosts: for the Lord is good; for his mercy endureth for ever. . . . Bring the sacrifice of praise into the house of the Lord" (Jeremiah 33:11).

MAKE THE TEMPLE THE CENTER OF YOUR LIFE

For these reasons, the temple was from the beginning of the restoration of the gospel the center of Latter-day Saint life. It was the focus of everything Joseph Smith taught and built in his life.

After the Saints had found refuge in 1839 at Commerce, Illinois, on the Mississippi River, Joseph renamed the settlement Nauvoo, which, he said, "is of Hebrew origin, and signifies a beautiful situation, or place, carrying with it, also, the idea of *rest*; and is truly descriptive of this most delightful situation."[3]

Joseph might have said more on this subject. *Nauvoo* is indeed a form of a Hebrew word (*naveh*) that often refers to the dwelling place of God, or the temple. In Exodus, Moses sings praise to God for leading Israel out of bondage and up to the *naveh*, or His "holy habitation" (15:13); and Isaiah says that when Messiah reigns, the Saints will dwell in the *shalom naveh*, or the peaceable habitation of God (32:18).

It was fitting, then, for Joseph to call this place Nauvoo to signify the peaceful habitation of God, the place where He will reign and reveal Himself to His people.

Anywhere a temple is built is, therefore, a "nauvoo." Every temple is the beautiful habitation of the Lord Himself, made holy by His presence. It is a gathering place for the Saints to come into His presence and receive his highest and holiest blessings. A "nauvoo" is a place where the Atonement of Christ is experienced in its fulness.

Doctrine and Covenants 124:26–27. Come ye, with all your gold, and your silver, and your precious stones . . . and with all your precious things of the earth; and build a house to my name, for the Most High to dwell therein.

Everything that was done by the Latter-day Saints at Nauvoo, Illinois, was in service of this goal. The receipt of the revelation we now know as Doctrine and Covenants 124 "was the Prophet's most significant recorded in nearly three years."[4] The heart of this revelation was the commandment to the Saints to "come from afar" and dedicate themselves totally to the construction of the holy house.

Much has been made of the dedicated industry of the Saints at Nauvoo, of their building a genteel city on the frontier, of the courtly brick homes and gardens, of the prosperity and peace enjoyed there. But all of this was to enable their real work: The real center—both geographical and spiritual—of the "City Beautiful" was the temple.

Thousands of Saints fulfilled the commandment to come from afar and help build the house of the Lord and enjoy the fulness of priesthood blessings. Even the martyrdom of the Prophet Joseph Smith failed to slow the gathering: "the population of Nauvoo actually grew during the year following the murders at Carthage."[5] The task of completing the temple was the key responsibility of the Saints at Nauvoo, as at all times and in all places.[6] Through the winter of 1845–46, the Saints crowded the temple to receive the ordinances and would not disperse even at night—they were that determined to experience the fulness of the Atonement of Jesus Christ in His temple.

The immense sacrifice of the early Saints stands as a lesson for us. Shouldn't the temple be the "center place" of our lives as well? We have scores of temples, many within easy distances. Shouldn't we be "crowding" the temple as the early Saints did?

Most of the cities of the world are centered on the financial district, which just tells you that we live in Babylon—geographically—but we must not live there spiritually. The city of Nauvoo was centered on the temple, and it should be the center of everything we do. We build homes, we work hard, we serve—to what end?

So that we can gather our loved ones and friends to the house of the Lord and enjoy His embrace, which is the very definition of eternal life.

LET THE WORK OF MY TEMPLE CONTINUE
AND NOT CEASE

Given the advantages we have today, this commandment the Lord gave to the early Saints must be even more applicable to us:

Doctrine and Covenants 127:4. Let the work of my temple, and all the works which I have appointed unto you, be continued on and not cease; and let your diligence, and your perseverance, and patience, and your works be redoubled, and you shall in nowise lose your reward, saith the Lord of Hosts.

The "work of my temple" is to carry out the ordinances of exaltation for our loved ones both living and dead.

Family history has become a worldwide obsession, technology for finding our ancestry has exploded, TV shows about ancestors make people cry. But for many Latter-day Saints, family history seems a complex, time-consuming process that can wait, perhaps, until we're retired (if that day ever comes).

Doctrine and Covenants 128:15. Now, my dearly beloved brethren and sisters, let me assure you that these are principles in relation to the dead and the living that cannot be lightly passed over, as pertaining to our salvation. For their salvation is necessary and essential to our salvation . . . they without us cannot be made perfect—neither can we without our dead be made perfect.

Given the high value the Lord puts on this work, we no doubt postpone it at our peril. Ironically, doing family history work is a joy that we deprive ourselves of if we don't "get around to it" because of our job or other activities.

I have a good friend, Rich, who has a busy family and a full-time job. He says, "For us, family history is a way of life." I was startled to hear this and wanted to know more.

"Not a day goes by that I don't think about family history work," He says. "It's ongoing. It's happening right now." He, his brothers, and his cousins have turned research into their family into a worldwide effort, tracking their ancestors through Internet research and correspondence. It's so engaging that it feels almost like a game.

They've been particularly concerned about a loose end in their family tree, a distant ancestor named Hugh. They knew he was from Ireland, but that was about all. The problem was that there were too many Hughs with his family name in Ireland at the time, so they couldn't tell which Hugh was theirs.

They now have a website called In Search of Hugh, where they post known information, links to official and Church documents, updates and discoveries. They hold regular conference calls. They are constantly posting questions for anyone to investigate—"How did Hugh's son Thomas join the Church?" "Why were Hugh's children baptized in the Protestant church when the rest of the family was Catholic?" Rich says, "We think like three-year-olds—they're always asking 'Why?' It's the questions that prompt the answers."

The family also prays about Hugh. At one point, Rich and his brothers felt a distinct impression from Hugh himself: "I'll help you when you help me." The brothers realized that they already had a great deal of information about Hugh's children other than their own ancestor—but they had done no temple work for those that were not in that direct line. That impression has led to an outpouring of ordinances for the people in the lateral family lines. Hugh will be pleased.

By entering known information into Google Maps, Rich has been able to isolate the village and even the farm where Hugh was a tenant. This in turn helped him pinpoint other family members: "Here's a Doyle farm right down the lane," he says, showing me the map. "We know Hugh married a Doyle. Could this tenant farmer be her father?" By connecting many dots like these, a picture of Hugh is gradually coming clear.

Rich's advice: "Make a family tree or a fan showing your family line. Where are the holes? Those spaces represent real people who need you now. You can collaborate with other family members and use their strengths to fill those holes, to add the foliage to your family tree. If you don't know computers, someone in your family does."

Rich says, "There are throngs of people beyond the veil who want us to do something—anything—for them. Those who care will begin working with your mind—they will lead you to the information you never thought existed." If we do our part with tools we now have, family history can become fascinating—and perhaps replace some of the less joyful things we do in our leisure time.

I submit that we could do many things without a great deal of extra effort—or even slightly change things we are already doing—to engage the hearts of our families in their own history. I have told stories about my grandparents for family home evening. Valerie's ancestor was a prominent Mormon pioneer who left a lot of writings behind; we have studied some of those together. Some family members have painted ancestor portraits and scenes associated with the story of our family. One of my grown children gave everyone framed "fans" showing our ancestry to hang on the wall. My sister's hobby is making scrapbooks full of photos and family memorabilia, which have become valued treasures.

> Doctrine and Covenants 138:57. The faithful elders of this dispensation, when they depart from mortal life, continue their labors in the preaching of the gospel of repentance and redemption, through the sacrifice of the only Begotten Son of God, among those who are in darkness and under the bondage of sin in the great world of the spirits of the dead.

Hugh's family is laboring now to bring redemption to him and other loved ones. We can't very well *continue* a work after this life that we haven't been doing while in this life. For a faithful Latter-day Saint, all life—mortal and immortal—is a mission to serve and save our Father's beloved children. For us now, in this mortal moment, the temple is the focus of that great work.

HEAR THE VOICE OF THE LORD IN THE TEMPLE

Finally, the temple is not only the locus of this sacred priesthood service but also our refuge from a fragile, strained mortal life. In the silent rooms, enclosed in the white walls of the Lord's house, I find the kind of peace and new understanding I need. I have found the temple to be, in reality, the answer to my problems.

Doctrine and Covenants 128:23. How glorious is the voice we hear from heaven, proclaiming in our ears, glory, and salvation, and honor, and immortality, and eternal life.

Not long ago, I was facing a new church calling and had a serious concern about how to carry it out. I went to the temple one evening having prayed hard about it for some time and fasting that day. As I sat quietly before the service, I prayed again, and then opened my eyes as the session began. The insights I needed began to flood my mind. Each moment opened up a new vision, a new step I could take to approach the problem. The Spirit literally warmed me and filled me with inspiration—and joy.

So who am I? Just another member of the Church with a problem. Any one of us who enters the temple with a deep need is a child going home to Father, and there He will take us under His loving arm and lift our hearts and counsel our minds with a voice from heaven. Why would we postpone that kind of help? Or try to do everything on our own in our uncertain, stumbling way?

President Boyd K. Packer observes, "At the temple the dust of distraction seems to settle out, the fog and the haze seem to lift, and we can 'see' things that we were not able to see before and find a way through our troubles that we had not previously known."[7]

Our home faces a temple. Early in the morning when Valerie and I leave the house for our walk, we can look up and see the figure of an angel and the gleaming steeple of the temple. We've seen it against a white snowy hillside, the rose clouds of dawn, and the dewy green of spring. We've seen it standing like a fortress against threatening clouds and under dismal rain. We've barely grasped its outline in blinding fog.

But always, we see the light. The temple shines in the sun; it illuminates the night; it is a beacon in the storm. It is perhaps most comforting in the fog of winter. I can be totally disoriented, geographically lost, but I know that the soft, dazzling cloud in the distance surrounds the house of the Lord—and then I know exactly where I am.

NOTES

1. Gordon B. Hinckley, cited in George I. Cannon, "Holiness to the Lord, the House of the Lord," BYU-Idaho Devotional, June 17, 2003. http://www.byui.edu/Presentations/transcripts/devotionals/2003_06_17_cannon.htm

2. Russell M. Nelson, "Celestial Marriage," *Ensign*, November 2008, 94.

3. Cited in Glen M. Leonard, *Nauvoo: A Place of Peace, a People of Promise*, Deseret Book, 2002, 59.

4. Ibid., 235.

5. Ibid., 445.

6. *History of the Church* 7:234; Doctrine and Covenants 124:39.

7. Quoted in "Inside the Temple," LDS.org, http://www.lds.org/church.temples/why-we-build-temples/inside-the-temple?lang=eng.

TWENTY

TESTIMONY

How can I gain a stronger testimony of the gospel?

I've collected the following concerns from various blogs and question sites on the Internet, but I've heard similar feelings expressed before, and you probably have too:

> "I've attended church all my life. I've read the Book of Mormon. Now I want a *real* testimony."

> "I don't know if I have a testimony or not. I honestly don't know what I believe."

> "I had a talk with my wife and she was in tears, for she is struggling with something. . . . She is starting to wonder if the Church is true or not."

> "I wish I had a stronger testimony. I have a lot of doubts."

> "I'm about to go on a mission. I wonder if my testimony is strong enough. How do I know I'm not just fooling myself? How can I know the Church is true?"

These questions are fundamental and heartfelt, and the Doctrine and Covenants provides divine answers.

One of the most tender revelations in that book is given to Oliver Cowdery, who, within days after meeting the Prophet Joseph Smith, sought confirmation from God that Joseph was His prophet. Doctrine and Covenants section 6 explained to Oliver the confirming experience he had had and to the rest of us how to seek a testimony:

Doctrine and Covenants 6:14–15, 20. Blessed art thou for what thou hast done; for thou hast inquired of me, and behold, as often as thou hast inquired thou hast received instruction of my Spirit. . . . Thou knowest that thou hast inquired of me and I did enlighten thy mind; and now I tell these things that thou mayest know that thou hast been enlightened by the Spirit of truth. . . . Behold, thou art Oliver, and I have spoken unto thee because of thy desires; therefore treasure up these words in thy heart. Be faithful and diligent in keeping the commandments of God, and I will encircle thee in the arms of my love.

We learn from this revelation that we must *ask* for a confirming revelation about the truth of the gospel. We must *want to know.*

This may sound obvious, but I'm convinced that deep down many people don't really want to know. Their prejudices or fears are so great that they recoil at even the thought of seeking a testimony. For some, the whole idea is a laughing matter—for others, it's beneath them. Still others sense that a revelation from God would jar their comfortable lives so forcefully that they won't consider it.

Once on my mission my companion and I knocked on a door in southern France. We explained who we were to the gentleman who answered the door, and he looked soberly at us and asked us to step in. He wanted us to meet his mother.

The mother was an elderly woman, bedridden and apparently dying. Several people were grouped around her bed. We felt awkward standing at the foot of the bed, but the woman's son asked her to tell us her story.

"Last night," she said to us, "I was awakened by a man dressed in a brilliant white robe. He stood where you are standing right now. In his hands was a book made of shining golden metal, and he slowly turned the pages so that I could see each one. But I could not read the writing."

That was her story. The people in the room looked at us as if they were expecting us to explain it. My companion seemed oddly impatient about all of this, but I was excited. I immediately launched into the story of the Book of Mormon and the Restoration. I suggested to the woman that she had received a witness of the Book of Mormon in an unusual way and that her family needed to listen to our message.

Slowly, politely, the old woman responded that she was a Catholic and had always been a Catholic and would die a Catholic. This was clearly the end of the discussion, and the son showed us to the door.

I was astonished. The old woman had a vision, told her family, and they didn't recognize a miracle when they experienced it? They weren't even curious to know more?

Afterward, my companion told me that he had felt odd about these events. This elder was senior to me and much wiser than I. The Spirit had let him know that there was no faith in the room, so the vision—if there had been a vision at all—was not likely to bear fruit: "The word preached did not profit them, not being mixed with faith in them that heard it" (Hebrews 4:2).

So we went on our way. I learned that day that to get answers from God we have to *desire* those answers: "I have spoken unto thee because of thy desires," the Lord said to Oliver Cowdery. This desire must be more than idle curiosity like wanting to know who won the football game or what the weather is going to be. This desire must be from the heart.

Do we really *want* to know? Do we ask with real intent to act on our knowledge? Or don't we really care? That's the first question. It stands to reason that a precious testimony from God does not come cheaply.

SEEK THE SPIRIT THROUGH THE PRAYER OF FAITH

We also learn from section 6 that God blesses us with instruction from His Spirit "as often as we inquire." We should expect revelation if we ask with real intent. The scripture calls such inquiries "prayers of faith."

Doctrine and Covenants 42:14. And the Spirit shall be given unto you by the prayer of faith.

Because faith is a principle of action, a prayer of faith is offered by a person who is honestly seeking the guidance of the Spirit and intends to follow any counsel received. *Every heartfelt prayer of faith is answered with instruction.* Once we learn to recognize the voice of the Spirit, we must be prepared to act on those instructions.

A person who asks for a witness merely out of intellectual curiosity can expect no answers. The Lord requires the "prayer of faith."

We also learn that when we receive words from the Lord, we are to "treasure up the words in our hearts." It is a great thing to hear truth from the Spirit of God, whether by His own voice or by confirming the words of His servants. The testimony is to be treasured, guarded, protected, and nurtured. It can easily die away through neglect.

If we treasure the testimony we receive, bear it, and act on it, we qualify for an even greater confirmation: "Be faithful and diligent in keeping the commandments of God [those we receive in our hearts as well as those we receive through His servants], and I will encircle thee in the arms of my love." We learn from this verse that a testimony is more than data communicated to the mind—it is also a relationship of the heart. We will feel His arms around us, warming and safeguarding us, if we act with faith and diligence. We will feel His love, and we can testify of that love.

In section 6, the Lord sensed that Oliver needed a stronger testimony, so He gave to Oliver and to us a key for recognizing truth from God:

> *Doctrine and Covenants 6:22–23. If you desire a further witness, cast your mind upon the night that you cried unto me in your heart, that you might know concerning the truth of these things. Did I not speak peace to your mind concerning the matter? What greater witness can you have than from God?*

These verses are personally important to me. When I first went into training as a missionary, my testimony was shaky. I prayed more intensely and more humbly for strength than I ever had in my life because now I was "up against it." I really needed help or I would not be able to serve the right way.

One morning we got on a bus and went to the Manti Temple for an endowment session. Impressed with the beauty of the temple but still struggling inside, I went through that session with a serious prayer in my heart. I needed to be pushed over the edge, to have my doubts relieved.

I will never forget the celestial room of the temple. The walls were a soothing blue with white trim, and a soft light came from the chandeliers above. I went to a corner of the room, where I could be alone, and finished my prayer. I stood there for a long time, and gradually my mind filled with a silence that was more than just the absence of noise. I recognized it as the "peace that passeth understanding." The Lord had spoken peace to my mind, and for me at that time, it was enough.

That sacred peace of mind that I experienced is the fruit of the Spirit (Galatians 5:22). A mind baffled by doubts and confusion is not at peace, although it's very human. The gift of peace of mind is an extraordinary gift indeed in our age of turmoil, and it is one of the effects of revelation from God.

> Doctrine and Covenants 8:2. Yea, behold, I will tell you in your mind and in your heart, by the Holy Ghost, which shall come upon you and which shall dwell in your heart.

"In modern revelation God promises us that we will receive 'knowledge' by His telling us in our mind and in our heart 'by the Holy Ghost,'" says Elder Dallin H. Oaks. "One of the greatest things about our Heavenly Father's plan for His children is that each of us can know the truth of that plan for ourselves. That revealed knowledge does not come from books, from scientific proof, or from intellectual pondering. . . . We can receive that knowledge directly from our Heavenly Father through the witness of the Holy Ghost."[1]

Understanding truth intellectually differs from understanding it "in your mind and in your heart." "I know it's Monday": this is intellectual truth. "I know I love my wife Valerie": this is truth of the heart. Both the heart and the mind are engaged when God reveals truth.

Stephen R. Covey tells of a time he was speaking to a group of college students about sexual morality. They argued fiercely that abstinence before marriage was an unreasonable and outworn principle. Rather than debating the point with them, he asked them to do an experiment: To close their eyes and ponder the question silently "in their hearts" for a few minutes. When he invited them to open their eyes, nearly everyone in the group had changed their minds. Something had spoken to them in the silence. Something had spoken to the tender heart and the humble spirit about the sacredness of love. Regardless of what they had "known" before, they now "knew" something else.

So it was in my search for a testimony. I saw no visions and heard no voices, but I did begin to hear . . .

Doctrine and Covenants 85:6. The still small voice, which whispereth through and pierceth all things, and often times it maketh my bones to quake while it maketh manifest.

In the original Hebrew, that voice is "quiet and thin" (see 1 Kings 19:12). In the French Bible, it's a "sweet, light murmur." In the German Bible, it's a "soft, peaceful, gentle whisper." If we want a stronger testimony, we must learn to listen for and recognize that unique voice. Elder Oaks teaches:

Visions do happen. Voices are heard from beyond the veil. I know this. But these experiences are exceptional. . . . Most of the revelation that comes to leaders and members of the Church comes by the still, small voice. . . . I testify to the reality of that kind of revelation, which I have come to know as a familiar, even daily, experience to guide me in the work of the Lord.[2]

LISTEN FOR THE GENTLE VOICE OF THE SPIRIT

We can expect the Lord to speak to us not with thunderous manifestations but with his gentle voice, the voice of the Spirit:

Doctrine and Covenants 97:1. Verily I say unto you my friends, I speak unto you with my voice, even the voice of my Spirit, that I may show unto you my will.

Personally, I believe that God is very conservative about revealing Himself too forcefully because He knows spectacular manifestations won't help us. We're in a mortal school taking a test. If the professor walks into the room in person and announces all the answers to the test, what's the point of the test? But God is willing to whisper to us ever so softly just enough to nudge us in the direction of His will.

The voice of the Spirit is also an intimate voice. There is love, gentleness, and tenderness in that voice, urging us on so that we can continue in faith.

But we object. "Joseph Smith saw visions. He didn't need faith because he *saw*. Why don't I get to see visions? Then I could be sure."

Joseph Smith's calling was unique as prophet of a new dispensation. There was literally no other way for God to initiate His marvelous work in our day without the visits of heavenly messengers. Joseph Smith's experiences are typical only of dispensational prophets like Adam, Enoch, or Moses; but even with these grand experiences, Joseph still needed faith. And he became very familiar with the still, small voice as well.

I've had some experience as an actor on the stage. One of the scariest things for an actor is to forget a line—and this has happened to me. Believe me, it makes you sweat. I even have nightmares about it. What a blessing it is to have a prompter. This is a person who stands out of view of the audience and follows the script with you. If you forget a line, she will whisper the first few words softly, just audibly enough that you can hear them but the audience can't. Usually, this quiet prompting is all you need to pick yourself up and move on.

The voice of the Spirit is like that. God is not going to play your role for you or you would not grow; but He is always there like the backstage prompter, following the action intently, ready to urge you on with just the right amount of direction when you need Him.

These small divine interventions are the miracles I've come to rely on to strengthen my testimony. I now understand that these interventions must be quiet, not only because gentleness is God's nature, but also because more strident miracles might intrude on our need to learn for ourselves.

Doctrine and Covenants 63:9. Behold, faith cometh not by signs, but signs follow those that believe.

So the great principle of testimony is that "ye receive no witness until after the trial of your faith" (Ether 12:6). A spiritual witness cannot come before the trial, or the trial would be useless. Too many demand the witness before they will try faith, but a testimony simply doesn't work that way, any more than the correct answers to the test can be handed out before the learning happens.

Going to France on a mission was a big trial for me. My first day in the big city of Bordeaux was not just nerve-wracking but downright frightening—because of the traffic! I had never ridden a motorbike before, and when I pulled into the French traffic (where the rule is every man for himself), I was terrified. I remember thinking, "I will never live to see home again."

I managed, shakily, to follow my companion around the hectic streets, but it was a strain. And at the end of the day, disaster happened. As we approached a busy intersection on our way home, he roared through a yellow light and left me behind at the red. In an instant, he was gone.

While I stood at that red light, I felt like the world fell on me. It was my first day, I didn't know the language, I didn't know the way back to the apartment, I was intensely homesick, I was surrounded by crazy drivers, I didn't want to be in France, and I honestly didn't know if I would survive the intersection.

Suddenly, someone spoke to me. It was a young man standing next to me on a motorbike like mine, also waiting for the light. He smiled at me in that ironic French way and asked me in English, "Are you lost?" I said I was. "Do you live at the Voltaire?" I was dumbstruck—the Voltaire was our apartment house. I said yes. "I live there too. Follow me."

The light turned, and I followed the young man all the way home.

Of course, I reasoned later, he recognized me as one of the Mormon missionaries who lived in his building. It was evening, and everybody was going home. So it wasn't such a miraculous thing that he would speak to me.

But to me it was a miracle. A small one, to be sure, but just what I needed at a moment when I was truly lost—and not just geographically. I had tried my faith, and as my faith reached its limit, God moved. From then on, I knew He was watching out for me. Countless such little miracles have strengthened my witness over the years, but always and only after the trial of faith.

STUDY IT OUT IN YOUR MIND; THEN ASK IF IT IS RIGHT

The trial of faith can be a real trial. As Oliver Cowdery learned, we must be prepared to work hard to get a confirming witness of the

Spirit. When Oliver tried to translate from the Book of Mormon plates, he found he could not. He couldn't understand it—he had prayed for guidance. Why couldn't he receive it? The Lord explained:

Doctrine and Covenants 9:8–9. Behold, I say unto you, that you must study it out in your mind; then you must ask me if it be right, and if it is right I will cause that your bosom shall burn within you; therefore, you shall feel that it is right. But if it be not right you shall have no such feelings, but you shall have a stupor of thought that shall cause you forget the thing which is wrong.

At a crucial point in my own life, I made a decision that would affect my entire future. At the time, I thought it was a good, acceptable course of action. I had worked out all the angles and evaluated the decision for a long time. I had often prayed about it. I had "studied it out in my mind." But once I made the decision, almost immediately I felt depressed. It was a growing gloom. I even went to the cellar, turned out the lights, and sat cross-legged on the drain, the lowest place in the house, to think it over. I was literally in darkness, tasting despair almost tangibly.

Another small miracle occurred. My mother was in the house, and she happened to come looking for me. She was surprised to find me squatting in the dark on the cellar floor. I explained to her what I was feeling, and she gently suggested that perhaps I had made the wrong decision and the Spirit of the Lord was telling me that.

My mother's counsel took hold immediately. Of course, I thought—I was experiencing the "stupor of thought" God promised to those who sought his direction and took a wrong path. The next day I reversed my decision and went an entirely different direction. The second path involved much greater uncertainties and challenges than the first path; but as I look back, and knowing what I know now, I can see with great clarity that my first decision would have been disastrous. I thank God for his *disconfirming* guidance.

I recognize also how valuable it was for me to study the issue out first. I learned that my own judgment could be flawed, that the criteria for my decision weren't trustworthy. I learned to distinguish between a "good, acceptable course of action" and a truly valuable course of action. I also learned not to settle for the less demanding choice when an opportunity for real growth lies before me. I learned that I could trust God to give a well-considered decision his stamp of approval—or disapproval.

The opposite of what I experienced is the comforting, serene warmth that confirms a right choice. It is the spiritual equivalent of a trusted counselor who puts an arm around your shoulder and says, "You're on the right track now." Elder Boyd K. Packer teaches, "This burning in the bosom is not purely a physical sensation. It is more like a warm light shining within your being."[3] I have experienced that sensation as well.

When I first met my wife, I had that feeling (it's probably important to point out that she didn't at first.) My feeling of peace and serenity grew over the months of our courtship. Her presence warmed my soul, and it still does. In the most momentous decision I ever made— to ask Valerie to marry me—I thank God for his *confirming* guidance. And I thank her for accepting.

Unfortunately, people who are seeking a witness from God will run into many barriers. The adversary will make sure of that. When Joseph Smith first asked God for answers, he found out just how powerful that opposition can be. The Doctrine and Covenants can help us break through the common obstacles of intellectualism, false doctrine, and neglect of our covenants that can impede the development of a testimony.

INTELLECTUALISM

The barrier of intellectualism can defeat people who are trying to gain a testimony. I know several really gifted people who have left the Gospel behind because it doesn't satisfy their scientific or philosophical concerns. Of course, I know others equally gifted who bear a rich testimony of the Gospel.

The intellectual concerns of those who reject the gospel are countless. However, in every case, the real reason for their rejection is not that they have learned too much but that they haven't learned enough.

Something in Church history bothers them, but instead of examining the issue carefully, they denounce the Church. The Joseph Smith story sounds totally outlandish to them, so they refuse to give it a thoughtful hearing. A French writer who published an article about the Church was baffled that the Mormon people could be so kind and generous to him and still believe a doctrine he found *déroutant et niais* (confusing and silly).

These people practice the very thing they pretend to oppose—*a priori* reasoning. They reason that the gospel can't be true before they examine it. They will not accept the Savior's simple invitation:

Doctrine and Covenants 88:63. Draw near unto me and I will draw near unto you; seek me diligently and ye shall find me; ask, and ye shall receive; knock, and it shall be opened unto you.

If through intellectual arrogance we decline to draw near unto Him in humble prayer; if we seek Him casually instead of diligently; if we fail because of pride to ask Him for answers, we will get exactly what we pay for. Not much.

To gain any worthwhile knowledge, we must pay the price. Every scientist, every philosopher, every serious student knows this.

As a college student, I was constantly under pressure to substitute my testimony for the "philosophies of men." I had a part-time job as a clerk in the Church Historical Department in Salt Lake City, so I took the opportunity to do a lot of reading in Church history. I systematically went through "anti-Mormon" books in the library; over a couple of years I read them all. I found that they were repetitious and full of falsehood and "spin," but some things did bother me.

Instead of letting these things fester, I reserved judgment and examined them even further. In virtually every case, careful study turned what I thought was a weakness in the Church position into a strength. I like what Hugh Nibley reportedly said: "We need more anti-Mormon books. They keep us on our toes."

It's funny how people are bothered by different things. As a graduate English student, I was bothered by Doctrine and Covenants 88:15, "The spirit and the body are the soul of man." The verse made no sense to me because in English "spirit" and "soul" are nearly synonymous. How could this be an inspired verse? Eventually, I learned that in other relevant languages these two words are completely different;

for example, the Hebrew word for "soul" is *nefesh* and the word for "spirit" is *ruah*. So Joseph Smith's revelation was right, and my smug little objection was wrong.

This keeps happening to me. The more I investigate the gospel, the more riches of truth I discover. Small problems have a way of turning into surprising insights that make my testimony stronger.

FALSE DOCTRINE

Sometimes poorly informed media spread false ideas about what we teach, and these ideas are usually easy to refute. Others purposely distort our teachings to oppose us. Then some of the things people teach in the Church are "folk doctrines," that is, commonly shared notions that aren't really justified by scripture or modern revelation. These false doctrines can become a barrier to testimony.

Over the years, I've become a lot more sensitive to "folk doctrines" within the Church. I've realized that many of the "Mormon-culture" assumptions I grew up with are not only wrong but hurtful:

> *Doctrine and Covenants 10:63. Satan doth stir up the hearts of the people to contention concerning the points of my doctrine; and in these things they do err, for they do wrest the scriptures and do not understand them.*

I believe there are people in the Church, some well-meaning, others wanting to stand out in some way, who rush in to "explain" what the Lord has chosen not to explain. They give rise to folk doctrines about things like the age of the earth, the means of creation, the origins of race, the geography of the Book of Mormon, or the role of government. In their misguided efforts, they "wrest" the scriptures, twisting or distorting them away from their basic meanings.

These people, according to Elder Oaks, "pursue their searchings beyond the fringes of orthodoxy, seeking answers to obscure mysteries rather than seeking a firmer understanding and a better practice of the basic principles of the gospel."[4]

Such people can do real harm. In my youth, I was sad when some of my friends left the Church over speculative "doctrines" taught to them by people who assumed an authority they did not have and who should have known better.

Of such people, the Lord asks this question:

Doctrine and Covenants 50:13–15. Unto what were ye ordained? To preach my gospel by the Spirit, even the Comforter which was sent forth to teach the truth. And then received ye spirits which ye could not understand, and received them to be of God; and in this are ye justified?

The Spirit of the Lord will not confirm speculative teachings. Such teachings produce contention, doubt, and darkness. People who abuse the scriptures to justify their peculiar social, political, or scientific views—without paying the price of sound gospel scholarship and humbly inquiring of the Lord—cast up stumbling blocks to the testimonies of others.

By contrast . . .

Doctrine and Covenants 50:21–23. He that receiveth the word by the Spirit of truth receiveth it as it is preached by the Spirit of truth. Wherefore, he that preacheth and he that receiveth, understand one another, and both are edified and rejoice together. And that which doth not edify is not of God, and is darkness.

As a teacher, I have made a practice of praying that the Lord will help me to teach by the Spirit of truth so that we can all be edified and rejoice together. The goal is to *understand* the gospel together, not to sell my point of view. I can testify that many times prayer has been answered and testimonies strengthened—particularly my own.

NEGLECT

Another obstacle to a strong testimony is simple neglect. Like any living thing, a testimony must be constantly nourished to thrive.

Doctrine and Covenants 84:54. Your minds in times past have been darkened because of unbelief, and because you have treated lightly the things you have received.

Treating our gospel obligations lightly will lead to a darkening of the mind or a loss of testimony. Those who are too busy with work, family, or school to pray and study the scriptures faithfully "treat lightly the things they have received." Those who go through the Sunday motions thoughtlessly rather than intently preparing themselves to take the sacrament covenant are light-minded. In these ways, they starve their own testimonies.

To me, the scriptural commandment to "cease from light-mindedness" (see Doctrine and Covenants 88:121) is about taking covenants too lightly. The natural consequence is to descend into unbelief and eventual condemnation.

> *Doctrine and Covenants 84:57. They shall remain under this condemnation until they repent and remember the new covenant, even the Book of Mormon and the former commandments which I have given them, not only to say, but to do according to that which I have written.*

Close reading of the Book of Mormon, along with keeping our covenants, will revive a fading testimony. In my own experience, opening the Book of Mormon is like opening a window to blinding, healing sunlight. Continual exposure to it builds up resistance to the infections of the heart that thrive in darkness. It is like no other book.

I want to testify to you that our Heavenly Father is real and that Jesus Christ is my Savior. Through His atoning power, He has saved me countless times, most importantly from myself. I testify of the Prophet Joseph Smith and his calling to restore and refresh an exhausted world. The Doctrine and Covenants is above all a witness of that calling.

Recently a dear friend who left the Church long ago asked me if my testimony was not just wishful thinking on my part. I smiled, mostly to myself, because of the surprising reality of the things I have experienced and cannot dismiss as my own imaginings. As Joseph Smith once said, "I don't blame anyone for not believing my history. If I had not experienced what I have, I would not have believed it myself."[5]

I have been "guided out of the traffic," so to speak, too many times. I have seen too many fruits, both the ripe and fresh and the decayed and withered, in the lives of too many people. And I have felt the warmth of the loving, atoning arms of the Savior around me too often.

The wish of my heart is that my friend and so many others fatigued by the strain of life in a hope-starved world might also seek and find that embrace.

NOTES

1. Dallin H. Oaks, "Testimony," *Ensign*, May 2008.

2. Dallin H. Oaks, "Teaching and Learning by the Spirit," *Ensign*, March 1997.

3. Boyd K. Packer, "Personal Revelation: The Gift, the Test, the Promise," *Ensign*, November 1994.

4. Dallin H. Oaks, "Our Strengths Can Become Our Downfall," *Ensign*, October 1994.

5. *Teachings of Presidents of the Church: Joseph Smith*, 527.

DEW IN THE DESERT

A lot of people are out there, willing to help solve your problems, for a fee of course (the self-help industry rakes in about $10 billion a year). There's been an explosion of gurus, books, websites, columnists, media psychologists, and TV evangelists—all anxious to help you change your life. Insofar as these people teach true principles, they may do a lot of good.

But if you want direct, clear answers to the big questions of your life, the doctrines of Christ are open to you. The book of Doctrine and Covenants is a tender mercy of the Lord that gives divine guidance *for us, today*—guidance that is far more valuable than the ideas of any human counselor. For our benefit, the Lord advises:

Doctrine and Covenants 1:19. Man should not counsel his fellow man, neither trust in the arm of flesh.

I think too often we wrestle with our problems without help, or we rely too much on well-meaning people or sources that are just not up to the challenge. By nature, the "arm of flesh" is too weak to support us in our trials. Meanwhile, the scriptures, the best possible source of help, too often lie untouched.

How much more do we need the support of the arm of the Lord, which is stretched out to us all day long?

Doctrine and Covenants 136:22. My arm is stretched out in the last days, to save my people Israel.

Who of us doesn't need saving? I don't know about you, but I constantly need to be saved from sin, temptation, error, and my own weak judgment. In the long spiritual drought that constitutes mortal life, where we are separated from our Father in Heaven, we desperately need to cling to the divine arm that can lead us beside the still waters.

A teacher I revere once said, "Observe how often the 'dews of heaven,' or 'the rains' or 'pools'—moisture and water of any form—comprise the most precious part of God's special blessings to his chosen people, for without water there will always be deserts."[1]

I believe that only the doctrines of God can satisfy our thirst for answers and guidance. And we have a sacred responsibility to open those doctrines up to other people—our children, our friends, our associates—all of whom thirst as well.

Doctrine and Covenants 88:77. I give unto you a commandment that you shall teach one another the doctrine of the kingdom.

Please note that this is not a suggestion but a requirement. Why? Because it is the most charitable and merciful thing we can do for each other. What greater comfort can come to the troubled than to have the "dews of heaven" distil upon their souls? What greater gift is there than hope in the Atonement of Jesus Christ?

President Spencer W. Kimball observed this about people who turn to the doctrines of Christ in times of trouble: "A great, sweet peace settles down upon them like the dews of heaven. And innumerable times hearts that were weary in agonizing suffering have felt the kiss of that peace which knows not understanding."[2]

A wise man I know taught the gospel individually to each of his children once a week in an hour-long session. He used the Doctrine and Covenants heavily because so many sections address particular topics, which helped him teach the gospel by theme or subject. At dinnertime he would call out a section number, and whoever knew the topic of that section got a prize. This practice, he says, "has helped our children realize that learning the gospel is essential in order to live the gospel."[3] I suspect his children know where to look in a world thirsting for answers.

When I visited Palestine, I learned that little rain falls there between April and October; and if it were not for substantial dew that forms during the hot months, few plants could survive. Anciently, before modern irrigation, all life there depended on the dew. At times, the Lord withheld the dew from the children of Israel because of their wickedness: "Therefore the heaven over you is stayed from dew, and the earth is stayed from her fruit" (Haggai 1:10).

If we fail to learn doctrine and neglect our covenants, we can expect that the dews of heaven will dry up for us, along with the fruitfulness of our lives.

In the north of Palestine, a beautiful green mountain known as Carmel juts out into the Mediterranean. Because Carmel is so high and close to the sea, heavy dews water a mountaintop forest of oaks and fir trees each night. It's no wonder in that dry land that the dews of Mount Carmel should become a lasting symbol of the healing, refreshing water of life found in the doctrines of Christ. Those who cherish the doctrines and keep their covenants will, I have found, receive the answers they need—

Doctrine and Covenants 128:19. As the dews of Carmel, so shall the knowledge of God descend upon them.

NOTES

1.   Reed C. Durham, Jr. "And Blossom as the Rose," *Ensign*, May 1972. http://www.lds.org/ensign/1972/05/and-blossom-as-the-rose?lang=eng&query= "the+dews+of+heaven".

2.   Spencer W. Kimball, "The Certainty of the Resurrection," *Ensign,* April 2010. http://www.lds.org/ensign/2010/04/the-certainty-of-the-resurrection?lan g=eng&query="the+dews+of+heaven.

3.   James W. McConkie II, *Looking at the Doctrine and Covenants Again for the Very First Time* (West Valley City, UT: Temple Hill Books, 2010), xix-xx..

DOCTRINE
AND
COVENANTS
REFERENCES

Reference	Page	Reference	Page
30:2	161	65:5	178
33:16	191	68:31	121
38:39	121, 123	72:3	165
42:14	213	76:23-24	76, 96
42:43	113	76:24	2
42:45	63	76:55–57	184
45:10	45	76:64	183
49:16	64	76:81	193
49:18	113	78:18	63
50:10	144	78:5	103
50:13–15	223	82:1	13
50:21–25	223	82:19	159
50:22	132	84:6–28	181
50:40	4	84:26	180
58:27	85, 93	84:33	167, 184
58:28	23	84:54	223
58:42–43	18	84:57	224
58:56	144	84:66	182
59:18–19	112	84:88	173
59:20	112	85:6	216
63:9	217	88:6	8, 26
63:66	46	88:15	221
64:8	14	88:40	127
64:9–10	11	88:62–63	196
64:10	15	88:63	221
65:1, 3	171	88:68	91, 93

REFERENCE	PAGE	REFERENCE	PAGE
88:76	111	93:36	99, 135, 197
88:77	185, 228	93:40	100
88:78–79	133	93:45	8
88:84–85	185	96:3	144
88:80	162, 167	97:1	149, 216
88:84	158, 185	97:12, 16	124
88:118	149, 193	97:15–16	202
88:119	91, 129	98:4–6	137
88:121	224	98:8–10	142
88:123	66, 18	98:11	23
88: 123, 125	66	98:40	13
88:124	110	100:6	132
89:4	114	101:23	160
89:5, 7–9	108	101:77–78	138
89:10–12	109	104:4	50, 152
89:16–17	110	104:11–12	167
89:18–21	109	104:21	144
89:20	110	104:52	152
90:17	150	104:59	158
93:1	37	104:78	120
93:13	2	107:18	181
93:20	3	107:99	163
93:21, 23	2	107:99–100	187
93:24	147	109:7	99, 122, 131
93:29	127	109:72–74	178
93:30	134	109:76	203

INDEX

conspiring men 113–14
Cook, Quentin L. 39, 44
Cook, Sir Francis 75
Copernicus, Nicolaus 150–51
covenant xi
covetousness 67, 118–19, 125
Covey, Sean x
Covey, Stephen R. 66, 215

D

Dawkins, Richard 152, 154
Declaration of Independence 138
Declaration of the Rights of Man
        and of the Citizen 138
depression 74, 80
divorce 47, 64
doctrine xi
Doctrine and Covenants x, xii

E

education
    "house of learning" 129, 131
    neglect of 129
    purpose of 135
    secular 134
    seeking diligently 131–33
    the purpose of life 127
Einstein, Albert 151
Eliot, T.S. 91
employment 92
Evans, Richard L. 93
Eve, great and mighty one 95
Eyring, Henry 155
Eyring, Henry B. 38, 65, 68

F

family history 201, 206–8
financial problems 39, 117
    bankruptcy 117, 120
    debt 117, 119, 120–21
    fraud 123
    pride 123
    tithing and 123–26
folk doctrine 103, 105, 222
forgiveness
    for self 17–18
    love of God and 16–17
    repentance and 18
    "until seventy times seven" 13–14

G

Galilei, Galileo 150
Garrett, Dean 123
gospel
    and enduring 37
    Doctrine and Covenants and xi
    ultimate reward of 37–38
grace, as enabling power 2, 7
gratitude 35, 112

H

Hafen, Bruce C. 6
Hales, Robert D. 126, 179, 180
Hallowell, Edward 86
Harris, Martin 125
health
    behaviors and 107–8
    fasting and 111
    Mormon record of 107
    sleep and 110, 111–12
    unproven remedies and 113–14
high-minded 150, 155

ABOUT
THE
AUTHOR

B reck England is writer-in-chief for FranklinCovey Co., a provider of leadership and personal effectiveness training for businesses worldwide. He has consulted with companies from Switzerland to Saudi Arabia and has written training materials on management and communication skills, as well as on strategy execution. For seven years he was an adjunct professor in the Marriott School at Brigham Young University.

Breck has published widely, most recently *The 3rd Alternative: Solving Life's Most Difficult Problems* and *Predictable Results in Unpredictable Times*, cowritten with Stephen R. Covey. Some years ago, he released an award-winning biography of a prominent pioneer apostle, *The Life and Thought of Orson Pratt*, and a number of biographical and historical articles in the *Ensign*.

In the Church, Breck has served as a gospel doctrine teacher, elders quorum president, high priests group leader, and a bishop's counselor. He sang with the Mormon Tabernacle Choir for five years. As a member of the joint Melchizedek Priesthood and Relief Society curriculum committee, he helped produce the series Teachings of the Presidents of the Church. He and his wife, Valerie Goodrich England, are the parents of five and grandparents of twelve.